IFIP Advances in Information and Communication Technology

555

IFIP – The International Federation for Information Processing

IFIP was founded in 1960 under the auspices of UNESCO, following the first World Computer Congress held in Paris the previous year. A federation for societies working in information processing, IFIP's aim is two-fold: to support information processing in the countries of its members and to encourage technology transfer to developing nations. As its mission statement clearly states:

IFIP is the global non-profit federation of societies of ICT professionals that aims at achieving a worldwide professional and socially responsible development and application of information and communication technologies.

IFIP is a non-profit-making organization, run almost solely by 2500 volunteers. It operates through a number of technical committees and working groups, which organize events and publications. IFIP's events range from large international open conferences to working conferences and local seminars.

The flagship event is the IFIP World Computer Congress, at which both invited and contributed papers are presented. Contributed papers are rigorously refereed and the rejection rate is high.

As with the Congress, participation in the open conferences is open to all and papers may be invited or submitted. Again, submitted papers are stringently refereed.

The working conferences are structured differently. They are usually run by a working group and attendance is generally smaller and occasionally by invitation only. Their purpose is to create an atmosphere conducive to innovation and development. Refereeing is also rigorous and papers are subjected to extensive group discussion.

Publications arising from IFIP events vary. The papers presented at the IFIP World Computer Congress and at open conferences are published as conference proceedings, while the results of the working conferences are often published as collections of selected and edited papers.

IFIP distinguishes three types of institutional membership: Country Representative Members, Members at Large, and Associate Members. The type of organization that can apply for membership is a wide variety and includes national or international societies of individual computer scientists/ICT professionals, associations or federations of such societies, government institutions/government related organizations, national or international research institutes or consortia, universities, academies of sciences, companies, national or international associations or federations of companies.

More information about this subseries at http://www.springer.com/series/16606

Leon Strous · Roger Johnson ·
David Alan Grier · Doron Swade (Eds.)

Unimagined Futures –
ICT Opportunities
and Challenges

 Springer

Editors
Leon Strous
De Nederlandsche Bank
Amsterdam, The Netherlands

Roger Johnson
Birkbeck University of London
London, UK

David Alan Grier🆔
Djaghe LLC
Washington, DC, USA

Doron Swade
Kingston upon Thames, UK

ISSN 1868-4238   ISSN 1868-422X   (electronic)
IFIP Advances in Information and Communication Technology
ISSN 2730-5759   ISSN 2730-5767   (electronic)
IFIP AICT Festschrifts
ISBN 978-3-030-64248-8   ISBN 978-3-030-64246-4   (eBook)
https://doi.org/10.1007/978-3-030-64246-4

This Springer imprint is published by the registered company Springer Nature Switzerland AG
The registered company address is: Gewerbestrasse 11, 6330 Cham, Switzerland

Foreword

IFIP – the International Federation for Information Processing – was founded in 1960 following the first World Computer Congress, and under the auspices of UNESCO. Its aim was to support and advance the work of the then fledging societies dealing with information processing (which we now refer to as information and communication technology, or ICT) and the nascent computing industry.

Today, IFIP is the global federation of ICT societies and associations committed to advancing the professional and socially-responsible application of technology. IFIP's members are national, regional, and international ICT societies. In turn, their members are ICT professionals, practitioners, researchers, academics, educators, and policy-makers, who are focused on: developing and advancing ICT knowledge and expertise; promoting digital equity; educating and enhancing public understanding of technology and its potential (both for good and, occasionally, ill); and increasing professionalism and professional standards.

IFIP is a strong advocate for digital equity ("all of the Internet, for all of the people, all of the time", access to technology for minorities, particularly those in remote areas, and gender equality). Along with its member societies, it works closely with the United Nations and its agencies (UNESCO, ITU, and UNCTAD being the most prominent ones), and many other international bodies, to promote understanding of issues related to technology. It aims to collaborate on solutions to help in the achievement of the United Nations Sustainable Development Goals (SDGs).

IFIP organizes more than 100 events every year to bring together international experts on various ICT-related topics, to share the latest developments, explore possibilities, and to discuss the latest issues of relevance to the ICT profession.

Events, such as the World Computer Congress (WCC) – which spawned the creation of IFIP in the first instance – bring together thought leaders from across the globe to share their knowledge and expertise and to share information about emerging technology issues and policies. The World IT Forum (WITFOR) is specifically focused on means of enhancing access to technology for developing nations to enable them, and their citizens, to play an active role in the global digital economy.

IFIP's International Professional Practice Partnership (IP3) is the leading group driving professional practice for technologists around the world. It has been responsible for having the importance of professionalism as a key enabler of the SDGs being recognized and discussed at the United Nations General Assembly.

IFIP also seeks to raise awareness and understanding among the wider community about where technology is headed, how it can enhance the quality of all our lives, and how to ensure that all people have equal access and equal opportunity. We must also, of course, be aware that as in the natural sciences, many new technologies that have much potential for good also have potential for harm.

IFIP is uniquely placed to achieve these outcomes through its global network of 13 Technical Committees and more than 130 Working Groups, that bring together experts in different fields in order to share and enhance their knowledge, and to focus attention on key areas related to technology.

IFIP member societies, and their individual members, have access to the largest network of technical expertise in the world. This enables them to make valuable connections, grow their knowledge and skills, and contribute to the development of global insights and standards for ICT and ICT professionals.

This collection is a celebration of IFIP on the occasion of its diamond jubilee. The authors have almost all – at some point or other – made significant contributions to IFIP and IFIP member societies, as well as to their own respective technical areas. As a result, they understand both the organization and the issues well. The contributions in this book highlight those developments and challenges that society, in general, and IFIP and other ICT-related societies around the world (including IFIP's own members), in particular, are facing. They consider contributions and developments in a number of key and emerging technical areas and address IFIP's and other ICT societies' important role in policy, professionalism, and professional ethics. These are all significant issues for the ICT industry as it evolves to consider new technologies, new areas of application, and the increasing influence of technology on almost every aspect of our lives. Indeed, as that influence grows, it becomes more of an issue for all of us.

Unimagined Futures: ICT opportunities and challenges reminds us briefly of IFIP's past; it addresses its present context, and its future challenges in a variety of areas. Many of these, of course, are challenges for all of us, and are not unique to IFIP. This excellent collection is written and edited by some of those who know IFIP best. It stands as a record of what the ICT industry—and ICT community as a whole—should be, and can become.

September 2020

Mike Hinchey
IFIP President (2016-2022)

Preface

The International Federation for Information Processing (IFIP) was formally established in 1960. Like many organizations it has celebrated its "significant birthdays"
with a publication. Looking at a number of examples from different organizations on
our bookshelves, most contain two elements in varying proportions – firstly reviewing
the progress made since the last birthday volume and secondly looking to the future.

For this volume, the first of two planned 60th anniversary books, IFIP invited
experts in different aspects of the contemporary ICT scene to contribute essays from
their specialist areas. While addressing the contemporary challenges facing the ICT
community today, the book provides the opportunity to look back to help understand
the contemporary scene and identify appropriate future responses to them. As such, the
book aims to contribute to the ICT community worldwide, as well as IFIP and its
member societies, on setting their policy priorities and agendas for the coming decade.
We hope to provoke discussion about appropriate responses to the challenges by
individuals as well as by national and international bodies including IFIP.

The title *Unimagined Futures: ICT opportunities and challenges* reflects the fact
there were many futures in the past that happened without our having envisaged them,
and there are multiple futures that we now speculate about. Often the way things turned
out exceeded our wildest imaginings and we can be sure that this will be no different
for things to come.

In a conversation with Eunika Mercier-Laurent for the chapter "The future of AI or
AI for the future," the term Imaginative and Creative Technology[1] was used as the
meaning of ICT instead of Information and Communication Technology. Maybe by
becoming more imaginative and creative, we can create even better unimagined futures.

ICT's capabilities have been transformed beyond recognition since 1960 and ICT
practitioners have had a substantial role in transforming the world in which we all live.
The ICT workforce since 1960 has changed from programmers, analysts, and operators
numbering a few tens of thousands worldwide into the highly diverse multi-million
strong body we see today. For the end user, there are no longer levels of intermediaries
between them and the computer–programmers to create software and operators to run
the programs. Users have direct access to their PC or mobile device providing access to
applications undreamt of in 1960.

While there are still software developers and operations staff – now concerned with
networking as much as processing – the workforce has diversified to include new
activities such as the graphic design, building, and maintenance of myriad web sites.

In 1995, at the opening ceremony of the IFIP Secretariat office in Laxenburg just
outside Vienna, Austria, Prof. Heinz Zemanek, then the IFIP Historian, reminded the
audience of the story of the early days of the telephone service when it started to dawn
on telephone company executives in the USA that eventually half the population would

---

[1] While difficult to find who coined the term, a Google search resulted in a few hits.

be making telephone calls while the other half would be employed as telephone operators connecting their calls. He went on to observe that telephone technology rapidly set about automating the connection process so that every telephone user was transformed into an operator by giving us all initially a dial and latterly a keypad. Zemanek was an important computer pioneer but, as an indicator of the speed of change, he had no idea that 25 years later it would be normal for people to carry a "mobile" which would be a portable computer, one of whose many functions would be a telephone, and that people would often use texts and social media to communicate with other people rather than making telephone calls to one individual.

While the contributions were invited and not peer-reviewed like in conference proceedings, all chapters were reviewed by two editors to assure its quality by providing feedback to authors. This volume is the first Festschrift in the IFIP *Advances in Information and Communication Technology* (AICT) series. Festschrifts honor individual researchers and their scientific work, or they honor institutions or fields like IFIP Technical Committees, Working Groups, or other initiatives. Historical and even personal aspects may show up. They present internationally relevant technical contributions with a reasonable topical focus. As such, the Festschrifts also contribute to the principal aim of the IFIP AICT series to encourage education and the dissemination and exchange of information about all aspects of computing.

The editors accept full responsibility for the choice of topics, realizing that many more topics would have deserved a chapter in the book. We are especially grateful to the authors willing to give freely of their expertise and time to contribute to this book during the very difficult period of the first half of 2020.

We are very pleased with the rich content of the contributions and by making the volume open access, we trust that it will be read and enjoyed by many.

September 2020

Leon Strous
Roger Johnson
David Alan Grier
Doron Swade

Authors

Wil van der Aalst

Prof. Dr. ir. Wil van der Aalst is a Full Professor at RWTH Aachen University leading the Process and Data Science (PADS) group. He is also part-time affiliated with the Fraunhofer-Institut für Angewandte Informationstechnik (FIT) where he leads FIT's Process Mining group. His research interests include process mining, Petri nets, business process management, workflow management, process modeling, and process analysis. Wil van der Aalst has published over 800 articles and books and is typically considered to be in the top 15 of most cited computer scientists with an H-index of over 150 and more than 100,000 citations. Next to serving on the editorial boards of over 10 scientific journals, he is also playing an advisory role for several companies, including Fluxicon, Celonis, Processgold, and Bright Cape. Van der Aalst received honorary degrees from the Moscow Higher School of Economics (Prof. h.c.), Tsinghua University, and Hasselt University (Dr. h.c.). He is also an elected member of the Royal Netherlands Academy of Arts and Sciences, the Royal Holland Society of Sciences and Humanities, the Academy of Europe, and the North Rhine-Westphalian Academy of Sciences, Humanities and the Arts. In 2018, he was awarded an Alexander-von-Humboldt Professorship.

Wil is proud to be an IFIP Fellow.

Ron Berndsen

Prof. Ron Berndsen is an independent director of LCH and chairs the LCH Risk Committees. He is also attached to the Tilburg School of Economics and Management at Tilburg University as Full Professor of Financial Market Infrastructures and Systemic Risk. Ron is Editor-in-Chief of the *Journal of Financial Market Infrastructures* and a member of the Advisory Council of the SWIFT Institute.

The author has been active in the field of payments and market infrastructures for over 17 years. He was Head of the Oversight Department and Head of the Market Infrastructures Policy Department at De Nederlandsche Bank. Ron also served as a member on the Market Infrastructure Board at the European Central Bank and as member of the Committee on Payments and Market Infrastructures at the Bank of International Settlements. He also co-chaired the FSB Group on Cross-Border Crisis Management for Financial Market Infrastructures and was a member of the Oversight Committees of CLS, EuroCCP, Euroclear, LCH, SWIFT, and TARGET2.

He was awarded a doctorate of Tilburg University in 1992 for his PhD thesis in Economics and Artificial Intelligence.

Regina Bernhaupt

Regina Bernhaupt's main research passion is to make people's lives better. Her research focus is on understanding how, when, and why interactive systems fail and how to evaluate the impact of new technologies on people's everyday lives. Her main contributions have been in areas like interactive television, games, and entertainment-oriented applications. Her special topic is how to allow people to stay in control of a system, but as well as to stay in control over their data (privacy) and their lives. Regina was introduced to IFIP during the Interact conference 2003, and became a member of the Working Group 13.2 Methodologies for User-Centred System Design of IFIP in 2005. Today she is the president of this Working Group. She also serves as the Dutch representative of IFIP TC-13. She has been actively involved in the TC-13 Interact conference since 2005 in various roles and was Papers Chair for Interact in 2017.

Vinton G. Cerf

Vinton G. Cerf co-designed the TCP/IP protocols and the architecture of the Internet and is Chief Internet Evangelist for Google. He is a former member of the National Science Board and current member of the US National Academies of Engineering and Science and is a Foreign Member of the British Royal Society and Swedish Royal Academy of Engineering. He is a Fellow of ACM, IEEE, AAAS, and BCS. Cerf received the US Presidential Medal of Freedom, US National Medal of Technology, Queen Elizabeth Prize for Engineering, Prince of Asturias Award, Japan Prize, ACM Turing Award, Legion d'Honneur, the Franklin Medal, the Catalunya International Prize, and 29 honorary degrees.

Robert Davison

Robert Davison is a Professor of Information Systems at the City University of Hong Kong and Fellow of the Association for Information Systems. His research focuses on the use and misuse of information systems, especially with respect to problem solving, guanxi formation, and knowledge management in Chinese organizations. He has published over 200 articles in a variety of the premier IS journals and conferences. He is particularly known for his scholarship in the domain of action research. Robert chairs IFIP's Working Group 9.4 (Social Implications of Computing in Developing Countries), is a member of Working Group 8.2 (Information Systems and Organizations), and is also a member of the IFIP Digital Equity Committee. He serves as the Editor-in-Chief of the *Information Systems Journal* and the *Electronic Journal of Information Systems in Developing Countries*. Robert seeks to enhance the inclusion of scholars from the global south within our community and frequently visits developing countries where he offers research seminars and workshops, engaging with PhD students and scholars. As a researcher and as an editor, he champions local and indigenous perspectives. Home Page: http://www.is.cityu.edu.hk/staff/isrobert.

Moira de Roche

Moira de Roche is an independent consultant. She is the Chair of IFIP IP3, and a member of the IFIP board. She is also a Director on the Global Industry Council, an IFIP think-tank comprised of senior people from all parts of the globe who are involved with ICT. Moira was awarded the IFIP Silver Core in 2016.

Moira is an accomplished speaker and has presented at conferences around the world, including South Africa, on diverse subjects such as Technology and Learning, IT Leadership, Future Skills, and more. Her speaking engagements on behalf of IP3 have seen her speaking on Professionalism, Trust, and the Duty of Care in Digital, as well as people-related issues with Industry 4.0. She has attended and presented at the World Summit for Information Society since 2012.

A Past President of IITPSA (Institute of IT Professionals South Africa) Moira is a Professional Member and Fellow, and currently serves as a Non-Executive Director. She received the IITPSA Distinguished Service in ICT Award in 2009.

Moira is also a member of ACM and the South African Institute of Directors. She serves as a Councilor on the board of the South African National Museum and is a member of the Board Committees on HR, Governance, and Legal as well as Core Business and IT.

Erik DeBenedictis

Erik has a background in Computer Science and Engineering, starting with BSc and PhD degrees in Electrical Engineering and Computer Engineering from Caltech in 1978 and 1983, and an MA degree in Computer Engineering from Carnegie Mellon University in 1979. He worked at Bell Laboratories on hypercube parallel computers, Ansoft Corporation (now Ansys) developing the sparse matrix solver for the High Frequency Structure Simulator (HFSS, mentioned in the article), and in a project management role. He then worked at nCUBE corporation on hypercube parallel supercomputer before founding NetAlive, Inc., a startup with a wireless internet software application framework. He later joined Sandia National Laboratories performing research on supercomputers, cryogenic computers, quantum computing, and spacecraft computing. He is now the principal of Zettaflops, LLC.

He is a Senior Member of the IEEE and has had volunteer leadership roles as a co-lead of the Rebooting Computing initiative, the Quantum initiative, and is Editor-in-Chief of IEEE *Transactions on Quantum Engineering*.

Per Fors

Per Fors is a postdoctoral scholar at the Department of Civil and Industrial Engineering at Uppsala University. His main research interests are topics related to technology, sustainability, and ethics, and he is teaching ethics, and sustainability to engineering students. Per is a member of the IFIP WG 9.9 (ICT and Sustainable Development).

David Alan Grier

David Alan Grier is the Technology Principal at Djaghe LLC and is the author of *When Computers Were Human*. He is an IEEE Fellow and has served as president of the IEEE Computer Society, Editor-in-Chief of *Computer*, Editor-in-Chief of the *Annals of the History of Computing*, editorial columnist for *Consumer Electronics Magazine* and the *Communications of the Chinese Computing Federation*.

Roger Johnson

Dr. Roger Johnson is a Fellow of the British Computer Society and a Chartered Engineer. He worked for 30 years in the School of Computer Science at Birkbeck University of London following a period as a software engineer developing software mainly in the financial services industry. He published extensively on database management and later the history of computing. He is a leading authority on the work of Andrew Booth, who invented the Booth multiplier, and was the first person to successfully connect a magnetic storage device to a computer.

Roger is a Past President of the British Computer Society and was the UK representative to IFIP from 1992 to 2010. He served as IFIP Honorary Secretary from 1999–2010. He was also a UK member of the Council of European Professional Informatics Societies (CEPIS) and served as President from 1997–99. He was a founding member of the Computer Conservation Society in 1989, the UK's computer history society, serving as Chair from 2003–2007 and is currently its Program Secretary. He is Secretary of the Turing-Welchman Bombe Rebuild Trust which owns, maintains, and demonstrates the replica of Turing's Bombe to visitors to the National Museum of Computing on the Bletchley Park Campus, UK.

David Kreps
David Kreps is a Reader in Philosophy of Information Systems. His books include *Against Nature: The Metaphysics of Information Systems* (Routledge); *Bergson, Complexity and Creative Emergence* (Palgrave); *Gramsci and Foucault: A Reassessment* (Routledge); *This Changes Everything: ICT and Climate Change – What We Do?* (Springer); and *Technology and Intimacy: Choice or Coercion?* (Springer), and he has published in the *European Journal of Information Systems; Information Communication and Society; First Monday; Information Technology and People; Journal of Information, Communication and Ethics in Society; and Ethics and Information Technology*, and is a regular contributor to the International Conference on Information Systems and other conferences in the field.

After many years involvement with IFIP Working Group 9.5 on Virtuality and Society, including two terms as Chair, in 2018 David became Chair of the IFIP's Technical Committee 9 on ICT and Society (IFIP TC-9). David has Chaired three of the Human Choice and Computers conference series: HCC12 "Technology and Intimacy: Choice or coercion" Salford, Manchester, 2016; HCC13 "This Changes Everything," Poznan, Poland, 2018; and HCC14 "Human-Centred Computing in a Data-Driven Society," which was to have taken place in Tokyo, Japan, 2020, but had to be canceled due to the COVID-19 pandemic. He was Editor of the proceedings for all three conferences, including the eBook of HCC14, which went ahead.
In his role as TC Chair, David is proud to have led on the creation of an IFIP Position Paper on E-Waste and the creation and adoption of the IFIP Code of Ethics.

Christopher Leslie
Christopher Leslie, the Chair of IFIP's Working Group 9.7 on the History of Computing, is a Lecturer in the School of Foreign Languages at the South China University of Technology in Guangzhou. A two-time winner of a Fulbright fellowship, he has taught at Hunter College, John Jay College, New York University, Universität Potsdam, and the South China University of Technology. Dr. Leslie was born and raised in a village in the western part of New York State, but he took his MA and PhD from the City University of New York Graduate Center in New York City. His research interests include the interactions among science, technology, and culture.

Gabriela Marín Raventós
Gabriela Marín Raventós received a MSc in Computer Science from Case Western Reserve University in 1985 and a PhD in Business Analysis and Research from Texas A&M University, USA, in 1993. She has been a Computer Science faculty member at

Universidad de Costa Rica (UCR) since 1980. She was Dean of Graduate Studies and Director of the Research Center for Communication and Information Technologies (CITIC), both at UCR. Currently, she is the UCR Graduate Program in Computer Science and Informatics Chairperson.

She has organized several international and national conferences, and has been, and still is, Chair of several Program and Editorial Committees. From 2012 to 2016, she was President of the Latin American Center for Computer Studies (CLEI), becoming the first woman to occupy such a distinguished position. Since September 2016, she is Vice President of the International Federation for Information Processing (IFIP), in charge of the Digital Equity Committee. Her research interests include Smart Cities, Human Computer Interaction, Decision Support Systems, Gender in IT, and Digital Equity.

Eunika Mercier-Laurent

Eunika Mercier-Laurent is an electronic engineer, holds a PhD in Computer Science, is an expert in Artificial Intelligence (AI), and is an Associate Researcher at the University of Reims Champagne Ardennes as well as Professor at EPITA International Masters and SKEMA. Her teaching and MOOC includes Knowledge Management and Innovation powered by AI, Ethical Development of AI Systems, Innovation Ecosystems, and Innovation Week Challenges.

After working as researcher in INRIA and a computer designer and manager of innovative AI applications with Groupe Bull, she founded Global Innovation Strategies devoted to all aspects of Knowledge Innovation. Among her research topics are: Knowledge and Eco-innovation Management Systems, methods and techniques for innovation, knowledge modeling and processing, complex problem solving, AI for sustainability, and eco-design and impacts of AI.

She has over 15 years of involvement with IFIP including the Chair position of Technical Committee 12 on AI since 2019 and Chair of WG 12.6 (AI for Knowledge Management). She is representative of TC-12 in France since 2018.

Eunika is President of Innovation3D, International Association for Global Innovation, expert for EU programs, and author of over hundred scientific publications and books.

Bertrand Meyer

Bertrand Meyer is Provost and Professor of Software Engineering at the Schaffhausen Institute of Technology in Switzerland and holds associated positions at Innopolis University and Politecnico di Milano. He is also Chief Technology Officer at Eiffel Software (Santa Barbara, California). He was previously Professor of Software Engineering and Department Chair at ETH Zurich. His works spans several areas of software engineering including software verification, programming languages, object technology, requirements engineering, and concurrent programming. His contributions include the concept of "Design by Contract," the Eiffel development method and programming language, and a number of widely used books.

Chris Rees

Chris Rees was President of the British Computer Society, The Chartered Institute for IT, in 2018–2019. During his presidential year he chose the Ethics of AI as his theme, and lectured on the topic to professional and lay audiences in the UK, Europe (including at the IFIP World Computer Congress in Poznan in 2018), Sri Lanka, Mauritius, and Australia. He is a Liveryman of the Worshipful Company of Information Technologists and Chaired its Ethical and Spiritual Development Panel. He advises charities which benefit from the WCIT Charity on the ethical development of AI systems.

Before his retirement in 2015 he was a Director of Charteris plc for 18 years and before that a Partner in Deloitte Consulting for 12. At Deloitte he led the Knowledge Based Systems Centre, a unit developing knowledge-based systems, including the first working fraud detection system for Barclaycard and systems to detect fraudulent share applications in government privatization issues. He practised as a management consultant and as an expert witness in large scale IT disputes. His earlier career was with IBM UK, National CSS (later Dun & Bradstreet) in the USA, and Logica. He has an MA from the University of St Andrews.

He is co-author of *From Principles to Profit – The Art of Moral Management* (Duckworth, London, 2006).

Liesbeth Ruoff-van Welzen

Liesbeth Ruoff-van Welzen acquired expertise in various fields. After starting as a marketeer in education at the predecessor of the Rotterdam School of Management and IT firms in the hardware and services sector, she became CEO of IDC Benelux. She played an important role in the development and growth of the company and its market research in different sectors like services, channels, and networks. Her last role was Group Vice President IDC EMEA. In 2002 she decided to leave IDC and to start her own company LRWA. In the beginning she worked closely with Paul Strassmann and Tom Pisello. Topics LRWA addressed lay in the area of the added value of IT, how to achieve that within organizations, and how to deliver as an IT company added value. It became more and more clear that skills, attitude, and competences of human capital within organizations were the differentiator between a positive or negative result. That topic is LRWA's main focus.

She currently spends most of her time ensuring that professionalism of the ICT world and digital skills of professional users and citizens are taken seriously, and adequate actions are taken. She does that in her role as chairman of the Interest Group (IG) Digital Skills of the KNVI, the Dutch organization for the information professional, member of CEN TC-428, the European Standardization Committee for ICT Professionalism and Digital Competences and board member of IP3, a part of IFIP.

Adrian Schofield

Adrian began his career in the UK petroleum industry, followed by some years in casino administration. He spent 25 years in various executive and consulting roles in the South African ICT sector prior to joining the Joburg Centre for Software Engineering at the University of the Witwatersrand in 2008 as Manager: Applied Research Unit. In 2018, he was appointed Production/Program Consultant at IITPSA (Institute of Information Technology Professionals South Africa).

He has lectured about the Management of Technology and Systems Thinking and is a regular commentator in the trade media. Adrian has spent more than 30 years promoting standards and growth in the ICT sector. Adrian has served as President of the Information Technology Association in South Africa and as Vice Chairman of the Africa ICT Alliance. He received the 2012 Distinguished Service in ICT Award from Computer Society South Africa (now IITPSA). In 2015, he was appointed as a Councillor for the Broad-Based Black Economic Empowerment (B-BBEE) ICT Sector Council, until March 2020.

He currently serves as Vice Chairman (Standards and Accreditation) of IP3 (the International Professional Practice Partnership at the International Federation for Information Processing).

Adrian is a Fellow and Professional Member of IITPSA, having served terms as its Vice President and President.

Leon Strous

Leon has a background in business economics, business informatics, and a postgraduate degree in IT-Audit. He worked eight years for Philips Electronics in The Netherlands with a focus on internal control and information security. Since 1993, Leon is with De Nederlandsche Bank (DNB), the reserve bank of The Netherlands. Previous positions in the internal audit department, in the oversight department, and in a policy department of the cash and payments division. Currently his main job is advancing business continuity and crisis management arrangements with the key players in the payments and securities processes in the financial sector in The Netherlands. He is also liaising between the financial sector and the government concerning critical infrastructure protection programs.

His more than 25 years of involvement with IFIP include being Chair of Technical Committee 11 on Information Security and Privacy Protection (2001–2007) and President of the Federation (2010–2016). He was the representative for The Netherlands in TC-11 from 1995–2007 and in the General Assembly from 2001–2017.

He has co-authored and co-edited publications in the area of information security and has been involved in various roles in the organization of many conferences, including IFIP World Computer Congresses and the IFIP World IT Forum (WITFOR).

Leon was awarded Knight of the Order of Orange-Nassau in 2015. He is an Honorary Member of IFIP.

Doron Swade

Doron Swade is an engineer, historian, and museum professional. He was Curator of Computing for many years at the Science Museum, London, and later Assistant Director and Head of Collections. He has studied physics, mathematics, electrical engineering, control engineering, philosophy of science, and man-machine studies at various universities including University of Cape Town, University of Cambridge, University of Essex, and University College London. He designed digital hardware for 10 years and consulted for the microcomputer industry in the UK and USA. He lectures widely and has published four books (one co-authored) and many scholarly and popular articles on history of computing, curatorship, and museology. He is a leading authority of the life and work of Charles Babbage and is responsible for the construction of Charles Babbage's Difference Engine No. 2 built to original nineteenth-century designs. He founded the Computer Conservation Society in 1989, which is dedicated to the preservation and restoration to working order of historic computing machines. He is an Honorary Fellow of the British Computer Society (2019) and of Royal Holloway University of London (2018). He was awarded an MBE in 2009 for services to the history of computing.

Ruth Wandhöfer

Dr. Ruth Wandhöfer operates at the nexus of finance, technology, and regulation, and is passionate about creating the digital financial ecosystem of the future. She is an expert in the field of banking and one of the foremost authorities on transaction banking regulatory and innovation in financial technology matters. After a distinguished career of over a decade with Citi, Ruth is now an independent Non-Executive Director on the boards of Permanent TSB and Digital Identity Net as well as a Partner at Gauss Ventures. She is a Strategic Adviser of the European Third Party Provider Association (ETPPA) and Adviser at Coinfirm. Until recently, she has served as independent Non-Executive Director on the Board of the London Stock Exchange Group and Pendo Systems Inc.

Ruth was named as one of 2010s 'Rising Stars' by Financial News; named in Management Today's 2011 '35 Women under 35' list of women to watch, and identified as one of the 100 Most Influential People in Finance 2012 by the Treasury Risk Magazine. She received the 'Women in Banking and Finance Award for Achievement' in 2015 and in 2016, 2017, and 2018 she was named on the global 'Women in Fintech Powerlist' of Innovate Finance. She is a 2018, 2019, and 2020 Top 10 Global Fintech Influencer (Fintech Power 50).

She speaks five languages, has completed studies in Financial Economics (MA, UK), International Politics (MA, FR), and an LLM in International Economic Law (UK). She was awarded a doctorate by CASS Business School, London, and Tilburg University in 2019 for her PhD thesis in Finance on the topic of "Technology Innovation in Financial Markets."

She published two books: "EU Payments Integration" (2010) and "Transaction Banking and the Impact of Regulatory Change" (2014), is a Fellow of CASS Business School City University London, a Visiting Professor at the London Institute of Banking and Finance, and also lectures at Queen Mary London School of Law.

Ulrika H. Westergren

Ulrika H. Westergren is an Associate Professor of Informatics at Umeå University, Sweden, and a faculty member of the Swedish Center for Digital Innovation. She specializes in the digitalization of society with a focus on organizational change, new business models, value creation, and issues of trust, in relation to the introduction of new technology. She has led numerous collaborative projects with companies within the manufacturing and processing industries and is currently focusing on exploring viable business models for firms that are operating within an Internet of Things ecosystem and on IoT for societal benefit. Ulrika is the Swedish representative in IFIP Technical Committee 9: ICT and Society and serves as a member of the Domain Committee IFIP IoT. She has published her work at numerous conferences and in journals, such as the *European Journal of Information Systems, Information Systems Journal, Information and Organization, Business Horizons, and Information Systems and E-business Management Journal*, and is co-author of The IoT Guide (www.iotguiden.se). Ulrika is also an appointed member of the advisory council to Sweden's national accreditation body, Swedac. She is passionate about creating knowledge about new technology and the opportunities and challenges that digitalization offers, both in terms of the emergence of new business logic and in the social implications that follow. Ulrika holds an A.B. in International Relations from Bryn Mawr College, USA, and a PhD in Information Systems from Umeå University.

Anthony Wong

Anthony has double degrees in Computer Science and Law from Monash University, Master of Laws in Media, Communications and IT from University of New South Wales (UNSW), and a Master of Intellectual Property from University Technology Sydney (UTS), Australia.

He has also held senior management positions in multinational corporations and government. His multidisciplinary career traversed legal practice, multinationals in both IT vendor and customer capacities, including with Philips, The Netherlands, as CIO of the Australian Tourist Commission during the Sydney 2000 Olympics, and led the digital transformation of Thomson in the Asia Pacific.

Anthony is the Managing Director of AGW Lawyers & Consultants, a multidisciplinary legal and advisory practice in many areas of law and technology across financial services, media and publishing, education, tourism, insurance, start-ups, business services and consulting, and the data and digitization industries.

He is Vice President of the International Federation for Information Processing (IFIP) and Vice Chair of IFIP IP3. He is Past President of the Australian Computer Society (ACS) and Past President of SEARCC.

Anthony is an industry thought leader and has served on the IT Industry Innovation Council for the Australian Government. He chaired the New South Wales (NSW) Government ICT Advisory Panel and served on the NSW Digital Transformation Taskforce.

He is a Fellow and Honorary Life Member of the ACS and a member of the International Technology Law Association (ITechLaw), Australian Society for Computers and Law, Australian Institute of Company Directors (AICD), International Association of Privacy Professionals (IAPP), and the Law Society of New South Wales.

He is a regular commentator and presenter on topical issues on various print and online media, radio, and TV, as well as a speaker at various national and international forums.

Contents

Challenge for Society of Scale and Speed of Technological Change

Vinton G. Cerf[(✉)]

Google, LLC, 1900 Reston Metro Plaza, Suite 1400, Reston, VA 20190, USA
vgcerf@gmail.com

Let us imagine that it is 1895. Telegraphy and telephony are well established. Common forms of transportation include ships, canals, railroads, horses and horse drawn carts. Automobiles are still a rarity but mass production lies about a decade ahead. A year ago, Guglielmo Marconi demonstrated short range radio transmission and this year has just shown that it works at ranges over two miles. Six years from now, he will demonstrate trans-Atlantic transmission and in 1912, the sinking of the Titanic will underscore the enormous importance of wireless telegraphy. Henri Becquerel is about to discover radioactivity. Einstein's four miraculous papers[1] will appear in just ten years. The Wright Brothers heavier-than-air Kittyhawk flight is only 8 years away. Charles Lindbergh will make his famous trans-Atlantic flight in 1927. John Logie Baird will demonstrate television ("Televisor") in early 1926.

While we may think of today's technology as speeding faster than we can keep up, it's fair to say that over 100 years ago, people's heads were spinning with new technologies also arriving with unexpected speed and effect. People, practices, laws and norms adapted to these new technologies and the products and services they enabled. Nor should we be surprised. Thinking of fire, the wheel, roads and aqueducts, water wheels, windmills and electric power, reaching back thousands of years in some cases, humanity has managed to accommodate and adapt to a wide range of inventions. It may be hubris to believe that today's technologies are somehow more profound and have had greater impact on society than today's latest developments.

When you are living in the maelstrom, however, it is not hard to feel as if change is overwhelming. This is especially true of inventions that serve as the basis for a cornucopia of consequential inventions. Digital technology, first with mechanical calculators, vacuum tubes but more recently with semiconductors since the 1947 invention of the transistor, has created an unprecedented opportunity for the creation of new products and services. The animating force behind these products is software. Programmable devices appear to have infinite malleability - limited only by what human intellect can program. Some forms of AI may even take over some of that task in the future!

Mainframe computers running in "batch" mode gave way to timesharing in the 1960s. By the early 1970s, packet-switched networks of computers emerged in the form of the ARPANET[2] which became the progenitor of the Internet[3] which was formally launched

---

[1] Brownian motion, photo-electric effect, special relativity and mass-energy equivalence.

[2] https://en.wikipedia.org/wiki/ARPANET [retrieved 8/27/2020].

[3] https://en.wikipedia.org/wiki/Internet [retrieved 8/27/2020].

© IFIP International Federation for Information Processing 2020
Published by Springer Nature Switzerland AG 2020
L. Strous et al. (Eds.): Unimagined Futures, IFIP AICT 555, pp. 1–4, 2020.
https://doi.org/10.1007/978-3-030-64246-4_1

into operation in January 1983 after a ten year development cycle. Commercial operation of Internet service began in the United States in 1989 with three networks (UUNET[4], PSINET[5], CERFNET[6]). In 1991, the World Wide Web was launched at CERN[7]. The MOSAIC[8] browser, with its graphical user interface, arrived from the National Center for Supercomputer Applications (NCSA)[9] in 1993. That, in turn, morphed into the Netscape Navigator[10] made popular by the Netscape Communications Corporation.

At this point in 1995, 100 years after our starting point in this essay, Internet-related companies, applications and technologies were rapidly proliferating. The so-called "dot-boom" was on with billions of dollars being thrown at startups that appeared to have some, often tenuous, relationship to the Internet. This came to an abrupt halt in April 2000 when most of these companies ran out of capital and had no revenue. But the Internet continued to grow. Companies like Google[11], Yahoo![12], MySpace[13] among many others continued to grow as did countless Internet Service Providers, and, often, cable television or telephone companies that had gotten into the Internet service business.

Going back into history, Martin Cooper, then at Motorola, demonstrated a handheld mobile phone in April 1973[14]. Of course, mobile telephony had a long history by that time, but this was the first handheld unit, thanks to miniaturization of components. About that time, Robert Metcalfe and David Boggs were inventing Ethernet[15] at Xerox PARC and Robert Kahn and I were meeting at Stanford to discuss the design of the Internet[16]. There must have been something in the air in 1973! Computer networking and mobile telephone evolved on independent paths for several decades until in 2007, Steve Jobs at Apple announced the iPhone[17]: a handheld smartphone that could interact with servers on the Internet by way of applications ("apps") running in the smartphone. These two technologies, Internet and the smartphone, were hypergolic. The smartphone made the Internet readily accessible from wherever you could get a mobile signal and the Internet made the smartphone more useful by supplying it with access to the world's knowledge, online.

In the thirteen years since the arrival of Apple's iPhone, many competing products have arrived and all of them have been increasing their processing and memory capacity, communication speeds and improving their accessories, notably cameras and motion

---

[4] https://en.wikipedia.org/wiki/UUNET [retrieved 8/27/2020].

[5] https://en.wikipedia.org/wiki/PSINet [retrieved 8/27/2020].

[6] https://en.wikipedia.org/wiki/PSINet [retrieved 8/27/2020].

[7] https://home.cern/ [retrieved 8/27/2020].

[8] https://en.wikipedia.org/wiki/Mosaic_(web_browser) [retrieved 8/27/2020].

[9] http://www.ncsa.illinois.edu/ [retrieved 8/27/2020].

[10] https://en.wikipedia.org/wiki/Netscape [retrieved 8/27/2020].

[11] https://en.wikipedia.org/wiki/Google [retrieved 8/27/2020].

[12] https://en.wikipedia.org/wiki/Yahoo! [retrieved 8/27/2020]

[13] https://en.wikipedia.org/wiki/Myspace [retrieved 8/27/2020].

[14] https://en.wikipedia.org/wiki/History_of_mobile_phones [retrieved 8/27/2020].

[15] https://en.wikipedia.org/wiki/Ethernet [retrieved 8/27/2020].

[16] https://www.internetsociety.org/internet/history-internet/brief-history-internet/   [retrieved 8/27/2020].

[17] https://en.wikipedia.org/wiki/IPhone [retrieved 8/27/2020].

sensors. They carry multiple radios to include 3G, 4G and 5G mobile telephone capability, Bluetooth, NFC[18] and Wi-Fi. But the most notable expansion has been the library of applications available for downloading. There are millions of applications. A recent statistic says there are 2.2 million apps for the iPhone and 2.8 million apps in the Google Playstore.[19]

This brings us to the key question: is innovation coming at us more rapidly than ever before? It is surely tempting to say so, but perhaps it just feels that way. The ease with which apps are built for smartphones, pages created for the World Wide Web, software is produced for Internet-enabled devices (Internet of Things[20]) all contribute to the feeling that we are rushing into a future in which we are being overwhelmed with change. There is some truth to this. In a "consumer economy" getting the next and newest thing is in some ways the reason the economy is sustainable or growing. New features can be added to software without necessarily changing hardware and that adds to the feeling and reality of rapid change. There is something Einsteinianly relative about this feeling. If software were delivered in the air from a fan, we could be standing still and the fan increasing in its speed making us feel like we are moving faster and faster when, in fact, we are standing still but the world is rushing past.

There are many reactions to this phenomenon. Some pine for the "good old days" when things did not seem to change so quickly. But see the opening paragraphs of this essay! Some people see this as a challenge to learn more and more quickly. Just-in-time learning is a skill and we can see interesting evidence of this phenomenon. A Google search quickly answers "how do I X?" for some value of X. I learned recently that "young folks" [that's everyone younger than I am which is almost everyone in the world now!] often turn to YouTube for advice. I tried this out recently when my wife and I decided we wanted to make Chinese eggplant; a spicy and delicious dish. We turned to YouTube: "How do you make spicy Chinese eggplant?", we asked. Instantly we found a 12 min video[21] showing us exactly how to do it. We followed directions. It was delicious!

This notion of just-in-time learning has implications that are relevant for our future. If our life spans are increasing, this implies that our work lives may extend for sixty or seventy years. We are not likely to learn enough in the first couple of decades of our lives to sustain our productivity and relevance for such a long period. We will have to learn new things if only to adapt to the new technologies that arise at a steady if not increasing pace. Learning online as needed has the advantage of immediate utility and relevance. This is not to say that a more organized form of learning is irrelevant. Rather, it suggests that online learning may be increasingly relevant. In mid-life it may not be feasible to drop everything and go back to school full time. Short courses and certificate training are useful alternatives. Self-guided and paced learning is increasingly feasible and available.

The 2020 COVID-19 pandemic has underscored the value and importance of online learning. At a time when "social distancing" is necessitated for health reasons, learning online has become a necessity. Universities are adapting to this. Georgia Institute of

---

[18] https://en.wikipedia.org/wiki/Near-field_communication [Retrieved 8/27/2020].

[19] https://buildfire.com/app-statistics/ [retrieved 8/27/2020].

[20] https://en.wikipedia.org/wiki/Internet_of_things [retrieved 8/27/2020].

[21] https://www.youtube.com/watch?v=q3V_ibwxBXg [retrieved 8/27/2020].

Technology's online masters program in applied systems engineering[22] is a good example. It is the same program as is taught in residential settings but costs much less per student because class sizes can be much larger. New universities have been created for online, large scale learning such as Udacity[23] and Coursera[24]. A quick search of the WWW for online degrees produces a plethora of responses. Universities are adapting rapidly to these new formats. With high probability, these systems will evolve to be increasingly student-centric with self-pacing and adaptive remediation becoming the norm.

So, where does that leave us in this debate over the pace of change? I think digital technology has enabled more rapid discovery and development in virtually all disciplines. We hear the term "computational-X" for many values of X: astronomy, biology, chemistry, linguistics, to name a few. The consequence is that we really are experiencing more rapid evolution of knowledge, tools, techniques, products and services. This need not lead to despair! This same technology is also helping us cope with the need for adaptation and learning. We will become all the more productive in consequence.

---

[22] https://info.pe.gatech.edu/pmase/ [retrieved 8/27/2020].

[23] https://www.udacity.com/ [retrieved 8/27/2020].

[24] https://www.coursera.org/ [retrieved 8/27/2020].

The Data Science Revolution

How Learning Machines Changed the Way We Work and Do Business

Wil M.P. van der Aalst[1,2]([✉])

[1] Process and Data Science, RWTH Aachen University, Aachen, Germany
wvdaalst@pads.rwth-aachen.de
[2] Fraunhofer FIT, Sankt Augustin, Germany
http://www.vdaalst.com

Abstract. Data science technology is rapidly changing the role of information technology in society and all economic sectors. Artificial Intelligence (AI) and Machine Learning (ML) are at the forefront of attention. However, data science is much broader and also includes data extraction, data preparation, data exploration, data transformation, storage and retrieval, computing infrastructures, other types of mining and learning, presentation of explanations and predictions, and the exploitation of results taking into account ethical, social, legal, and business aspects. This paper provides an overview of the field of data science also showing the main developments, thereby focusing on (1) the growing importance of learning from data (rather than modeling or programming), (2) the transfer of tasks from humans to (software) robots, and (3) the risks associated with data science (e.g., privacy problems, unfair or nontransparent decision making, and the market dominance of a few platform providers).

Keywords: Data science · Machine learning · Artificial Intelligence · Responsible data science · Big data

1 Introduction

The International Federation for Information Processing (IFIP) was established in 1960 under the auspices of UNESCO as a result of the first World Computer Congress held in Paris in 1959. This year we celebrate the 60th anniversary of IFIP. IFIP was created in 1960 because of the anticipated impact and transformative power of information technology. However, the impact of information technology over the past 60 years has been even larger than foreseen. Information technology has dramatically transformed the lives of individuals and businesses. Over the last 60 years, *data science*, i.e., extracting knowledge and insights from structured and unstructured data, has become the main driver of such transformations. In this paper, we reflect on the impact of data science and key developments.

© IFIP International Federation for Information Processing 2020
Published by Springer Nature Switzerland AG 2020
L. Strous et al. (Eds.): Unimagined Futures, IFIP AICT 555, pp. 5–19, 2020.
https://doi.org/10.1007/978-3-030-64246-4_2

In [2], data science is defined as follows: *"Data science is an interdisciplinary field aiming to turn data into real value. Data may be structured or unstructured, big or small, static or streaming. Value may be provided in the form of predictions, automated decisions, models learned from data, or any type of data visualization delivering insights. Data science includes data extraction, data preparation, data exploration, data transformation, storage and retrieval, computing infrastructures, various types of mining and learning, presentation of explanations and predictions, and the exploitation of results taking into account ethical, social, legal, and business aspects."* Data science can be seen as an umbrella term for machine learning, artificial intelligence, mining, Big data, visual analytics, etc. The term is not new. Turing award winner Peter Naur (1928–2016) first used the term 'data science' long before it was in vogue. In 1974, Naur wrote [15]: "A basic principle of data science, perhaps the most fundamental that may be formulated, can now be stated: The data representation must be chosen with due regard to the transformation to be achieved and the data processing tools available". In [15], Naur discusses 'Large Data Systems' referring to data sets stored on magnetic disks having a maximum capacity of a few megabytes. Clearly, the notion of what is large has changed dramatically since the early seventies, and will continue to change.

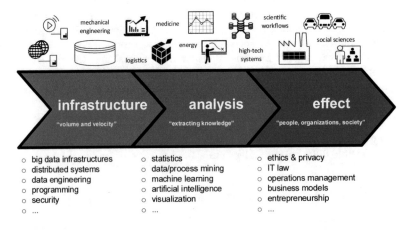

Fig. 1. Overview of the key ingredients of data science [4].

Figure 1 visualizes the above definition. The top part shows that data science can be applied in many different areas, i.e., most data science approaches are generic. The middle part shows that there are three main ingredients: *infrastructure* (concerned with the huge volume and incredible velocity of data), *analysis* (concerned with extracting knowledge using a variety of techniques), and *effect* (concerned the impact of data science on people, organizations, and society). The diagram shows the *interdisciplinary nature* of data science. As an example, take a self-driving car. To build a self-driving car one needs an *infrastructure* composed of sensors (camera, lidar, radar, etc.), hardware controllers, networking capabilities, powerful processing units, and *analysis* techniques for perception (e.g., convolutional neural networks), localization, prediction, planning, and control using this infrastructure. However, one also needs to consider the *effect*. The self-driving car has to be economically feasible and may require new business models. While creating such a car, one also needs to consider legal and ethical implications. In July 2016, Tesla reported the first fatality of a driver in a self-driving car triggering heated debates. Who is responsible when the car crashes? What decisions should be taken when a crash is unavoidable (e.g. protect passengers or pedestrians)? Who owns the data collected by the self-driving car? Due to the huge impact of data science on people, organizations, and society, many legal, ethical, and financial aspects come into play.

As Fig. 1 shows, the field of data science is broad, building on multiple scientific disciplines. How does data science relate to hyped terms such as Big data, Artificial Intelligence (AI), and Machine Learning (ML)? Big data seems to be out of fashion and AI and ML are the new buzzwords used in the media. AI may mean everything and nothing. On the one hand, the term AI roughly translates to "using data in an intelligent manner" looking at its use in the media. This means that everything in Fig. 1 is AI. On the other hand, the term is also used to refer to very specific approaches, such as deep neural networks [13]. The same applies to the term ML. All subfields of data mining (classification, clustering, patterns mining, regression, logistic regression, etc.) can be seen as forms of machine learning. However, ML is also used to refer to only deep learning.

John McCarthy coined the term AI in 1955 as "the science and engineering of making intelligent machines". Today, the field of AI is typically split in symbolic AI and non-symbolic AI. *Symbolic AI*, also known as Good Old Fashioned AI (GOFAI), uses high-level symbolic (i.e., human-readable) representations of problems, logic, and rules. Experts systems tend to use symbolic AI to make deductions and to determine what additional information it needs (i.e., what questions to ask) using human-readable symbols. The main disadvantage of symbolic AI is that the rules and knowledge have to be hand-coded. *Non-symbolic AI* does not aim for human-readable representations and explicit reasoning, and uses techniques imitating evolution and human learning. Example techniques include genetic algorithms, neural networks and deep learning. The two main disadvantages of non-symbolic AI are the need for a lot of training data and the problem of understanding why a particular result is returned. Symbolic AI is still not widely adopted in industry. Although non-symbolic AI performed worse than symbolic AI for many decades, by using back-propagation in multi-layer neural networks, non-symbolic AI started to outperform conventional approaches [13,17]. As a result, these techniques are now also used in industry for tasks such as speech recognition, automated translation, fraud detection, image recognition, etc.

The successes of non-symbolic AI are amazing. However, AI is only a small part of data science, often tailored towards specific tasks (e.g., speech recognition) and using specific models (e.g., deep convolutional neural networks). The same applies to ML (which is often considered to be a subfield of AI). When the term AI or ML is used in the media, this often refers to data mining, pattern/process mining, statistics, information retrieval, optimization, regression, etc.

This paper aims to 'demystify' data science, present key concepts, discuss important developments. We also reflect on the impact of data science on the way we work and do business. The paper is partly based on a keynote given at the IFIP World Computer Congress (WCC 2018) on 18 September 2018, in Poznan, Poland. It extends the corresponding keynote paper [4].

The remainder is organized as follows. Section 2 metaphorically discusses the four essential elements of data science: "water" (availability, magnitude, and different forms of data), "fire" (irresponsible uses of data and threats related to fairness, accuracy, confidentiality, and transparency), "wind" (the way data science can be used to improve processes), and "earth" (the need for data science research and education). Section 3 discusses the shift from modeling and programming to data-driven learning enabled by the abundance of data. Due to the uptake of data science, traditional jobs and business models will disappear and new ones will emerge. Section 4 reflects on these changes. Data science can make things cheaper, faster, and better. However, also negative side-effects are possible (see the "fire" element mentioned before). Therefore, Sect. 5 discusses the topic of responsible data science in the context of the growing dominance of digital platforms. Section 6 concludes this paper.

2   The Four Essential Ingredients of Data Science

In this section, we define the four essential elements of data science [4]. As metaphors, we use the classical four elements: "water", "fire", "wind", and "earth" (see Fig. 2). According to Empedocles, all matter is comprised of these four elements. Other ancient cultures had similar lists, sometimes also composed of more elements (e.g., earth, water, air, fire, and aether) that tried to explain the nature and complexity of all matter in terms of simpler substances. To explain the essence of data science, we use "water" as a placeholder for the availability of different forms of data, "fire" as a placeholder for irresponsible uses of data (e.g., threats to fairness, accuracy, confidentiality, and transparency), "wind" as a placeholder for the way that data science can be used to improve processes, and "earth" as a placeholder for education and research (i.e., the base of data science) underpinning all of this. Note that Fig. 2 complements Fig. 1, allowing us to emphasize specific aspects.

2.1   The "Water" of Data Science

The first essential element of data science ("water") is the data itself [4]. The exponential growth of data and data processing capabilities since the establishment of IFIP in 1960 is evident:

– Things are getting exponentially *cheaper*, e.g., the price of storage dropped from one million euros per MB in the 1960-ties to 0.00002 cents per MB today.

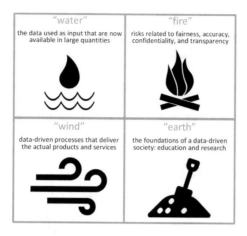

Fig. 2. The "water", "fire", "wind", and "earth" of data science [4].

- Things are getting exponentially *faster*, e.g., the number of floating-point operations per second increased from a few kFLOPS (10^3 floating-point operations per second) to hundreds of PFLOPS (10^{15} floating-point operations per second).
- Things are getting exponentially *smaller*, e.g., the size of a transistor decreased from a few centimeters (10^{-2} m) to a few nanometers (10^{-9} m).

The reductions in price and size and the increase in speed apply to *processing* (i.e., CPU and GPU processors), *storage*, and *communication*. A GPU may have thousands of processors and a company like Google has over one million servers.

The above numbers illustrate our increased capabilities to process large amounts of data. These are used to align the digital world and the physical world. For example, organizations are collecting 'events' at a large scale [2]. Events may take place inside a machine (e.g., an X-ray machine, an ATM, or baggage handling system), inside an enterprise information system (e.g., an order placed by a customer or the submission of a tax declaration), inside a hospital (e.g., the analysis of a blood sample), inside a social network (e.g., exchanging e-mails or twitter messages), inside a transportation system (e.g., checking in, buying a ticket, or passing through a toll booth), etc. The uptake of the so-called Internet of Things (IoT) resulted in many connected devices ranging from light bulbs to wearable heart monitors [18]. Events may be 'life events', 'machine events', or 'organization events'. These may be stored in traditional relational databases (e.g., Microsoft SQL Server, Oracle Database, MySQL, and IBM DB2), NoSQL databases (e.g., CouchDB, MongoDB, Cassandra, and HBase), or distributed ledgers using blockchain technology (e.g., Ethereum, NEO, Cardano). The term *Internet of Events* (IoE), coined in [1], refers to the omnipresence of event data in all application domains.

In 2001, Doug Laney introduced the first three V's describing challenges related to Big data: Volume, Velocity, and Variety [12]. Later, additional V's were added: Veracity, Variability, Visualization, Value, Venue, Validity, etc. The above refers to the first 'V' (Volume) describing the incredible scale of some data sources. The second 'V' (Velocity) refers to the speed of the incoming data that need to be processed. In many applications, it has become impossible to store all data and process it later. Such streaming data needs to be handled immediately. The third 'V' (Variety) refers to the different types of data coming from multiple sources. Structured data may be augmented by unstructured data (e.g. free text, audio, and video).

2.2   The "Fire" of Data Science

The second essential element of data science ("fire") refers to the dangers of using data in an irresponsible way [4]. Data abundance combined with powerful data science techniques has the potential to dramatically improve our lives by enabling new services and products, while improving their efficiency and quality. Many of today's scientific discoveries (e.g., in health) are already fueled by developments in statistics, mining, machine learning, artificial intelligence, databases, and visualization. At the same time, there are also great concerns about the use of data. Increasingly, customers, patients, and other stakeholders are concerned about irresponsible data use. Automated data-based decisions may be unfair or non-transparent. Confidential data may be shared unintentionally or abused by third parties.

When IFIP was created sixty years ago, one could not foresee the possible risks related to data science. The Facebook-Cambridge Analytica scandal in 2018 and many other scandals involving unacceptable uses of data heavily influenced public opinion. Also books such as "Weapons of Math Destruction: How Big Data Increases Inequality and Threatens Democracy" [16], created increased awareness of the risks associated with data science. The European General Data Protection Regulation (GDPR) [8] is a response to such risks. However, legislation such as GDPR may also inhibit certain applications. Hence, technological solutions involving distribution and encryption are needed. In Sect. 5, we elaborate further on the topic of responsible data science.

2.3   The "Wind" of Data Science

The third essential element of data science ("wind") is concerned with the way data and processes interact. Storing and processing data is typically not a goal in itself. Data are there to support processes. Data science can help organizations to be more effective, to provide a better service, to deliver faster, and to do all of this at lower costs. This applies to logistics, production, transport, healthcare, banking, insurance, and government.

Data science can be used to *improve tasks within the process*; e.g., certain checks can be automated using a neural network trained on many examples. Data science can also be used to *improve the design or management of the whole process*, e.g., using process mining, one can identify root causes for specific bottlenecks and deviations. Data science can also be used to *create new products and services*, e.g., Spotify is able to recommend music based on the listener's preferences.

Clearly, there is a tradeoff between "water" and "wind". Giving up privacy concerns may lead to better processes, services, and products.

2.4   The "Earth" of Data Science

The fourth essential element of data science ("earth") is concerned with the foundations of a data-driven society: *education* and *research* [4]. Education (in every sense of the word) is one of the fundamental factors in the development of data science. Data science education is needed at all levels. People need to be aware of the way algorithms make decisions that may influence their lives. Hyped terms such as Big data, Artificial Intelligence (AI), and Machine Learning (ML) are not well understood and may mean anything and nothing (see Sect. 1). Some examples of phenomena that illustrate the need for education.

- *Correlation is not the same as causality.* It may be that ice cream sales and crime rates strongly correlate. However, this does not imply that one causes the other. The so-called hidden variable is the weather. Higher temperatures lead to higher ice cream sales and higher crime rates. It makes no sense to try to reduce crime by putting a ban on ice cream sales.
- *Simpson's paradox.* It may be that within different subsets of data a variable has a positive influence, whereas it as a negative influence when considering all the data. For example, in each study program, females are more likely to pass. However, when considering all students, males are more likely to pass. Another example is that for both young patients and old patients, exercising has a positive effect on one health. However, when looking at all patients, there is a negative correlation between exercising and health.
- *Hacking deep neural networks.* Given a well-trained neural network that is able to separate cars and horses, it is possible to add a bit of 'noise' to the images (invisible to the human eye) such that horses are classified as cars and cars are classified as horses. The same applies to speech recognition.
- *Homomorphic encryption.* It is possible to do computations on encrypted ciphertexts such that the encrypted result, when decrypted, matches the result of the operations as if they had been performed on the non-encrypted data.
- *Secure multi-party computation.* It is possible to jointly compute a function over multiple parties that all keep their data private. Hence, one can apply data science techniques without sharing the actual data.

The above example phenomena and the oversimplified coverage of AI in the media illustrate that policy and decision makers need to know more about data science. This cannot be left to "the market" or solved through half-hearted legislation like the GDPR [8]. To remain competitive, countries should invest in data science capabilities. This can only be realized through education and research.

3   Learning Versus Modeling and Programming

Currently, many fields of science are undergoing a paradigm shift. A new generation of scientists emerges that focuses on the analysis and interpretation of data rather than models detached from data. This shift is caused by the availability of data and easy-to-use data-science tooling.

The fields of science can be roughly split into:

- *Formal sciences* (logic, mathematics, statistics, theoretical computer science, etc.) that are based on a priori knowledge or assumptions that are independent of real/life observations.
- *Natural sciences* (physics, chemistry, biology, etc.) that study natural phenomena (atoms, molecules, gravity, magnetism, cells, planets, etc.).
- *Social sciences* (psychology, sociology, economics, literature, etc.) that study human and societal behavior.
- *Applied sciences* (engineering, medicine, software engineering, etc.) that apply scientific knowledge to practical applications (e.g., creating systems).

Natural, social, and applied sciences heavily depend on observations of natural phenomena, people, and systems. In *inductive research*, the goal of a researcher is to infer models and theories (i.e., theoretical concepts and patterns) from observed data. In *deductive research*, the goal of the researcher is to test models and theories using new empirical data. The importance of data has grown in all of these fields. This is a direct result of our ability to observe natural phenomena, people, and systems much more directly.

Consider, for example, the social sciences with research methods such as surveys (i.e., questionnaires), laboratory experiments, field experiments, interviews, and case studies. Traditional surveys may have low response rates and a sample bias (the set of participants that was invited and accepted may not be representative). Laboratory experiments are often too small and also have a sample bias. Interviews and case studies tend to be subjective. Therefore, most scientific results cannot be reproduced. This is commonly referred to as the "replication crisis" [11]. Therefore, younger social science researchers prefer to use research methods that use objective larger-scale observations. For example, directly recording the activities of participants rather than relying on self-reporting or more field experiments with many subjects rather than lab experiments with a only few subjects.

Another example is the uptake of computational biology and bioinformatics where large collections of biological data, such as genetic sequences, cell populations or protein samples are used to make predictions or discover new models and theories.

Also the field of computer science is changing markedly. There seems to be less emphasis on theoretical computer science due to the desire to relate models and theories to real-world phenomena. It is no longer fashionable to create new modeling languages and to prove properties in self-created artificial settings. Instead, sub-disciplines related to data science are rapidly growing in the number of students and researchers. Automated learning (e.g., machine learning, different forms of mining, and artificial intelligence) are replacing parts of programming. Rules are no longer programmed but learned from data. This is changing computer science. For example, how to verify the correctness a system that uses neural networks?

The shift from modeling and programming to automated learning is affecting science and also the economies that build upon it. Consider for example the way that marketing changed. Today's marketeer is expected to have data science skills. In fact, many professions have become much more data-driven or are about disappear (see next section).

4 Machines Versus People

The uptake of data science will continue to change the way we work, the way we move, the way we interact, the way we care, the way we learn, and the way we socialize [4]. As a result, many professions will cease to exist [9,10,14]. At the same time, new jobs, products, services, and opportunities emerge.

The frontier between the tasks performed by humans and those performed by machines and algorithms is continuously moving and changing global labor markets. In [9], Frey and Osborne provide predictions for the computerization of 702 occupations. They estimate that 47% of jobs in the US will be replaced by (software) robots.

In [14] three types of roles are identified: stable roles (work that remains), new roles (new types of work that did not exist before), and redundant roles (work that is taken over by e.g. robots). Examples of redundant roles are clerical work (e.g., data entry), factory work (e.g., assembly), postal service, and cashiers. Of the new roles mentioned in [14], most are related to data science.

In [10] three waves of automation are predicted: (1) *algorithmic wave* (replacing simple computational tasks in data-driven sectors such as banking), (2) *augmentation wave* (replacing more complex clerical work and materials handling closed environments such as warehouses), and (3) *autonomous wave* (replacing physical work in transport, construction, and healthcare). The algorithmic wave is currently in full swing. The augmentation wave has started with the uptake of *Robotic Process Automation* (RPA) and robots in production and warehouse. This wave is likely to come to full maturity in the next decade. The autonomous wave uses technologies that are already under development, but, according to [10], will only come to full maturity on an economy-wide scale in the2030 s.

As a concrete example, consider the uptake of *Robotic Process Automation* (RPA) [5]. RPA software provided by vendors such as UIPath, Automation Anywhere, and Blue Prism provides software robots (bots) replacing humans. In the 1990-ties Workflow Management (WFM) software already aimed to realize Straight Through Processing (STP), i.e., handling cases with no or little human involvement. However, in many cases, this was not cost-effective because existing systems needed to be changed. Moreover, WFM often failed because of a limited understanding of the complexity of the actual processes performed by people.

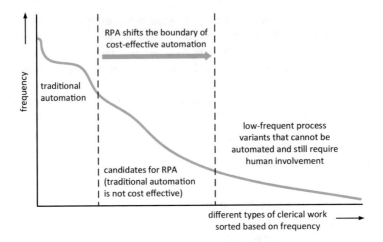

Fig. 3. Robotic Process Automation (RPA) has lowered the threshold for process automation [5].

The key difference between RPA and traditional WFM is that RPA does not aim to replace existing (back-end) information systems. Instead, software robots interact with the existing information systems in the same way as humans do. RPA software interacts with the pre-existing applications through the user interface directly replacing humans, i.e., automation is realized by taking over tasks from workers without the back-end systems knowing. A typical RPA scenario is a sequence of copy-and-paste actions normally performed by a human. Compared to WFM, RPA lowers the threshold for automation. As shown in Fig. 3, the focus of traditional automation is on high-frequent clerical work. For less frequent work, automation is not cost-effective. RPA shifts the boundary where automation is still cost-effective. Machine learning, artificial intelligence, and process mining are enabling technologies making RPA possible. The software robots need to learn from humans and need to be monitored continuously. Process mining [2] can be used to identify repeating work. Moreover, if a software robot malfunctions due to technical glitches, exceptions, changing user interfaces, or changing contextual factors, then this can be detected using process mining. Machine learning and artificial intelligence can be used to learn specific tasks. In more advanced applications of RPA, work is flexibly distributed over workers and software robots. For example, tasks are initially performed by robots and are escalated to workers the moment there is a complication or exception. Similarly, workers can hand off work to robots using an 'auto-complete' option. Moreover, the RPA solution may adapt due to changes in the underlying process (e.g., concept drift). This illustrates that the border between humans and (software) robots will continue to shift.

Reports such as [9,10,14] analyze the impact for specific groups (e.g., based on gender, education, or nationality). Although it is difficult to predict such phenomena accurately, it is clear that the impact of data science on the work of people is accelerating and will be larger than ever before.

5 Responsible Data Science in a Platform Economy

The distribution of work between humans, machines, and algorithms is changing due to the uptake of data science. Moreover, the growing importance of data is also changing the economy and leads to new concerns related to privacy and fairness.

In recent years we have witnessed the rise of the platform economy [6]. The world's most valuable public companies are five American technology firms: Microsoft, Amazon, Apple, Alphabet (Google), and Facebook. These companies are closely followed by Chinese tech giants such as Alibaba, Tencent, Baidu, and Xiaomi, and many more US-based internet companies such as Netflix, eBay, Uber, Salesforce, and Airbnb. These organizations were able to grow extremely fast due to the digital platforms they provide. Some (e.g., Amazon, Alibaba, Airbnb, Uber, and Baidu) provide a transaction platform that matches supply and demand, others provide a technical infrastructure that other people can build upon (e.g., the App stores of Google and Apple), and some provide both (e.g., Amazon also offers cloud services). Successful digital platforms have the characteristic that they tend to grow very fast and, in the end, often one winner remains. For example, Amazon and Alibaba are dominating the way we buy products, Google is controlling the way we search, and Facebook is controlling the way we socialize. Apple, Alphabet, and Microsoft are controlling the platforms we use (iOS, Android, and Windows). After a platform becomes the market leader, it is very difficult to compete for organizations that started later, e.g., for a new company it is difficult (if not impossible) to compete with Google's search engine or with Amazon's marketplace. Large tech companies use profits generated with one platform to create other platforms. See, for example, the current competition to become the leading digital platform for smart homes (e.g., Amazon Alexa, Apple Homekit, Google Assistant, Philips Hue, and Samsung SmartThings). Often "the winner takes it all" due to low marginal transaction costs and so-called network effects [6]. The resulting monopoly may stifle innovation and makes society dependent on a few technology providers. Moreover, the platform providers may use their profits to extend their platforms in other directions. For example, Google is using its profits from search engine marketing to invest in many other services and products (e.g., autonomous driving) and Amazon is using its marketplace to promote its own products (smartphones, televisions, speakers, TV-series, diapers, etc.).

Next to the large-scale economic concerns, there are also smaller-scale concerns impacting individuals. The *Responsible Data Science* (RDS) initiative initiated by the author in 2015, aims to address problems related to *fairness, accuracy, confidentiality*, and *transparency* [3]. Figure 4 shows the key challenges of RDS:

- *Data science without prejudice* – How to avoid unfair conclusions even if they are true?
- *Data science without guesswork* – How to answer questions with a guaranteed level of accuracy?

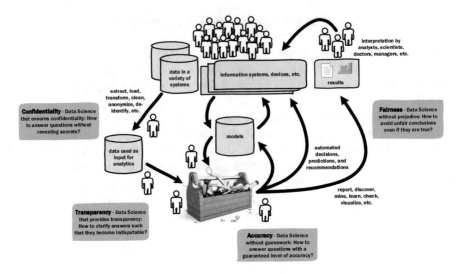

Fig. 4. *Fairness, Accuracy, Confidentiality,* and *Transparency* (FACT) are the main concerns of *Responsible Data Science* (RDS).

– *Data science that ensures confidentiality* – How to answer questions without revealing secrets?
– *Data science that provides transparency* – How to clarify answers such that they become indisputable?

To sustain the use of data science, it will become increasingly important to address concerns related to fairness, accuracy, confidentiality, and transparency.

Data science techniques need to ensure *fairness*: Automated decisions and insights should not be used to discriminate in ways that are unacceptable from a legal or ethical point of view. This may conflict with the goal of applying data science, e.g., discriminating between students that will be successful in their studies or not, discriminating between customers that will be able to pay back the loan or not, or discriminating between patients that will benefit from treatment or not. These decisions can all be seen as classification problems: The goal is to explain a response variable (e.g., the person will pay back the loan) in terms of predictor variables (e.g., credit history, employment status, age, etc.). Ideally, the learned model explains the response variable in terms of predictor variables. However, these may correlate with sensitive attributes such as gender, nationality, age, etc. As a result, the learned classifier may effectively reject cases from certain groups of persons. This explains the question "How to avoid unfair conclusions even if they are true?".

Data science techniques also need to ensure *accuracy*: Most data science techniques return an answer even when there is not enough evidence in the data. When using many variables relative to the number of instances, classification may result in complex rules overfitting the data [3]. This is often referred to as the curse of dimensionality: As dimensionality increases, the number of combinations grows so fast that the available data become sparse. With a fixed number of instances, the predictive power reduces as the dimensionality increases. Using cross-validation most findings (e.g., classification rules) will get rejected. However, if there are many findings, some may survive cross-validation by sheer luck.

Data science techniques also need to ensure *confidentiality*: The results should not reveal certain types of personal or otherwise sensitive information. The importance of protecting personal data is widely acknowledged and supported by legislation such as the General Data Protection Regulation (GDPR) [7] which states that *"The principles of data protection should apply to any information concerning an identified or identifiable natural person. Personal data which have undergone pseudonymisation, which could be attributed to a natural person by the use of additional information should be considered to be information on an identifiable natural person. To determine whether a natural person is identifiable, account should be taken of all the means reasonably likely to be used, such as singling out, either by the controller or by another person to identify the natural person directly or indirectly. To ascertain whether means are reasonably likely to be used to identify the natural person, account should be taken of all objective factors, such as the costs of and the amount of time required for identification, taking into consideration the available technology at the time of the processing and technological developments. The principles of data protection should therefore not apply to anonymous information, namely information which does not relate to an identified or identifiable natural person or to personal data rendered anonymous in such a manner that the data subject is not or no longer identifiable."* Organizations that violate the the GDPR can be fined to up to 20 million euro or up to 4% of the annual worldwide turnover. The regulations have been criticized for the administrative overhead they generate and the unclear compliance requirements.

There are many techniques to anonymize data, e.g., data masking, generalization, pseudonymization, swapping, perturbation, and sampling. The problem is that also anonymized data may unintentionally reveal sensitive information, e.g., by combining results and background information. There are also more advanced approaches using (homomorphic) encryption or secure multi-party computation. Unfortunately, legislation and policy makers are lagging behind. Therefore, confidentiality concerns may lead to inaccurate, non-optimal, and even unfair decision making [3].

Finally, data science techniques need to ensure *transparency*: It should be clear how the data were processed and that the stakeholders correctly understand the results. Often results highly depend on data cleaning, selection, and parameters of the techniques used. It is easy to change the outcome by altering the analysis-pipeline. Moreover, users that do not understand the phenomena described in Sect. 2.4 will have difficulties interpreting data science results accurately. Black-box machine learning techniques such as deep neural nets provide results (e.g., decisions) without explanation. In many application domains this is unacceptable (e.g., sending people to prison, rejecting job applications, or medical decisions). Explainable AI refers to methods and techniques enhancing artificial intelligence such that the results of the solution can be understood by human experts. However, explanations may be very complex and full transparency may not always be possible or required.

The above challenges show that there is a need for data science techniques that are responsible (i.e., "green") by design. This will be one of the main data science challenges of the coming years.

6   Conclusion

Data science has become one of the main ingredients of information processing and is changing the way we use and think about IT. Data science includes data extraction, data preparation, data exploration, data transformation, storage and retrieval, computing infrastructures, various types of mining and learning, and the presentation of explanations and predictions. Moreover, given the impact of data science, also ethical, social, legal, and business aspects play a major role. The multidisciplinary nature makes data science particularly challenging.

In this paper, we used the classical four elements ("water", "fire", "wind", and "earth") as metaphors for the essential ingredients of data science. Moreover, we zoomed in on the growing importance of learning from data (rather than modeling or programming) and the transfer of tasks from humans to (software) robots. We also elaborated on the risks associated with data science, e.g., the dominance of digital platforms and concerns related to fairness, accuracy, confidentiality, and transparency.

In 1943, IBM's president, Thomas J Watson, apparently said: "I think there is a world market for about five computers." Up until the 1950-ties many people thought that a handful of computers per country would suffice. This illustrates that, in 1960, the year that International Federation for Information Processing (IFIP) was established, it was impossible to foresee the importance of data science. However, data science has become the main driver of transformation in society and business, and is likely to remain a key topic for IFIP in the next 60 years.

Acknowledgments. We thank the Alexander von Humboldt (AvH) Stiftung for supporting our research.

References

1. van der Aalst, W.M.P.: Data scientist: the engineer of the future. In: Mertins, K., Bénaben, F., Poler, R., Bourrières, J.-P. (eds.) Enterprise Interoperability VI. PIC, vol. 7, pp. 13–26. Springer, Cham (2014). https://doi.org/10.1007/978-3-319-04948-9_2
2. van der Aalst, W.M.P.: Process Mining: Data Science in Action. Springer-Verlag, Berlin (2016)
3. van der Aalst, W.M.P.: Responsible data science: using big data in a "people friendly" manner. In: Hammoudi, S., Maciaszek, L., Missikoff, M., Camp, O., Cordiero, J. (eds.) Enterprise Information Systems. Lecture Notes in Business Information Processing, vol. 291, pp. 3–28. Springer-Verlag, Berlin (2017)

4. van der Aalst, W.M.P.: Responsible data science in a dynamic world: the four essential elements of data science. In: Strous, L., Cerf, V.G. (eds.) IFIPIoT 2018. IAICT, vol. 548, pp. 3–10. Springer, Cham (2019). https://doi.org/10.1007/978-3-030-15651-0_1

5. Scheppler, B., Weber, C.: Robotic process automation. Informatik Spektrum **43**(2), 152–156 (2020). https://doi.org/10.1007/s00287-020-01263-6

6. van der Aalst, W.M.P., Hinz, O., Weinhardt, C.: Big digital platforms - growth, impact, and challenges. Bus. Inf. Syst. Eng. **61**(6), 645–648 (2019)

7. Council of the European Union: General Data Protection Regulation (GDPR). Regulation (EU) 2016/679 of the European Parliament and of the Council of 27 April 2016 on the protection of natural persons with regard to the processing of personal data and on the free movement of such data, and repealing Directive 95/46/EC (2016)

8. European Commission: Proposal for a Regulation of the European Parliament and of the Council on the Protection of Individuals with Regard to the Processing of Personal Data and on the Free Movement of Such Data (General Data Protection Regulation). 9565/15, 2012/0011 (COD) (2015)

9. Frey, C.B., Osborne, M.A.: The future of employment: how susceptible are jobs to computerisation? Technol. Forecast. Soc. Chang. **114**(C), 254–280 (2017)

10. Hawksworth, J., Berriman, R., Goel, S.: Will robots really steal our jobs? An international analysis of the potential long term impact of automation. Technical report, PricewaterhouseCoopers (2018)

11. Ioannidis, J.P.A.: Why most published research findings are false. PLoS Med. **2**, e124 (2005)

12. Laney, D.: 3D data management: controlling data volume, velocity, and variety (research note 949). Technical report, META Group (2001)

13. Wick, C.: Deep learning. Informatik-Spektrum **40**(1), 103–107 (2016). https://doi.org/10.1007/s00287-016-1013-2

14. Leopold, T.A., Ratcheva, V., Zahidi, V.: The future of jobs report. Technical report, Centre for the New Economy and Society, World Economic Forum (2018)

15. Naur, P.: Concise Survey of Computer Methods. Akademisk Forlag, Kobenhaven (1974)

16. O'Neil, C.: Weapons of Math Destruction: How Big Data Increases Inequality and Threatens Democracy. Crown Publishing Group, New York (2016)

17. Rumelhart, D.E., Hinton, G., Williams, R.J.: Learning representations by back-propagating errors. Nature **323**, 533–536 (1986)

18. Strous, L., Cerf, V.G. (eds.): IFIPIoT 2018. IAICT, vol. 548. Springer, Cham (2019). https://doi.org/10.1007/978-3-030-15651-0

The Future of AI or AI for the Future

Eunika Mercier-Laurent[(✉)] ![ORCID]

Chair IFIP TC12, University of Reims Champagne Ardenne, Reims, France
eunika.mercier-laurent@univ-reims.fr

Abstract. The third hype of AI and enthusiasm for applying last techniques in all fields raise great interest and some important questions on the future directions in AI research and applications. Guiding by the principle of combing the best from human and computers capacities this chapter lists some important challenges to face and related directions in AI research. Multiple interrelated crises such as natural disasters, pandemics and other generated by humans require new approaches, combining existing techniques and set new directions for research. This chapter presents briefly the Artificial General Intelligence (AGI) concept and the challenges to face in sustainability, smart resources management, future connectivity, industry, agriculture, health, economy and education. The presented vision for the future of AI includes both researchers' dreams and emergencies.

Keywords: Artificial intelligence · Future · Planet protection

1 Artificial General Intelligence or/and AI for Human Purpose?

The third hype of AI triggered some trends, but above all, new definitions such as narrow AI and large AI, weak and strong AI, unconscious and conscious AI [1, 2]. All these new definitions are efforts to split AI into communities, while in fact intelligence is a whole system.

Like the first generation of AI founders, some researchers still work on trying to build a machine more intelligent than humans are. They claim to be able to build Artificial General Intelligence [3]. In his provocative video entitled: Machines playing God, Tegmark [4, 5] reduces AI to deep learning. However, what he mentions as future work has been already developed since 1970s by researchers in Machine Learning such as Michalski, Quinlan (EBG, generalization from examples) and some others [6].

Some build humanoid robots, but is it a priority in the world today while we have increasing number of unemployed and homeless? Or for super-intelligent killer-robots and drones [7]?

Do we need super-intelligence? What will be the place of humans in the artificial supra-intelligent society [4]?

Can such AI help facing today's complex challenges, mostly generated by human activities or influence people to be respectful?

Fighting Covid 19 pandemic, managing the economic crisis generated by confinement, understanding the new virus and elaborating vaccine are priorities. How can AI assist us in managing the Planet and biosphere protection?

L. Strous et al. (Eds.): Unimagined Futures, IFIP AICT 555, pp. 20–37, 2020.
https://doi.org/10.1007/978-3-030-64246-4_3

According to experts, we entered to Anthropocene epoch [8] and it is urgent to multiply the efforts to protect our planet Earth. It requires minimizing our footprint by minimizing the use of energy [9] and water and minimizing all kind of pollution in order to preserve the air we breathe, water we drink and quality of food. All fields of human activity are involved: growing cities, transportation, technology with race for performance, agriculture, health, industry, etc. The current situation requires evaluation and monitoring of the impact of human activities.

This chapter discusses two possible futures – AGI and AI for human and planet purpose.

1.1 Four Generations of AI

While Aristotle, Archimedes, Descartes and Leibnitz have laid theoretical foundations for AI, Norbert Wiener [10], Warren McCulloch, Walter Pitts, Donald Hebb [11] and Ludwig von Bertalanffy [12] have introduced cybernetics, artificial neural networks and a base for evolutionary algorithms before the official birth of AI in 1956. Alan Turing proposed the famous test in 1950.

First generation of AI is linked with the beginning of computers. Some call this period Early enthusiasm (1950–1970). First robot, called Perceptron, chess game, LISP, the first AI programming language designed by John McCarthy inspired the work on object programming and triggered the **second generation** of AI, those of Knowledge-based AI that has begun in the 1960s.

Object programming languages, Natural Language Processing (Prolog), various knowledge representation models, Case-based reasoning, Knowledge discovery techniques, constraint programming were born between 1970s and 1990. Many successful applications (1980–1994) demonstrated the usefulness of AI that since has been embedded in many applications in all fields [13].

In the middle of the 1990s Internet became the star and AI was temporarily shelved. Some talk about AI Winter (1995–2012).

Third generation of AI was born in 2012 from the necessity of exploring the exponentially growing amount of data generated by among others electronic commerce and social networks. This generation will not be possible without previous research and applications of known AI techniques such as Artificial Neural Networks enhanced with better computer performance, improvement of robots, humanoid robots, drones and Internet of Things (IoT).

Fourth generation is coming. It will combine deep learning exploration of unstructured data and knowledge-based AI to obtain the robust AI systems able to provide decision support and AI Systems as a service [14].

In his video John Launchbury (DARPA) illustrates the differences between three generations of AI (he forgot the first) by the capacities of Perceiving, Learning, Abstracting and Reasoning [15]. However, he forgot to include symbolic machine learning, initiated in the early 1970 by Ryszard S. Michalski, John R. Quinlan, Jaime G. Carbonell, Tom M. Mitchell and some others [6]. Figure 1 presents his 3rd generation (in fact 4th) of AI that will balance all four components.

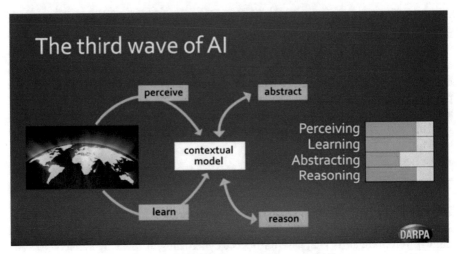

Fig. 1. DARPA third wave of AI, source [15]

2 Artificial General Intelligence

The founders of the AI fields were largely concerned with the creation of hardware and software acting as human, even more intelligent. Mark Gubrud proposed the expression of Artificial General Intelligence in military context [16]. What is the progress from General Problem Solver (Newell et al. 1959)? Certainly, computers' performance allows quicker processing but the available systems still lack intelligence. Forbes states "AI systems that can diagnose cancers with greater accuracy than human doctors, there are many other fields where specialized artificial intelligence is replicating human-like reasoning and cognition." [17]. Did Forbes journalist never try googling image search? The quality of diagnosis however depends on the accuracy of data used for learning model and on the quality of learning algorithm. If the accuracy is similar to the results of available search engines, a diagnosis can be erroneous, while experienced oncologist still diagnoses better than those by the best algorithm. Deep learning combined with expert system may give better results. Some work on this kind of applications was done in the late 1980s in the Faculté de Médecine, Paris.

Another limitation of deep learning is the exploring of past data to predict the future. It may work in linear world, but not in today's dynamic one.

One of the main actors of AGI is Open AI [18]. They focus on the development of highly autonomous systems that outperform humans and will be beneficial for humanity. They aim to build safe and beneficial AGI, but also consider their mission has been fulfilled if their work aids others to achieve this outcome. Among their projects, we find the following:

- a neural network based generator of music; similar work has been done by Sony CSL [19]
- Components of robots, robot hand able to solve Rubik's cube, robots learning dexterity
- exploring multi-agents learning capabilities

- automated text generation
- learning sentiments

They explore mainly various deep learning algorithms. This research lacks examples of overall projects combining all these elements in an artificial intelligent system. Exploring multi-agent learning capability is a topic of research since the beginning of multi-agent systems in the late 1980s. Automated text generation has been studied and practiced since the invention of Prolog in 1970 by Alain Colmerauer team, Marseille.

Military research is more advanced, but most of the projects are confidential. We can only guess what is inside of Kalashnikov robots, UAV and other military advanced equipment [20].

Before designing AGI systems, it is vital to understand what intelligence is and how such systems can effectively collaborate with humans.

In 2005 Kurtzweil states, "Singularity is Near". Robots still have no intuition and are unable to hypnotize human, but is it necessary?

Some researchers focus on the simulation of the brain. Is it possible to simulate something if we have only partial knowledge about it?

Neuroimaging technology can deliver images. Experiments such as specific activity in MRI helps discovering some functionalities [21]. The brain is NOT just a super-computer, it is much more than that and works in interaction with the other organs. According to multidisciplinary scientists [22], the brain is a system component of our body and interacts with the other organs. Some talk about connection between three "brains" equipped with neurons: brain, heart and gut or stomach, each plays a role in decision making.

Artificial neural network is simple implementation of biological neurons, which are much more complex.

The Human Brain Project [23] has begun in 2013. Sponsored by European Union it connects scientific and industrial researchers to advance our knowledge in the fields of neuroscience, computing, and brain-related medicine. It is composed of following platforms:

- Neuroinformatics (access to shared brain data)
- Brain Simulation (replication of brain architecture and activity on computers)
- High Performance Analytics and Computing (providing the required computing and analytics capabilities)
- Medical Informatics (access to patient data, identification of disease signatures)
- Neuromorphic Computing (development of brain-inspired computing)
- Neurorobotics (use of robots to test brain simulations)

The same year, 2013, White House announced the Brain Initiative. It is supported by several federal agencies as well as dozens of technology firms, academic institutions, scientists and other key contributors to the field of neuroscience [24].

The impact of such research may be beneficial in medicine, to cure serious diseases such as Alzheimer, other brain defects and in psychiatry.

In science fiction, AGI is associated with consciousness, sentience, sapiens and self-awareness. The current research is in its infancy for such capacities. Marketing is much more interested in "sentiment" analysis and eye tracking than in providing us with products that we really need. They never ask if someone did not find what he/she looked for. Is it so difficult to do or are they not interested?

Considering that it is more important to empower humanity by combining the best of human and best of computer we focus on AI for human and planet purpose.

3 AI for Human and Planet Purpose – What We Expect from Future AI?

Another trend in AI research and applications is collaborative intelligence human-machine. "*Computers are incredibly fast, accurate and stupid. Human beings are incredibly slow, inaccurate and brilliant. Together they are powerful beyond imagination*". This citation attributed to Einstein proposes certainly better future than those transforming human into slave of "intelligent" systems or into "shopping machine".

Years ago AI researchers and practitioners invented and have since experimented with various AI techniques such as natural language programming, expert systems, case based reasoning, constraint programming and multi-agent systems (Fig. 2).

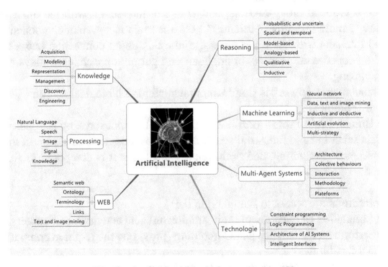

Fig. 2. Available AI techniques, source [9]

These techniques combined into hybrid systems and applied knowingly and wisely, allow solving the majority of complex problems generated by present challenges. However, it requires prior deep problem understanding and experience in applying the adequate AI techniques.

Today AI is "inside" numerous applications in all fields. The future of AI has to consider all these experiences to progress in right direction.

Between 1995 and today the AI research was awoken to business goals – sell more and quicker. This engine motivated development and improvement of various deep learning algorithms [25]. Most believe that it is possible to solve all kind of problems using deep learning; it has become "general problem solver" of the moment. Applied to navigation data to deduce client experience, for face recognition, eye tracking, chat bots, automated translation these algorithms give satisfactory results if the training set is correctly elaborated and if the algorithm is able to improve itself. For example, DeepL translator can learn from users who can correct the provided result if they know well a given language.

Nevertheless, sometimes the challenge is to find what is not in data. Life and intelligence is not about data.

In parallel, research in robotics progressed thanks to the innovation in electronics and miniaturization. The disasters such as Tchernobyl and Fukushima demonstrated the need for small flying robots able to evaluate the damage and act in the places that human cannot access. Similarly, for other risk management such as earthquakes and typhoons, where drones and flying robots provide great help to the human.

Surgical robots equipped with vision systems are also of significant help, especially in the situation when high precision is required. Disinfecting robots and vehicles demonstrated their usefulness during Covid 19 pandemics.

Industry 4.0 implemented the principle of collaboration human-machine in co-bots [26] and some factories of the future, such as those of Schneider Electric in Vaudreuil. AI powers the cyber physical systems and digital twins [27] (Fig. 3).

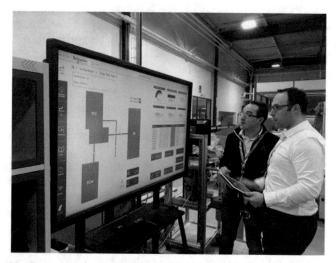

Fig. 3. Schneider factory of the future, Vaudreuil, source Schneider Electric [28]. https://www. lejournaldesentreprises.com/normandie/article/au-vaudreuil-le-numerique-transforme-lusine-sch neider-electric-228365. © Schneider Electric

Intuition and imagination combined with quick access to world base of problem solving give certainly better results than asking Sophia robot. We will still need truly intelligent personal assistants able to learn with the user, not necessary Alexa, Siri or more sophisticated robot.

In the nearest future, the AI approach to problem solving and combining deep learning with knowledge-based AI may bring significant help in many fields. It is very important and much more useful and ethical to build systems combining the best of human and of computer capacities instead of trying to reproduce human intelligence.

Deep understanding of inter-influences of human activity on environment may help finding acceptable co-designed solutions for preserving our biosphere and decelerating the Planet decline. (AI for sustainability)

Competition promoted by various ranking systems and research limited to a given field only are the barriers to progress by more collaborative and multidisciplinary research.

Technological innovation makes our lives easier. However, the progress without considering the impacts of human activities led to degradation of our living conditions. Many factors affect the sustainability. One of them is quick technological progress, considered as powerful engine of economy. It brings many benefits for humanity, but contributes also to Planet Crisis. Computers, smartphones, IoT and other devices are quickly outdated. The combination of various communicating software requires "up-to-date" hardware to run correctly. Most of hardware are not eco-designed and need raw material that has become scarce. Despite the large introduction of Corporate Social Responsibility, some companies still practice planned obsolescence to generate more revenues.

Social networks and various applications generate an exponential amount of data stored in data centers that need cooling. Fortunately, some apply circular energy to reduce impact on environment, but still those in Scandinavian countries clearly contribute to the rise of temperature and melting of ice.

What do we have that can be reused/improved and what needs to be invented?

3.1 Challenges to Face

Among the challenges for humans and for planet: fix existing disaster and make IT smarter and greener.

After health, time is probably one of the most important assets. Traditional IT can be smarter with AI inside. In her invited talk to 6th AI4KM, Helena Lindskog pointed out the importance of being "time rich" today and set up the challenge for AI is to help us have more time for innovation, for family, to discover and enjoy nature and other activities [29]. Make the IT friendly and intuitive, greening the software, smartening data centers are among the wishes. Computer learning with its user, his/her interests is the opposite of what we have today - pushing all kind of advertisement. AI should be able to understand the content of my emails, clean my email box and answer easy ones. I dream about intelligent assistant helping me find the file talking about a given topic or drawing/image to illustrate what I am writing.

Intelligent electronic commerce with immediate association of offer and demand, without categories; client describes his/her wishes or present a picture to "say" what I want.

Association of offer and demand such as job searching for me in my place, like restaurant on google map, service provider, spare pieces, repair café, 3D printer close to my place.

Imagine I switch on my computer or other device and immediately I get the results of relevant search proposed by embedded intelligence, knowing my profile.

Intelligent translator exists already, e.g. https://www.deepl.com/translator. The pronunciation of the translated text will be beneficial. When traveling, the real-time accurate conversation translator is of considerable help. Can such translators in the long term prevent us from learning languages (and using our brain)? Will our brain become lazy?

Today we have to face important challenges, such as those of UN for sustainability. AI can directly improve goal 6, 7, 9, 11 and next from Fig. 4. It may also influence improvement of others.

Fig. 4. Sustainable development goals, source un.org

According to Anthony Wang [30] it is over 70 various principles for AI ethics. One of the most repeated is that AI has to be beneficial for humanity. I add "and the planet".

3.2 From "Intelligent" Assistants to Helping the User

Intelligent assistants can take several forms:

- personal, working for one user
- for children protection
- linked to a company website or a platform answering the clients questions
- "street" assistant helping visitors/tourists
- in shop assistant, especially in big one guiding clients to the products they need
- inside of museum, expositions
- for people with disabilities

All have access to available resources and are designed to provide the user with immediate and relevant information, help, advice or a solution to a given problem. They have to "know" what the users do not know.

My dream is to have personal assistant able to learn my interests, scan all available and fake checked resources and provide me with the timely relevant information and this way participate in opportunity "hunting". It has to be capable of immediate finding a document in my computer related to the topic I ask, picture or drawing. Producer of Korean TV series "My holo love" imagined such an assistant, able to learn from user and improve its "knowledge". It is only visible and available for its user wearing special glasses. The only problem to solve is to preserve the user's intimacy when he/she is talking to invisible assistant [31].

The relevance of answers from automated assistant depends today on the quality of data and of learning algorithm. Both chat bots and connected assistants are involved. However, assistants available today need the capacity of "understanding" the question and provide relevant and verified answer. Equipped with multimodal interface it should follow me in my travels and "talk" languages that I do not talk, help finding the right word or expression in languages I talk, provide help for writing in other than the languages I master. Many comparator applications are available such as for tourism or insurance, but no one provides the optimal offer for the end user, because they work for their clients.

Having the access to medical cases, an intelligent assistant can provide the basic help before going to the doctor. It can also teach the user the preventive actions.

3.3   AI in School

Deep learning facilitated the development of intelligent assistants. For the most, they are helpful; however, they do not encourage people to think. Thinking and ability to use alternative cognitive approaches makes the difference between someone who just follow the school program and those able to solve problems using knowledge and limited resources. Thinking "without borders between fields" and ability to find alternative, greener solutions. Many professions change with technology and school has to prepare students for being flexible.

E-learning was introduced in schools at the beginning of 21st century. Many courses (MOOC) are now available online opening access to large knowledge at all levels and providing education to the rural zones without schools and to developing countries.

Digitalization of educational activities introduced tablets and now robots in schools. Educational games make learning more fun and attractive. What is missing is a sort of "super professor" able to evaluate a level of the student and to propose the best suited material from the web matching to the student profile and request. Still intelligent assistants can provide help explaining topic or exercise.

During Covid19 lockdown children had to learn at home. An i-teacher detecting difficulties of each, explaining and challenging is certainly helpful. It requires AI not only tracking activity but able to "understand" what child is doing and when he/she needs help. Challenging assistant – not switching off the brain, but stimulating thinking and suggesting various approaches.

Most of schools follow the teaching program, but few take care of the specific children talents with the aim of helping them to choose their professional future. We can imagine an AI –based Future Advice office combining the adequate AI techniques to evaluate talents, propose a game to test some professions with projection how it will evolve during the next ten or more years. Several years ago, the entertainment park Kidzania

[32] was open for children to make them try various professions. The IT and AI-related professions have to be added to the spectrum of those proposed.

3.4   AI & Food

In the age of processed food, the related industry aims to produce more food for less price regardless of nutritional quality. Pesticides and artificial fertilizers are massively used on the pretext of a duty to nourish the planet. Doing this they destroy and impoverish the soil, pollute water and pests become more resistant. Globalization allowed pests to travel longdistances hidden in goods; some are very harmful for local environment and difficult to fight with, because they are often unknown, as COVID is. According to Intel and some others, the world will need to produce 50% more food by 2050. Nevertheless pushed by food business, the food waste today is evaluated around 50% only in the United States [33]. Food is lost or wasted for a variety of reasons: bad weather, processing problems, overproduction and unstable markets cause food loss long before it arrives in a grocery store, while overbuying, poor planning and confusion over labels and safety contribute to food waste at stores and in homes. Uneaten food also puts unneeded strain on the environment by wasting valuable resources like water and farmland. Reducing food waste by just 15 percent could provide enough sustenance to feed more than 25 million people, annually. Food loss occurs on farms for a variety of reasons. To hedge against pests and weather, farmers often plant more than consumers demand. Food may not be harvested because of damage by weather, pests and disease. Market conditions off the farm can lead farmers to throw out edible food because the shape is out of the norms. If the price of product on the market is lower than the cost of transportation and labor, sometimes farmers will leave their crops un-harvested. This practice, called dumping, happens when farmers are producing more of a product that people are willing to buy, or when demand for a product falls unexpectedly.

During the COVID-19 pandemic, for example, farmers lost a major portion of their business due to restaurant and school lunchroom closures as well as a lack of workforce for gathering.

In the recent video entitles Sustainability European Space Agency (ESA) shows-up the satellite images demonstrating how far COVID affects the food production. They deplore the impact of border closures on the harvesting of fruits and vegetables [34]. Yet, because of the economic crisis, many people are partially unemployed and this workforce is not correctly managed. AI can help manage all kind of resource, but this potential is underused today.

AI system is able to detect from satellite images the zones to harvest or infected ones. Thinking – They have images of underexplored zones that can be cultivated to produce food locally. Some use harvesting robots; however, it should be cost effective.

Various AI techniques are already used to help farmers. Drones "decide" when coffee and oranges are ripe enough for picking (Hawaï, Bresil). They can also detect pests' invasion. Hopefully in the near future, we will have devices not only detecting, but selectively (pest recognition) absorbing them instead of using pesticides. Logistics planned with constraints programming to optimize time and trucks should be more widely used. Sensors connected to automated watering help optimizing the use of water.

Greenhouse tomatoes grow in a bed of pulped coconut husks, a nutrient-free environment that allows the growers controlling what goes into the plant. Sensors monitor the fruit's progress toward perfect ripeness, adjusting light to accelerate or slow the pace of maturation. However, this kind of farming requires considerable processing power.

We can imagine another approach combining the knowledge about soil and environment with knowledge about crop rotation, association of vegetable/fruits to avoid pests attack, chose the right period for sow and plant in function of available seeds. Such farmer advisor programmed applying green software principle can be powered with solar energy (Fig. 5).

Fig. 5. Connected farmer, source [35]. © European Union, 2017

While the harvesting machines have been used for years, they are now replaced by robots. Robotic harvesting equipment, partially in response to labor gaps that have left farmers scrambling to harvest crops like fruits and berries. Harvest Croo berry picker operate on the basis of machine vision and sensor fusion to "see" where harvest fruits and berries are. They use sophisticated directed movements to pick precisely [36].

Unmanned aerial vehicles or drones being outfitted with precision sensors, in order to run the fields and get the data that's needed. These airborne surveillance devices can look for stunted crops, signs of pest or weed damage, dryness and many other variables that are part of the difficulty of farming in general. With all of this data in hand, farmers can enhance their production models and their strategies across the lay of the land to decrease risk, waste and liability [37].

Main challenge is still protecting plants against weeds and various kinds of pests outdoors. Another alternative is to grow in greenhouses, which is being done as well, but some of the most amazing farming technology is being deployed outside. The "See & Spray" machines are an excellent example of combining artificial intelligence and computer vision [38]. Deploying mobile technologies with AI and computer vision built in, farmers can find weeds and eradicate them, instead of blanket spraying an entire crop. That makes the food cleaner, and it saves enormous amounts of money. It's just another example of real new technologies that are having a dramatic impact on yields and everything else.

The transition from conventional agriculture practices into a sustainable mode of growing food can lead to social and economic equity and a healthy environment.

In the nearest future we expect connecting the modern, AI powered systems with ancestral knowledge about how to cultivate without pesticides and with natural fertilizers. Maybe the future agriculture will be not about large farms but smart ones. Autonomous houses and farms can be monitored by AI ensuring optimized use of locally available resources and minimized impact on the planet.

3.5 AI for Risks/Crisis Management

Irresponsible human activities have led to Planet disaster. The increased frequency and magnitude of natural risks and those caused by humans requires new, quicker and more effective ways of managing them. Frequent fires mostly of criminal origin destroy forest, our lungs and its ecosystem. In many cases, AI demonstrated its potential to help managing these disasters [39, 40]. Earth observation systems can be applied for various risk management, whether caused by humans or natural risks. Fukushima, tsunami, earthquake, flooding require quick organizing of emergency actions involving people, hospitals, vehicles and other resources aligned to given disaster.

Facing Covid19 pandemic has multiple effects on health, on jobs, on economy, education, agriculture and environment. The researchers and medical staff are learning from examples and experiments. Handling such crises require related knowledge and smart managing of existing resources, real-time planning of hospital staff, equipment and quick finding of vaccine. Existing AI techniques can help in first stage diagnosis online to refer the patient to the right doctor. AI can optimize the allocation of beds, equipment, staff in function of their competencies and specialties. AI support exploration of clinical trials and accelerate finding of vaccine. Evaluation of efficiency of health policy [41] can be used as model for pandemic management and evaluation of induced risks.

In his TED Talk from 2015, Bill Gates states that pandemics are the greatest threat we will have to face in the future [42]. He said we need global alert system, technology, expertise, collaboration medical-military, simulation and diagnostic. Alternative is the understanding of real causes of pandemics and other serious risks in aim of avoiding and preventing them. Investments are necessary to fix the problem once it happens, but informed prevention avoids human, economic and environmental losses.

3.6   AI for Sustainability

Paradoxically AI needs devices, mostly designed with "planned obsolescence" principle to preserve continuous business. While "green software" has been slowly introduced, few really apply these principles. All fields are concerned and evaluation of impacts before doing should become mandatory. AI may play a greater role in simulation before doing, choosing the right raw material and design easy to update or to recycle [43]. IT and Information Systems should be eco-designed, which is not the case today. The management and storage of big data generated massively can be controlled by using conceptual models instead of storing all data. AI can effectively support optimization of hardware and software design. Neural computers are not new, but with the new hype researchers works again on this architecture. We do not know yet how far it can contribute to sustainability because nobody is in charge of this aspect. Similarly, designers of quantum computers focus on computation power and do not consider the eco-design.

Race for performance and connectivity pushes designers to 5G, which is not necessary the best choice because of the impact on living. AI-based decision support systems connected with innovative design methods such as TRIZ [44] may help designers finding alternative solutions. The trendy design thinking, known longtime before as "innovation with clients" [45] or extreme programming [46], has to integrate these principles.

Maybe researchers and designers by nature (biomimetics) take into consideration these aspects. Nevertheless, AI offers a spectrum of techniques helpful in optimization and verification of environmental and other constraints.

The case of Smart City, mainly based on technology offer a playground for water and energy (including renewable ones) optimization, smart eco-buildings, green and optimized transportation of people and goods, opportunity finding (job, service, training).

All human activity that have affected our biosphere and planet is concerned and AI can help minimizing this impact and do things smarter [8]. Preserving the balance in our biosphere will be beneficial for all living today and tomorrow.

3.7   AI and the Financial Service Industry

Without any doubt AI has a huge impact on the future of the financial services industry. This is widely acknowledged and described in many articles and reports [47–53], labelling it "revolutionizing/transforming/disrupting the industry". In an already highly digitized sector, AI adds an extra dimension in a number of areas. It offers new opportunities, both for new players and for incumbent institutions. It also brings threats, in particular to the established parties who have a legacy in their infrastructure and services.

Often mentioned areas where AI is transforming the industry are:

- Fraud detection and risk management. AI is extremely helpful in detecting and identifying fraudulent transactions, learning from past spending behaviors.
- Regulatory compliance. The financial services industry is heavily regulated. AI can help an institution to keep up to date with changing regulations and to be compliant with rules like Know Your Customer (KYC), anti-money laundering regulations, etc.
- Customer experience. Customers nowadays expect a more personalized offer of services. Developments like chatbots that, with the help of AI, can identify the individual customer, "understand" and interpret his or her emotions via voice and/or

facial recognition and subsequently can offer "tailormade" advice found in existing database.

- Managing personal finances. With the move to mobile banking and the use of wallets, AI offers opportunities to help customers make smart decisions on spending, saving and investing money. This can help improve the "financial health" of many people. Managing finance, AI simply accumulates all the data from your web and other footprints and creates your spending graph.

- Investment advisory. Here predictive analytics and recommendation engines turn into digital advisors that can even fully automate purchase and management of investments. The result is no longer a need for financial advisors/ relationship managers.

- Predict stock performance. Trading and investment depend on the ability to predict the future of (stock) markets accurately. Predicting this in a consistent way seems impossible for humans. Deep learning algorithms could perhaps achieve this as a result of using massive amounts of market data complemented with real-time economic and political data.

An example of the trading issue is high frequency trading (HFT). While not new in itself, since a little over a decade the execution time of transactions has moved from seconds to milli- and microseconds. HFT is a form of algorithmic trading which can arguably be labelled as an AI implementation of trading. The profits of HFT however seem to have passed their peak performance. Besides limitations caused by the infrastructure (hardware, networks) also the limitations of the algorithms play a role. Perhaps deep learning could give HFT a new boost. In [54, 55], as in many other articles, benefits but also risks are listed. Algorithms are not infallible, understanding how the algorithms and neural networks predict specific outcomes is difficult if not impossible (black box), high investments needed which could result in only a few players surviving (compare the world of the big tech firms).

All these developments will have a major effect on the workforce, not only in the number of employees but also in the types of jobs and skills needed for them. Another major impact is a change in the players in the financial landscape. The incumbents (current banks, insurance companies, pension funds, investment companies, etc.) already face strong competition from the so-called fintechs in some areas. But also the bigtechs (Amazon, Google, Facebook, Alibaba, …) are entering the financial services industry. We seem to move towards a platform economy where the bigtechs have an advantage with their strong customer base to easily offer additional (financial) services to their customers, knowing what their customers want thanks to AI.

Benefits of AI in the financial services industry are clear but so are the risks. Not only for a single financial institution but also for customers, for the trust in the financial system and for the financial stability in a country or even on a global scale. That is why in [48] it is stated that *"Financial firms using artificial intelligence (AI) should adhere to principles of sound and controlled business operations. A responsible use of AI in financial services means that firms should pay due attention to the soundness, accountability, fairness, ethics, skills and transparency aspects of the applications they develop."*

4   What Perspectives for Research – What Humanity Expects from Future AI?

Throughout this chapter we have already mentioned some needs, expectations and wishes for the future AI. In term of disruptive innovation, the current AI represents a little progress since its beginning. The AI techniques that we have today has been invented before and are recently extended to more powerful and to new applications. The wise combination of them in the hybrid systems allows facing today's challenges. What AI we need today and tomorrow?

Michael Zeldich (Artificial Labour Leasing) designs subjective robots. Such robots used for example for house cleaning learn with their users and are limited to perform what users ask for. He believes that our duty is to create an artificial society able to resist the planet's destruction and preserve our civilization.

Before we invent something else or all die, there are two main options for AI: to continue to progress with AGI or work on the challenges we have to face and then derive new theories and invent new approaches and techniques. The first requires deep understanding of how the human body works, how the organs are connected, how we interact with our environment. What future humans can expect from the AGI world?

According to WEF [53] *"Nevertheless, it is evident that more research needs to be done in order to better understand the opportunities and challenges brought about by the eventual mass adoption of AI in Financial Services. For instance, how can finance firms open up the 'black box' of AI and facilitate more explainable and transparent applications? As AI is becoming increasingly autonomous, what will the roles of humans be and how would an effective human-in-the-loop AI system manifest itself? What are some socioeconomic repercussions and ethical implications of AI-induced biases and risks? How can regulators and policymakers harness technology solutions to effectively regulate and supervise AI in finance?"*

These remarks about research trends, regulators and policymakers do not only apply to the financial industry but also to many others if not all sectors where AI is having or will have a major impact. So research is also needed to help regulators and policymakers, especially by providing them with simulators.

The issue of confidentiality of personal data is not easy to deal with. The same applies to our navigation and tracking data. Many websites refuse of access to information if the user does not accept them. However, it is much more relevant to obtain the right information from the user by asking instead bombing him/her with cookies and all sort of add-ons. AI can do much more than just analyze the data. Nevertheless, it requires a different way of thinking.

AI research should be multi- and interdisciplinary because intelligence is. We still need to progress in comprehension of our brain/body capacities.

Future AI research should balance needs and ambitions. The Covid 19 crisis clearly demonstrated that collaboration may lead to better and quicker results. World experience in AI applications for solving complex problems should be available allowing finding immediately the solution for the problem someone has to solve.

Information processing, still conceived using traditional methods such as categorization, "data thinking", processes should evolve not by adding AI layer, but "AI thinking".

We need systems able to adapt the configuration automatically working with the user, able to find immediately the file, image or video the user look for.

Hardware and software should be eco-designed and easy to recompose/recycle. AI based simulators help finding right components, minimize and "smartize" the software for the minimal energy use. MIT offers Climat Interactive simulator [56].

We need smart AI-powered search engines. For example, the EU database Cordis is a real "goldmine" containing information about the funded research projects and their results that may inspire researchers, industrial people and investors but it need to be equipped with smart, business free, search engine for immediate finding what visitor is looking for. It can be also useful for exploring the available results for quicker progress, for quick and relevant access to references in a given field.

We need decision support systems rather than fully automated decision making, that are not 100% reliable in case of missing data in critical situations.

Many challenging research problems can be found in sectorial applications such as in agriculture, health, education, banking and others. In the nearest future we expect connecting the modern, AI powered systems with ancestral knowledge about smart farming.

Health offers a great opportunity for AI research, especially in understanding and prevention of new viruses and serious and other diseases.

Education is among the pillars of modern society. Existing MOOC, e-learning and other online teaching and training systems may be improved by interactive e-teacher, however we still need a talent detector able to encourage learners to think and direct them to the area they are gifted for.

Planet protection, smart sustainability, innovation management offer also interesting challenges.

Detecting and tracking cyber and other criminals, identity thieves or global security are just a few fields of exploration for AI.

Multidisciplinary research without "borders" between fields and full exploring of all machine learning techniques, including symbolic, may help in elaborating of general solvers. Of course, this requires evolution of research evaluation criteria.

In this context, is it necessary to build a machine able of consciousness, sentience, sapiens and self-awareness?

Instead of splitting AI lets connect the research fields for more spectacular results and for human purpose.

We expect a global smartening of AI and IT researchers.

Acknowledgement. I would like to thank Leon Strous for his contribution to paragraph 3.7 AI and the Financial Service Industry.

References

1. Jajal, T.: Distinguishing between Narrow AI, General AI and Super AI, May 2028. https://med ium.com/@tjajal/distinguishing-between-narrow-ai-general-ai-and-super-ai-a4bc44172e22
2. Bersini, H.: The two A.I. – conscious and unconscious, Keynote at Data Driven Innovation, Rome (2018)

3. Artificial General Intelligence
4. Tegmark, M.: Life 3.0: Being Human at the Age of Artificial Intelligence (2017)
5. Tegmark, M.: Machines playing god: how AI will overcome humans, video, May 2018. https://www.youtube.com/watch?v=p9eLpRbRk4c
6. Michalski, R.S.: Machine Learning
7. Ten secret military technologies, video, June 2019. https://www.youtube.com/watch?v=LLYPDJTLr4I
8. Mercier-Laurent, E.: The Innovation Biosphere – Planet and Brains in Digital Era. Wiley, Hoboken (2015)
9. Kayakutlu, G., Mercier-Laurent, E.: Intelligence in Energy. Elsevier, Amsterdam (2017)
10. Wiener, N.: The Human Use of Human Being, Cybernetics and Society. Houghton Mifflin Company, Boston (1950)
11. Johnson, R.C.: Cognizers: Neural Networks and Machines That Think. Wiley, Hoboken (1988)
12. von Bertalanffy, L.: General System Theory (1968)
13. Rauch-Hindin, W.B.: Artificial Intelligence in Business, Science and Industry. Prentice-Hall, Upper Saddle River (1986)
14. Mercier-Laurent, E.: Implementing horizon Europe. 11th Innovation Summit, February 2020
15. Launchbury, J.: DARPA Perspective on Artificial Intelligence (2017). https://www.youtube.com/watch?v=-O01G3tSYpU
16. Gubrud, M.
17. Naveen, J.: How far we are from achieving general artificial intelligence? Forbes (2019)
18. Open AI. https://openai.com. Accessed 07 June 2020
19. Pachet, F.: Research https://www.francoispachet.fr/. Accessed 07 June 2020
20. Military (and others) robots. https://www.youtube.com/watch?v=OEIeS12TcWU. Accessed Feb 2018
21. Le Bihan, D.: Looking Inside the Brain: The Power of Neuroimaging. Princeton University Press, Princeton (2014)
22. Rajvanshi, A.K.: The Three Minds of the Body – Brain, Heart and gut. Speaking Tree, Gurgaon (2011)
23. https://www.humanbrainproject.eu/en/. Accessed 07 June 2020
24. https://www.darpa.mil/program/our-research/darpa-and-the-brain-initiative. Accessed 07 June 2020
25. Deep learning algorithms. https://www.predictiveanalyticstoday.com/deep-learning-software-libraries/. Accessed 07 June 2020
26. Co-bots. https://www.safran-group.com/media/20151218_cobots-collaborative-robots.Accessed 07 June 2020
27. Monsone, C., Mercier-Laurent, E.: Ecosystem of industry 4.0 – combining technology and human power. In: MEDES 2019 (2019)
28. Schneider Future Factory. https://www.se.com/fr/fr/about-us/newsroom/actualites/le-site-du-vaudreuil-de-schneider-electric-labellise-vitrine-industrie-du-futur-c155-636ff.html
29. Lindskog, H.: Globalization - understanding the correlations between attitudes towards globalization, time, resources and financial resources. In: Mercier-Laurent, E. (ed.) AI4KM 2018. IAICT, vol. 588, pp. 1–13. Springer, Cham (2020). https://doi.org/10.1007/978-3-030-52903-1_1
30. Wang, A.: Ethics and regulation of artificial intelligence. Keynote to NITC 2019, Colombo, Sri Lanka, October 2019
31. My holo love. https://www2.dramacool.movie/my-holo-love-episode-1.html
32. Kidzania. https://kidzania.com/en
33. Food waste. https://foodprint.org/issues/the-problem-of-food-waste/. Accessed 16 May 2020

34. A Sustainable Future, European Space Agency. http://www.esa.int/ESA_Multimedia/Videos/2020/05/A_sustainable_future. Accessed May 2020
35. Precision Farming – sowing the seeds of new agricultural revolution. https://cordis.europa.eu/article/id/400295-precision-farming-sowing-the-seeds-of-a-new-agricultural-revolution
36. Harvest croo. https://harvestcroo.com/. Accessed 29 May 2020
37. Gonzalez-De-Santos, P., Fernández, R., Sepúlveda, D., Navas, E., Armada, M.: Unmanned Ground Vehicles for Smart Farm, February 2020. https://doi.org/10.5772/intechopen.90683
38. See & Spray machines. http://smartmachines.bluerivertechnology.com/. Accessed 29 May 2020
39. Mercier-Laurent, E.: Preventing and facing new crisis and risks in complex environment. IJMDM **17**(2) (2018)
40. L'Heritier, C., Imussaten, A., Harispe, S., Dusserre, G., Roig, B.: identifying criteria most influencing strategy performance: application to humanitarian logistical strategy planning. Chapter in Information Processing and Management of Uncertainty in Knowledge-Based Systems, Applications. https://doi.org/10.1007/978-3-319-91479-4_10
41. Evaluation of efficiency of health policy. https://www.futura-sciences.com/sante/actualites/coronavirus-coronavirus-ia-evaluer-efficacite-politiques-sanitaires-80992/
42. TED Talk Bill Gates (2015). https://www.youtube.com/watch?v=QdSyKEBiOnE
43. Mercier-Laurent, E.: AI for Innovation Ecosystems
44. TRIZ. https://triz.org/triz
45. Amidon, D.: Innovating with clients. Chapter in The Innovation Strategy for the Knowledge Economy. Butterworth Heinemann (1997)
46. Extreme programming. http://www.extremeprogramming.org/
47. BAFIN2018 – Big Data trifft auf künstliche Intelligenz, Herausforderungen und Implikationen für Aufsicht und Regulierung von Finanzdienstleistungen, Bundesanstalt für Finanzdienstleistungsaufsicht (Bafin) (2018). https://www.bafin.de/SharedDocs/Downloads/DE/dl_bdai_studie.pdf?__blob=publicationFile&v=3
48. DNB2019 – General principles for the use of Artificial Intelligence in the financial sector. De Nederlandsche Bank (DNB), 25 July 2019. https://www.dnb.nl/en/binaries/General%20principles%20for%20the%20use%20of%20Artificial%20Intelligence%20in%20the%20financial%20sector2_tcm47-385055.pdf
49. FinTech2019 – How Data Analytics Backed By AI and ML is Transforming The BFSI Sector. FinTech News, Neeraj Goyal, 23 August 2019. https://www.fintechnews.org/how-the-financial-industry-is-affected-by-ai-and-ml/
50. Infosecurity2019 – How AI is Revolutionizing the Banking Sector. Infosecurity Group, Oliver Smith, 24 December 2019. https://www.infosecurity-magazine.com/opinions/ai-revolutionizing-banking/
51. Maruti2020 – 5 Ways AI is Transforming the Finance Industry. Maruti Techlabs (2020). https://marutitech.com/ways-ai-transforming-finance/
52. WEF2020-1 – AI has started a financial revolution - here's how. World Economic Forum (WEF), 04 February 2020. https://www.weforum.org/agenda/2020/02/how-ai-is-shaping-financial-services/
53. WEF2020-2 – Transforming Paradigms - A Global AI in Financial Services Survey. World Economic Forum/University of Cambridge, January 2020. http://www3.weforum.org/docs/WEF_AI_in_Financial_Services_Survey.pdf
54. Akioyamen, P.: Neural Networks & Deep Learning—The Revival of HFT? https://towardsdatascience.com/neural-networks-deep-learning-the-revival-of-hft-2bc2c271fba2. Accessed 7 June 2020
55. Seth, S.: The World of High-Frequency Algorithmic Trading. https://www.investopedia.com/articles/investing/091615/world-high-frequency-algorithmic-trading.asp. Accessed 7 June 2020
56. MIT Sloan Simulator Climat Interactive. https://vimeo.com/359091159

The Laws and Regulation of AI and Autonomous Systems

Anthony Wong[1,2(✉)]

[1] AGW Lawyers & Consultants, Sydney, Australia
anthonywong@agwconsult.com
[2] IFIP, Laxenburg, Austria

Abstract. Our regulatory systems have attempted to keep abreast of new technologies by recalibrating and adapting our regulatory frameworks to provide for new opportunities and risks, to confer rights and duties, safety and liability frameworks, and to ensure legal certainty for businesses. These adaptations have been reactive and sometimes piecemeal, often with artificial delineation on rights and responsibilities and with unintended flow-on consequences. Previously, technologies have been deployed more like tools, but as autonomy and self-learning capabilities increase, robots and intelligent AI systems will feel less and less like machines and tools. There is now a significant difference, because machine learning AI systems have the ability to learn, adapt their performances and 'make decisions' from data and 'life experiences'. This chapter provides brief insights on some of the topical developments in our regulatory systems and the current debates on some of the risks and challenges from the use and actions of AI, autonomous and intelligent systems [1].

Keywords: AI · Robots · Automation · Regulation · Law · Job transition · Employment · Data ownership · Data portability · Access · Control · Intellectual property · Legal personhood · Liability · Transparency · Explainability · Data protection · Privacy

1 Introduction

The base tenets of our regulatory systems were created long before the advances and confluence of new technologies including AI (artificial intelligence), IoT (Internet of Things), blockchain, cloud and others. With the rise of these new technologies we have taken many initiatives to address their consequences by recalibrating and adapting our regulatory frameworks to provide for new opportunities and risks, to confer rights and duties, safety and liability frameworks, and ensure legal certainty for business.

Sector-specific regulation has also been adopted and adapted to address market failures and risks in critical and regulated domains. These changes have often been reactive and piecemeal, with artificial delineation of rights and responsibilities. There have been many unintended consequences. More recently we have begun to learn from past

Published by Springer Nature Switzerland AG 2020
L. Strous et al. (Eds.): Unimagined Futures, IFIP AICT 555, pp. 38–54, 2020.
https://doi.org/10.1007/978-3-030-64246-4_4

mishaps, and these regulatory adaptations are now more likely to be drafted in techno-logically neutral way avoiding strict technical definition, especially when the field is still evolving rapidly.

AI and algorithmic decision-making will over time bring significant benefits to many areas of human endeavour. The proliferation of AI systems imbued with increasingly complex mathematical and data modelling, and machine learning algorithms, are being integrated in virtually every sector of the economy and society, to support and in many cases undertake more autonomous decisions and actions.

How much autonomy should AI and robots have to make decisions on our behalf and about us in our life, work and play? How do we ensure they can be trusted, and that they are transparent, reliable, accountable and well designed?

Previously, technologies have often been deployed more like tools, as a pen or paint-brush, but as autonomy and self-learning capabilities increase, robots and intelligent AI systems feel less and less like machines or tools. AI will equip robots and systems with the ability to learn using machine-learning algorithms. They will have the ability to interact and work alongside us or to augment our work. They will increasingly be able to take over functions and roles and, perhaps more significantly, the ability to make decisions.

When I reviewed AI ethical frameworks in 2019, there were more than 70 in exis-tence. The number continues to grow. In 2019, jurisdictions including Australia [2] and the EU [3] published their frameworks, adding to the lists of contributors includ-ing the OECD Principles on Artificial Intelligence [4], the World Economic Forum AI Governance: A Holistic Approach To Implement Ethics Into AI [5] and the Singapore Model AI Governance Framework [6]. The debates have matured significantly since then, beyond ethical principles to more detailed guidelines on how such principles can be operationalised in the design and implementation to minimise risks and negative outcomes. But the challenge has always been putting principles into practice.

Emerging technologies are rapidly transforming the regulatory landscape. They are providing timely opportunities for fresh approaches in the redesign of our regulatory systems to keep pace with technological changes, now and into the future. AI is currently advancing more rapidly than the process of regulatory recalibration. Unlike the past, there is now a significant difference—we must now take into consideration, machine learning AI systems that have the ability to learn, adapt their performances and 'make decisions' from data and 'life experiences'.

This chapter provides brief insights on some of the topical developments in our regulatory systems and the current debates to address some of the challenges and risks from the use and actions of AI, autonomous and intelligent systems [1].

2 Automation, Jobs and Employment Law Implications

Over the past few years we have been inundated with predictions that robots and automa-tion will devastate the workplace, replacing many job functions within the next 10 to 15 years. We have already seen huge shifts in manufacturing, mining, agriculture, adminis-tration and logistics, where a wide range of manual and repetitive tasks have been auto-mated. More recently, cognitive tasks and data analyses are increasingly being performed by AI and machines.

Historically, new technologies have always affected the structure of the labour market, leading to a significant impact on employment, especially lower skilled and manual jobs. But now the pace and spread of autonomous and intelligent technologies are outperforming humans in many tasks and radically challenging the base tenets of our labour markets and laws. These developments have raised many questions.

Where are the policies, strategies and regulatory frameworks to transition workers in the jobs that will be the most transformed, or those that will disappear altogether due to automation, robotics and AI?

Our current labour and employment laws, such as sick leave, hours of work, tax, minimum wage and overtime pay requirements, were not designed for robots. What is the legal relationship of robots to human employees in the workplace? In relation to workplace safety—what liabilities should apply if a robot harms a human co-worker? Would the 'employer' of the robot be vicariously liable? What is the performance management and control plan for work previously undertaken by human employees working under a collective bargaining agreement, now performed or co-performed with AI or robots? How would data protection and privacy regulations apply to personal information collected and consumed by robots? Who would be responsible for cyber security and the criminal use of robots or AI?

Are there statutory protection and job security for humans displaced by automation and robots? Should we tax robot owners to pay for training for workers who are displaced by automation, or should there be a universal minimum basic income for people displaced? Should we have social plans, such as exist in Germany and France, if restructuring through automation disadvantages employees?

There are many divergent views on all these questions. All are being hotly debated. Governments, policy makers, institutions and employers all have important roles to play in the development of digital skills, in the monitoring of long-term job trends, and in the creation of policies to assist workers and organisations adapt to an automated future. If these issues are not addressed early and proactively, they may worsen the digital divide and increase inequalities between countries and people.

ICT professionals are also being impacted as smart algorithms and other autonomous technologies supplement software programming, data analysis and technical support roles. With AI and machine learning developing at an exponential rate, what does the future look like?

2.1 Case Study - Line Between Human and Robo Advisers in Financial Services

FinTech (financial technology) start-ups are emerging to challenge the roles of banks and traditional financial institutions. FinTechs are rapidly transforming and disrupting the marketplace by providing 'robo-advice' using highly sophisticated algorithms operating on mobile and web-based environments. The technology is called robotic process automation (RPA) and is becoming widespread in business, and particularly in financial institutions. Robo-advice or automated advice is the provision of automated financial product advice using algorithms and technology and without the direct involvement of a human adviser [7].

Robo-advice and AI capabilities have the potential to increase competition and lower prices for consumers in the financial advice and financial services industries by radically reshaping the customer experience. They are designed, modelled and programmed by human actors. Often they operate behind the scenes 24/7 assisting the people who interact with consumers. There are considerable tasks and risks involved in writing algorithms to accurately portray the full offerings and complexity of financial products.

In 2017 Australia, after a number of scandals, introduced professional standards legislation for human financial advisers [8]. These regulations set higher competence and ethical standards, including requirements for relevant first or higher degrees, continuing professional development requirements and compliance with a code of ethics. The initiatives were introduced into a profession already under pressure from the robo environment.

Because robo-advice is designed, modelled and programmed by human actors, should these requirements also apply to robo-advice? Should regulators also hold ICT developers and providers of robots and autonomous systems to the same standards demanded from human financial advisers? What should be the background, skills and competencies of these designers and ICT developers?

Depending on the size and governance framework of an organisation, various players and actors could be involved in a collaborative venture in the development, deployment and lifecycle of AI systems. These might include the developer, the product manager, senior management, the service provider, the distributor and the person who uses the AI or autonomous system. Their domain expertise could be in computer science, or mathematics or statistics, or they might be an interdisciplinary group composed of financial advisers, economists, social scientists or lawyers.

In 2016 the Australian regulator laid down sectoral guidelines [9] for monitoring and testing algorithms deployed in robo-advice. The regulatory guidance requires businesses offering robo-advice to have people within the business who understand the "rationale, risk and rules" used by the algorithms and have the skills to review the resulting robo-advice. What should be the competencies and skills of the humans undertaking the role?

The EU General Data Protection Regulation (GDPR) [10] went further, by placing an explicit onus on the algorithmic provider to provide "meaningful information about the logic involved" [11]. In addition, GDPR provides an individual with explicit rights including the rights to obtain human intervention, to express their point of view and to contest the decision made solely by automated systems [12] that has legal or similarly significant impact. GDPR applies only when AI uses personal data within the scope of the legislation.

Revealing the logic behind an algorithm may potentially risk and disclose commercially sensitive information and trade secrets used by the AI model and on how the system works.

The deployment of robo-advice raises many new, interesting and challenging questions for regulators accustomed only to assessing and regulating human players and actors.

3 Do Robots and AI Dream of Owning Intellectual Property?

AI and machine-learning systems have already developed to the point where they can write music, generate automated reports, create art or even display human traits such as curiosity and conduct experiments to self-learn and develop [13]. Humans excel in creativity, imagination, problem solving, collaboration, management, and leadership which, at least for now, are very far off for AI and automation.

Will AI eventually outpace human capability and creativity? This may happen, but there is no consensus on when. Whatever the case, we are seeing more examples of original works created not by humans, but by autonomous AI. Businesses are increasingly investing in new AI and robotics technologies, and in research and innovation to enhance competitiveness.

AI has introduced extra dimensions to the complexity of intellectual property (IP). Investors should tread with caution while questions remain about the ownership of works generated or supplemented by AI. Who owns intangible outputs which could be perceived as IP when they are generated by a robot or AI? Who owns the IP—the manufacturer, the developer or the programmer? Could ownership fall to the user who provided the data for the robot to create the output? Or alternatively, could the robot own its creations?

But what happens when inventions, source code, objects or other assets are created autonomously and are directed by non-human entities, as will increasingly be the case in the future? The distinction between human-generated works and AI-generated works is emerging to be a controversial topic.

Our current regulatory framework generally assumes that IP is created by natural persons. The UK [14], European [15] and US [16] patent offices, recently rejected patent applications in which an AI machine 'DABUS' was designated as the inventor.

Commentators have long distinguished between computer-assisted [17] and computer-generated works. In many countries, including Australia, the former category has created few copyright problems, but computer-generated works with little or no human involvement pose a challenge to copyright's subsistence. Any works created by autonomous AI and robots will suffer serious hurdles in securing copyright protection. They might not have sufficient human authorial contribution for copyright to subsist. Given that technological research and progress are often driven by the promise of financial rewards, this uncertainty around IP ownership could be a disincentive for commercial entities to invest in AI development.

Some jurisdictions have implemented specific provisions to protect literary, dramatic, musical or artistic work which is computer-generated. [18] Sect. 178 of the UK Copyright Designs and Patents Act 1988 defines "computer-generated work" to mean work "generated by computer in circumstances such that there is no human author of the work". The author is the person who undertook the arrangements necessary for the creation of the work [19].

The WIPO's Second Session of the Conversation of Intellextual Property and Artificial Intelligence have disclosed the significance of the debate and that the "attribution of copyright to AI-generated works will go to the heart of the social purpose for which the copyright system exists" [20].

4   Data Fuels AI but Who Owns Data?

Data is at the centre of the operation of many AI machine learning models. Industrial and public data, as well as personal data, are important sources of input for the training and evaluation of AI machine learning models.

The deployment of advanced intelligent algorithmic software, in conjunction with the rapid declining cost of digital storage, is fuelling the assembly and combination of vast datasets (known as 'Big Data') for automated data processing and interrogation. These algorithmic programs are more cost effective and efficient than human readers and are being progressively deployed across all domains of our society. Their aims are to unlock and discover new forms of value, to connect previously unseen linkages, and provide insights to stimulate growth and innovation in the digital economy [21].

Economies have formed around data, irrespective of whether an adequate regulatory framework has been built around it. In their relentless technological development, the AI and Big Data phenomena have overtaken the slow march of our law and have embraced and encapsulated some of the facets of our concepts of property without giving due regard and serious thought to the implications of treating data as property. In an attempt to create order from a runaway phenomenon, should there be underlying policy reasons to accord some form of property rights in the context of Big Data, and if not, some 'bundles of rights'? [22].

Property rights evolve and change to address the practical needs of a given epoch in our society. Those needs change as our values and norms evolve. There is abundant literature on the different senses in which the term 'property' has been used to encapsulate the move from the traditional notions of property, such as land and chattels, to the notion of property in intangibles, such as artistic works. We are embarking on yet another significant leap, this time regarding property or 'property-like' considerations in data.

It is difficult to define property with any precision as the "notions of property inevitably change to reflect their context" [23]. Property law deals with rights and if recognised under established heads of law are claims 'good against the world', often described as 'rights to exclude others' [24].

Protecting value and proprietary rights in data involves a balancing act between many vested interests, including the interests of the purported owner, the interests of the custodian, the interests of competing third parties, and the interests of the public to access and use data. The debate on data ownership rights, and the layered complexities and issues pertaining to the granting of property rights in data, has intensified as the use and control of data assets become more and more critical to our economy and our ability to innovate. This requires a balancing of the commercial, private and public interests in data, as well as data protection and privacy concerns.

Existing laws in relation to copyright, patent, confidential information and trade secret, and trademark all relate to and protect rights involving information.

As observed by Nimmer, "copyright law has become a primary source of property rights in information in the 1990s" [25]. But existing copyright law is an inadequate framework for the consideration of property rights in data, because it provides owners with only a limited property right in the expression of the information [26]. Copyright law does not concern itself with the control or flow of ideas, facts or data per se. The data components contained in the copyrighted work may not be protected, no matter how valuable. Ideas and facts are generally regarded to be in the public domain [27].

The right to control use of information may also arise under patent or other laws. Patent protects the use of ideas or information contained in the patent, by restricting the practice of the invention for a period of time.

In Australia and elsewhere, the question of whether information can be properly characterised as property in the context of confidential information has been subjected to much academic and judicial commentary over the last half century [28]. But if the owner of the confidential information places it in the public domain and accessible for Big Data mining and analysis, the inherent 'secrecy' may be lost. In Australia, as in the United Kingdom, there is authority which supports the proposition that information is not property [29].

AI, Big Data and our society's dependence on the digital economy have emerged comparatively rapidly. This has heightened the debate on our ability and freedom to use and extract value from data without fear of prosecution as we try to gain insights into new discoveries, innovation and growth. Granting separate property rights to discrete collections of data (datasets) would create a substantial barrier to the evolution of Big Data and our ability to mine valuable information from these datasets.

In the world of Big Data these datasets can be created, collected and obtained (sometimes even verified) automatically, or as a by-product of another business function. Some will require the investment of time, capital and labour, while others may only require computer processing time. It will depend upon the types and forms of datasets, how they are derived, and the purpose they serve.

The different types and forms of Big Data will continue to challenge our thinking and concepts around the question of data ownership. They will also continue to create uncertainty about the boundaries of control and data ownership.

Rights in data come in many forms and from a variety of sources. For the most part, traditional intellectual property law has proven to be inadequate in providing protection. [30] These traditional intellectual property regimes do not provide adequate cover for data and information-based products. Indeed, these laws exclude most Big Data datasets (in whole or in part) from protection.

With the pervasive use of technology today, a rapidly growing percentage of our information is created automatically from the use of IoT devices, mobile and GPS devices, smart meters, systems collecting transactional data, and many other sources. Most of these sources generate factual information, so it is unlikely that they would be protected under our traditional intellectual property laws. Should rights be left to the realms of contract, confidential information, trade secrets, unfair competition laws and other mechanisms? Or should government provide the custodianship to enhance researchers' access to Big Data?

In 2006, the European Union adopted the Database Directive [31] in recognition of the fact that copyright is inadequate to protect the investment made by database owners. The database directive provides for two levels of protection:

a) a sui generis database protection where a substantial investment has been undertaken (financial, technical or human) in "obtaining, verifying, or presenting the contents of the database" [32].

b) in addition to that provided by copyright law, where by reason of the selection or arrangement of their contents constitute the author's own intellectual creation [33].

Article 1 of the directive defines a database as a "collection of independent works, data or other materials arranged in a systematic or methodical way and individually accessible by electronic or other means".

In the USA, the tort of misappropriation allows owners some control over the use that can be made of their databases.

4.1 Is It About Data Portability, Access and Control?

In the era of AI, machine learning models, data portability and the right to control access to data are also relevant. The right to control another's access to information can involve several distinct bodies of law, including contract law, the law of confidential information and trade secrets, computer and cyber crime law, communications law, and various laws relating to privacy.

Recently we have seen examples of government intervention using the regulatory framework to regulate interest in data in the digital environment, without the requirement to establish ownership in the data held or restricted by an access control system associated with a function of the computer.

The Australian Consumer Data Right (CDR) regulations [34] give individuals and businesses greater control over their data, including the ability to access particular data in a usable form and to direct a business to securely transfer that data to a trusted third party. The consumer right will roll out across sectors of the economy, commencing in the banking sector from July 2020 followed by the energy and telecommunications sectors. The data regulatory framework also imposes significant additional privacy and data sharing obligations and penalties for breach.

In the EU, the Free Flow of Non-Personal Data Regulation [35] and the General Data Protection Regulation [36] allow users of data processing services to use the data gathered in different EU markets to improve their productivity and competitiveness. Both EU Regulations refer to data portability and aim to make it easier to port data from one IT environment to another one, to enable switching of service providers and to foster competition.

5   Legal Personhoods for AI

Historically, our regulatory systems have granted rights and legal personhood to slaves, women, children, corporations and more recently to landscape and nature. Two of India's rivers, the Ganga and the Yamuna, have been granted legal status. In New Zealand legislation was enacted to grant legal personhoods to the Whanganui river, Mount Taranaki and the Te Urewera protected area. Previously, corporations were the only non-human entities recognised by the law as legal persons.

"To be a legal person is to be the subject of rights and duties" [37]. Granting legal personality [38] to AI and robots will entail complex legal considerations and is not a simple case of equating them to corporations.

Who foots the bill when a robot or an intelligent AI system makes a mistake, causes an accident or damage, or becomes corrupted? The manufacturer, the developer, the person controlling it, or the robot itself? Or is it a matter of allocating and apportioning risk and liability?

As autonomic and self-learning capabilities increase, robots and intelligent AI systems will feel less and less like machines and tools. Self-learning capabilities for AI have added complexity to the equation. Will granting 'electronic rights' to robots assist with some of these questions? Will human actors use robots to shield themselves from liability or shift any potential liabilities from the developers to the robots? Or will the spectrum, allocation and apportionment of responsibility keep step with the evolution of self-learning robots and intelligent AI systems? Regulators around the world are wrestling with these questions.

The EU is leading the way on these issues. In 2017 the European Parliament, in an unprecedented show of support, adopted a resolution on Civil Law Rules on Robotics [39] by 396 votes to 123. One of its key recommendations was to call on the European Commission to explore, analyse and consider "a specific legal status for robots ... so that at least the most sophisticated autonomous robots could be established as having the status of electronic persons responsible for making good any damage they may cause, and possibly applying electronic personality to cases where robots make autonomous decisions" [40].

The EU resolution generated considerable debate and controversy, because it calls for sophisticated autonomous robots to be given specific legal status as electronic persons. The arguments from both sides are complex and require fundamental shifts in legal theory and reasoning.

In an open letter, experts in robotics and artificial intelligence have cautioned the European Commission that plans to grant robots legal status are inappropriate and "non-pragmatic" [41].

The European Group on Ethics in Science and New Technologies, in its Statement on Artificial Intelligence, Robotics and Autonomous Systems, advocated that the concept of legal personhood is the ability and willingness to take and attribute moral responsibility. "Moral responsibility is here construed in the broad sense in which it may refer to several aspects of human agency, e.g. causality, accountability (obligation to provide an account), liability (obligation to compensate damages), reactive attitudes such as praise and blame (appropriateness of a range of moral emotions), and duties associated with social roles. Moral responsibility, in whatever sense, cannot be allocated or shifted to 'autonomous' technology" [42].

In 2020, the EU Commission presented its "White Paper on Artificial Intelligence— A European approach to excellence and trust for regulation of artificial intelligence (AI)" [43] and a number of other documents including a "Report on the safety and liability implications of Artificial Intelligence, the Internet of Things and robotics" [44] for comments. The White Paper is non-committal on the question of endowing robots with specific legal status as electronic persons. It proposes a risk-based approach to create an 'ecosystem of trust' as one of the key elements of a future regulatory framework for AI in Europe, so that the regulatory burden is not excessively prescriptive or disproportionate.

I concur with the conclusions reached by Bryson et al. [45] that the case for electronic personhood is weak and the negatives outweigh the benefits—at least for the foreseeable future.

As evidenced by the historical debates on the status of slaves, women, corporations and, more recently landscape and nature, the question of granting legal personality to autonomous robots will not be resolved any time soon. There is no simple answer to the question of legal personhood, and one size will not fit all.

Should legal personhood for robots or autonomous systems eventuate in the future, any right invoked on behalf of robots, or obligation enforced against them, will require new approaches and significant recalibration of our regulatory systems. Legal personhood could potentially allow autonomous robots to own their creations, as well as being open to liability for problems or negative outcomes associated with their actions.

6   Responsibility and Liability for Damages Caused by AI

How should regulators manage the complexity and challenges arising from the design, development and deployment of robots and autonomous systems? What legal and social responsibilities should we give to algorithms shielded behind statistically data-derived 'impartiality'? Who is liable when robots and AI get it wrong?

There is much debate as to who amongst the various players and actors across the design, development and deployment lifecycle of AI and autonomous systems should be responsible and liable to account for any damages that might be caused. Would autonomy and self-learning capabilities alter the chain of responsibility of the producer or developer as the "AI-driven or otherwise automated machine which, after consideration of certain data, has taken an autonomous decision and caused harm to a human's life, health or property" [46]?

Or has "inserting a layer of inscrutable, unintuitive, and statistically-derived code in between a human decisionmaker and the consequences of that decision, AI disrupts our typical understanding of responsibility for choices gone wrong"? [47] Or should the producer or programmer foresee the potential loss or damage even when it may be difficult to anticipate—particularly in unusual circumstances, the actions of an autonomous system? These questions will become more critical as more and more autonomous decisions are made by AI systems.

One of the more advanced regulatory developments in AI is in the trialling of autonomous vehicles [48] and in the regulatory frameworks for drones [49].

The rapid adoption of AI and autonomous systems into more diverse areas of our lives—from business, education, healthcare and communication through to infrastructure, logistics, defence, entertainment and agriculture—means that any laws involving liability will need to consider a broad range of contexts and possibilities.

We are moving rapidly towards a world where autonomous and intelligent AI systems are connected and integrated in complex IoT environments in the mesh and "the plurality of actors involved can make it difficult to assess where a potential damage originates and which person is liable for it. Due to the complexity of these technologies, it can be very difficult for victims to identify the liable person and prove all necessary conditions for a successful claim, as required under national law" [50]. The burden of proof in a tort fault-based liability system in some countries could significantly increase the costs of litigation.

We will need to establish specific protections for potential victims of AI-related incidents to give consumers confidence that they will have legal recourse if something goes wrong.

One of the proposals being debated is for the creation of a mandatory insurance scheme to ensure that victims of incidents involving robots and intelligent AI systems have access to adequate compensation. This might be similar to the mandatory comprehensive insurance that owners need to purchase before being able to register a motor vehicle [51].

Another approach is for the creation of strict liability rules to compensate victims for potential harm caused by AI and autonomous systems along the lines of current product liability laws in the EU and Australia. Strict liability rules would ensure that the victim is compensated regardless of fault. But who amongst the various players and actors should be strictly liable?

Whether the existing mixture of fault-based and strict liability regimes are appropriate is also subject to much debate.

Introducing a robust regulatory framework with relevant input from industry, policymakers and government would create greater incentive for AI developers and manufacturers to reduce their exposure by building in additional safeguards to minimise the potential risks to humanity.

7   Transparency and Explainability of AI

Algorithms are increasingly being used to analyse information and define or predict outcomes with the aid of AI. These AI systems may be embedded in devices and systems and deployed across many industries and increasingly in critical domains, often without the knowledge and consent of the user. Should humans be informed that they are interacting with AI, on the purposes of the AI, and on the data used for the training and evaluation?

To ensure that AI based systems perform as intended, the quality, accuracy and relevance of data are essential. Any data bias, error or statistical distortion will be learned and amplified. In situations involving machine learning—where algorithms and decision rules are trained using data to recognize patterns and to learn to make future decisions based on these observations, regulators and consumers may not easily discern the properties of these algorithms. These algorithms are able to train systems to perform certain tasks at levels that may exceed human ability and raise many challenging questions including calls for greater algorithmic transparency to minimise the risk of bias, discrimination, unfairness, error and to protect consumer interests.

Over the last few years legislators have started to respond to the challenge. In the EU, Article 22 of the General Data Protection Regulation (GDPR) [52] gives individuals the right not to be subject to a decision based solely on automated decision-making (no human involvement in the decision process), except in certain situations including explicit consent and necessity for the performance of or entering into a contract. The GDPR applies only to automated decision-making involving personal data.

In the public sector, AI systems are increasingly being adopted by governments to improve and reform public service processes. In many situations, stakeholders and users of AI will expect reasons to be given for transparency and accountability of government decisions which are important elements for the proper functioning of public administration. It is currently unclear how our regulatory frameworks would adjust to providing a meaningful review by our courts of decisions undertaken by autonomous AI systems, or in what circumstances a sub-delegation by a nominated decision-maker to an autonomous AI systems would be lawful. We may need to develop new principles and standards and "to identify directions for thinking about how administrative law should respond ... that makes sense from both a legal and a technical point of view [53].

As machine learning evolves, AI models [54] often become even more complex, to the point where it may be difficult to articulate and understand their inner workings—even to people who created them. This raises many questions: what types of explanation are suitable and useful to the audience? [55] How and why does the model perform the way it does? How comprehensive does the explanation need to be—is an understanding on how the algorithmic decision was reached required, or should the explanation be adapted in a manner which is useful to a non-technical audience?

In the EU, the GDPR explicitly provides a data subject with the following rights:

a) rights to be provided and to access information about the automated decision-making; [56]
b) rights to obtain human intervention and to contest the decision made solely by automated decision-making algorithm; [57] and
c) places explicit onus on the algorithmic provider to provide "meaningful information about the logic involved" in algorithmic decision, the "significance" and the "envisaged consequences" of the algorithmic processing [58].

But how would these rights operate and be enforced in practice? With recent and more complex non-linear black-box AI models, it can be difficult to provide meaningful explanations, largely due to the statistical and probabilistic character of machine learning and the current limitations of some AI models—raising concerns including accountability, explainability, interpretability, transparency, and human control.

What expertise and competencies would be required from a data subject to take advantage of the rights or for the algorithmic provider to provide the above rights?

"In addition, access to the algorithm and the data could be impossible without the cooperation of the potentially liable party. In practice, victims may thus not be able to make a liability claim. In addition, it would be unclear, how to demonstrate the fault of an AI acting autonomously, or what would be considered the fault of a person relying on the use of AI" [59].

This opacity will also make it difficult to verify whether decisions made with the involvement of AI are fair and unbiased, whether there are possible breaches of laws, and whether they will hamper the effective access to the traditional evidence necessary to establish a successful liability action and to claim compensation.

Should organisations consider and ensure that specific types of explanation be provided for their proposed AI system to meet the requisite needs of the audience before starting the design process? Should the design and development methodologies adopted have the flexibility to embrace new tools and explanation frameworks, ensuring ongoing improvements in transparency and explainability in parallel with advancement in the state of the art of the technology throughout the lifecycle of the AI system?

While rapid development methodologies may have been adopted by the IT Industry, embedding transparency and explainability into AI system design requires more extensive planning and oversight, and requiring input and knowledge from a wider mix of multi-disciplinary skills and expertise.

New tools and better explanation frameworks need to be developed to instill the desired human values and to reconcile the current tensions and trade-off between accuracy, cost and explainability of AI models. Developing such tools and frameworks is far from trivial, warranting further research and funding.

8 Summary and Looking Beyond

This chapter raises some of the major topical regulatory issues and debates relating to job transition and employment law; data ownership, portability, access and control; legal status of AI and personhood; intellectual property ownership by AI; AI liability; transparency and meaningful AI explanation; and aspects of data protection and privacy.

In the wake of the 2020 "black lives matter" protests, a number of technology companies have announced limitations on plans to sell facial recognition technology. There have also been renewed calls for a moratorium on certain uses of facial recognition technology that has legal or significant effects on individuals until appropriate legal framework has been established [60].

The need to address AI and autonomous system challenges has increased in urgency as the adverse potential impact could be significant in specific critical domains. If not appropriately addressed, human trust will suffer, impacting on adoption and oversight and in some cases posing significant risks to humanity and societal values.

From this brief exploration, it is clear that the values and issues outlined in the chapter will benefit from much broader debate, research and consultation. There are no definitive answers to some of the questions raised—as for many, it is a matter of perspective. I trust that this chapter will embark you on your own journey as to what our future regulatory systems should encapsulate. Different AI applications create and pose different benefits, risks and issues. The solutions that might be adopted in the days ahead, will potentially challenge our traditional beliefs and systems for years to come. We are facing a major paradigm shift which will require significant rethink of some of our long-established legal principles, as we must now take into consideration, machine learning AI systems that have the ability to learn, adapt and 'make decisions' from data and 'life experiences'.

ICT professionals understand better than most in relation to the trends and trajectories of technologies and their potential impact on the economic, safety and social constructs of the workplace and society. Is it incumbent on ICT professionals and professional societies to raise these issues and ensure they are widely debated, so that appropriate and intelligent decisions can be made for the changes, risks and challenges ahead? ICT professionals are well placed to address some of the risks and challenges during the design and lifecycle of AI-enabled systems. It would be beneficial to society for ICT professionals to assist government, legislators, regulators and policy formulators with their unique understanding of the strengths and limitations of the technology and its effects.

Historically, our regulatory adaptations have been conservative and patchworked in their ability to keep pace with technological changes. Perhaps the drastic disruptions that COVID-19 has caused in our work, life and play beyond the normal will provide sufficient impetus and tenacity to consider and re-think on how our laws and regulatory systems should recalibrate with AI and autonomous systems, now and into the future.

Acknowledgment. I would like to acknowledge and express my appreciation to Graeme Philipson for his editorial assistance. He is an ICT editor, writer and publisher, and author of 'The Vision Splendid: The History of Australian Computing'. www.philipson.info

References

1. This chapter is for general reference purposes only. It does not constitute legal or professional advice. It is general comment only. Before making any decision or taking any action you should consult your legal or professional advisers to ascertain how the regulatory system applies to your particular circumstances in your jurisdiction
2. Australian AI Ethics Framework (2019). https://www.industry.gov.au/data-and-publications/building-australias-artificial-intelligence-capability/ai-ethics-framework. Accessed 6 June 2020
3. European Commission: Ethics guidelines for trustworthy AI (2019). https://ec.europa.eu/digital-single-market/en/news/ethics-guidelines-trustworthy-ai. Accessed 6 June 2020
4. OECD: OECD Principles on Artificial Intelligence, 22 May 2019. https://www.oecd.org/going-digital/ai/principles/. Accessed 20 June 2020
5. World Economic Forum: AI Governance: A Holistic Approach to Implement Ethics into AI. https://www.weforum.org/whitepapers/ai-governance-a-holistic-approach-to-implement-ethics-into-ai. Accessed 20 June 2020
6. Singapore Model AI Governance Framework. https://www.pdpc.gov.sg/-/media/files/pdpc/pdf-files/resource-for-organisation/ai/sgmodelaigovframework2.pdf. Accessed 20 June 2020
7. Definition from the Australian Securities & Investments Commission: Regulatory Guide 255 - Providing Digital Financial Product Advice to Retail Client. https://asic.gov.au/regulatory-resources/find-a-document/regulatory-guides/rg-255-providing-digital-financial-product-advice-to-retail-clients/. Accessed 6 June 2020
8. Corporations Amendment (Professional Standards of Financial Advisers) Act 2017
9. Australian Securities & Investments Commission: Regulatory Guide 255 - Providing Digital Financial Product Advice to Retail Client. https://asic.gov.au/regulatory-resources/find-a-document/regulatory-guides/rg-255-providing-digital-financial-product-advice-to-retail-clients/. Accessed 6 June 2020
10. Regulation (EU) 2016/679 of the European Parliament and of the Council of 27 April 2016 on the Protection of natural persons with regard to the processing of personal data and on the free movement of such data, and repealing Directive 95/46/EC (General Data Protection Regulation), 2016 O.J. (L 119/1) [GDPR]

11. Ibid art. 15(1)(h)
12. Ibid art. 22(3)
13. This section is based on the article, Wong, A.: Do robots and artificial intelligence think about copyright? The Australian, 5 September 2017
14. UK Intellectual Property Office, refer patent decision BL O/741/19 of December 2019. https://www.ipo.gov.uk/p-challenge-decision-results/p-challenge-decision-results-bl?BL_Number=O/741/19. Accessed 10 July 2020
15. European Patent Office, refer decision of January 2020. https://www.epo.org/news-issues/news/2020/20200128.html. Accessed 10 July 2020
16. US Patent and Trademark Office, refer to decision of April 2020 on Application No. 16/524,350. https://www.uspto.gov/sites/default/files/documents/16524350_22apr2020.pdf. Accessed 10 July 2020
17. Here the computer is used as a tool equivalent of the painter's brush or the writer's pen by the author in the creation of the work
18. Similar provisions have been replicated in New Zealand, Ireland, India, Hong Kong and South Africa
19. Copyright Designs and Patents Act 2988 (UK) s 9(3)
20. World Intellectual Property Organisation (WIPO), Conversation of Intellectual Property and Artificial Intelligence, Revised Issues paper on Intellectual Property and Artificial Intelligence, May 2020, paragraph 23. https://www.wipo.int/meetings/en/doc_details.jsp?doc_id=499504. Accessed 20 July 2020
21. In recognition of the importance of the 'Digital Economy', the US President Obama requested a study to examine how the US can benefit from the data economy in January 2014. The report Big Data: Seizing Opportunities, Preserving Values concluded that data can be a driver for economic growth and innovation ('Big Data: Seizing Opportunities, Preserving Values')
22. For an overview on data ownership, refer to Wong, A.: Big data fuels digital disruption and innovation, but who owns data? In: Chaikin, D., Coshott, D. (eds.) Digital Disruption Impact of Business Models, Regulation & Financial Crime (ch. 2). Australian Scholarly Publishing, Australia (2017)
23. Beverley-Smith, H.: The Commercial Appropriation of Personality, p. 296. Cambridge University Press, Cambridge (2002)
24. Merges, R.P.: Justifying Intellectual Property, p. 100. Harvard University Press, Cambridge (2011)
25. Nimmer, R.T.: Information Law [2:8]. Thomson Reuters, May 2014
26. The nature of the copyright in a literary, dramatic or musical work is defined in copyright legislation in the respective jurisdictions and in Australia, under the Copyright Act 1968 (Cth) s 31
27. Samuelson, P.: Is information property? Commun. ACM **34**(3), 16 (1991)
28. For an introduction to the protection of information using the law of confidential information, see Lahore, LexisNexis: Patents, Trade Marks & Related Rights (at 25 April 2016) [30,000]
29. See, eg, *Federal Commissioner of Taxation v United Aircraft Corp* (1943) 68 CLR 525 at 534; *Moorgate Tobacco Co Ltd v Philip Morris Ltd. (No. 2)* (1984) 156 CLR 414 at 438; *Breen v Williams* (1996) 186 CLR 71 at 81, 90, 111, 125; and *Australian Broadcasting Corporation v Lenah Game Meats Pty Ltd.* (2001) 208 CLR 199 at 271
30. See Osenga, K.: Information may want to be free, but information products do not: protecting and facilitating transactions in information products. Cardozo Law Rev. **30**(5), 2099, 2101 (2009)
31. Directive 96/9/EC of the European Parliament and of the Council of 11 March 1996 on the legal protection of databases, OJ L 077, 27/03/1996
32. Ibid art 7

33. Ibid art 3
34. Treasury Laws Amendment (Consumer Data Right) Act 2019. https://www.accc.gov.au/focus-areas/consumer-data-right-cdr-0. Accessed 2 June 2020
35. Regulation (EU) 2018/1807 of the European Parliament and of the Council of 14 November 2018 on a framework for the free flow of non-personal data in the European Union, OJ L 303, 28.11.2018
36. Article 20 of the Regulation (EU) 2016/679 of the European Parliament and of the Council of 27 April 2016 on the protection of natural persons with regard to the processing of personal data and on the free movement of such data, and repealing Directive 95/46/EC (General Data Protection Regulation)
37. Smith, B.: Legal personality. Yale Law J. **37**(3), 283–299 (1928)
38. For a discussion on the concept and expression "legal personality" refer to Bryson, J.J., Diamantis, M.E., Grant, T.D.: Of, for, and by the people: the legal lacuna of synthetic persons. Artif. Intell. Law. **25**(3), 277 (2017)
39. European Parliament: European Parliament resolution of 16 February 2017 with recommendations to the Commission on Civil Law Rules on Robotics (2015/2103(INL)), https://eur-lex.europa.eu/legal-content/EN/TXT/?uri=CELEX%3A52017IP0051. Accessed 9 June 2020
40. Ibid paragraph 59(f)
41. http://www.robotics-openletter.eu/. Accessed 9 June 2020
42. European Group on Ethics in Science and New Technologies: Statement on Artificial Intelligence, Robotics and 'Autonomous' Systems, p. 10. European Commission, Brussels (2018). http://ec.europa.eu/research/ege/pdf/ege_ai_statement_2018.pdf. Accessed 9 June 2020
43. European Commission: White Paper on Artificial Intelligence - A European Approach to Excellence and Trust, COM (2020), vol. 65, 19 February 2020. https://ec.europa.eu/info/sites/info/files/commissionwhite-paper-artificial-intelligence-feb2020_en.pdf. Accessed 9 June 2020
44. European Commission: Report on the safety and liability implications of Artificial Intelligence, the Internet of Things and robotics, COM (2020), vol. 64, 19 February 2020. https://ec.europa.eu/info/files/commission-report-safety-and-liability-implications-ai-internet-thingsand-robotics_en. Accessed 9 June 2020
45. Bryson, J.J., Diamantis, M.E., Grant, T.D.: Of, for, and by the people: the legal lacuna of synthetic persons. Artif. Intell. Law **25**(3), 273–291 (2017)
46. The World Economic Forum: White Paper on AI Governance a Holistic Approach to Implement Ethics into AI, p. 6. Geneva, Switzerland (2019). https://www.weforum.org/whitepapers/ai-governance-a-holistic-approach-to-implement-ethics-into-ai. Accessed 9 June 2020
47. Selbst, A.D.: Negligence and AI's human users. In: Public Law & Legal Theory Research Paper No. 20-01, p. 1. UCLA School of Law (2018)
48. For a brief rundown of the regulatory frameworks and developments in selected countries refer to the Australian National Transport Commission 2020, Review of 'Guidelines for trials of automated vehicles in Australia': Discussion paper, NTC, Melbourne, pp. 16–18. https://www.ntc.gov.au/sites/default/files/assets/files/NTC%20Discussion%20Paper%20-%20Review%20of%20guidelines%20for%20trials%20of%20automated%20vehicles%20in%20Australia.pdf. Accessed 6 June 2020. For examples of Australian legislation refer to: Motor Vehicles (Trials of Automotive Technologies) Amendment Act 2016 (SA), Transport Legislation Amendment (Automated Vehicle Trials and Innovation) Act 2017 (NSW), Road Safety Amendment (Automated Vehicles) Act 2018 (Vic)
49. For the new European Union drone rules refer to: https://www.easa.europa.eu/domains/civil-drones-rpas/drones-regulatory-framework-background. For the Australia drone rules refer to: https://www.casa.gov.au/knowyourdrone/drone-rules and the Civil Aviation Safety Amendment (Remotely Piloted Aircraft and Model Aircraft—Registration and Accreditation) Regulations 2019

50. European Commission: Report on the safety and liability implications of Artificial Intelligence, the Internet of Things and robotics, COM (2020), vol. 64, p. 14, 19 February 2020. https://ec.europa.eu/info/files/commission-report-safety-and-liability-implications-ai-internet-thingsand-robotics_en. Accessed June 2020

51. Australian National Transport Commission 2020: Review of 'Guidelines for trials of automated vehicles in Australia': Discussion paper, NTC, Melbourne, pp. 26–27. https://www.ntc.gov.au/sites/default/files/assets/files/NTC%20Discussion%20Paper%20-%20Review%20of%20guidelines%20for%20trials%20of%20automated%20vehicles%20in%20Australia.pdf. Accessed 6 June 2020

52. General Data Protection Regulation (GDPR) art. 22; Recital 71; see also Article 29 Data Protection Working Party, 2018a, Guidelines on Automated individual decision-making and Profiling for the purposes of Regulation 2016/679, 17/EN WP251rev.01, p. 19. http://ec.europa.eu/newsroom/article29/item-detail.cfm?item_id=612053. Accessed 4 June 2020

53. Cobbe, J.: Administrative law and the machines of government: judicial review of automated public-sector decision-making. Legal Stud. 3 (2019)

54. For the interpretability characteristics of various AI models, refer to ICO and Alan Turing Institute: Guidance on explaining decisions made with AI (2020). annexe 2. https://ico.org.uk/media/for-organisations/guide-to-data-protection/key-data-protection-themes/explaining-decisions-made-with-artificial-intelligence-1-0.pdf. Accessed 6 June 2020

55. For the types of explanation that an organisation may provide, refer to ICO and Alan Turing Institute: Guidance on explaining decisions made with AI, p. 20 (2020). https://ico.org.uk/media/for-organisations/guide-to-data-protection/key-data-protection-themes/explaining-decisions-made-with-artificial-intelligence-1-0.pdf. Accessed 6 June 2020

56. General Data Protection Regulation (GDPR) art. 15

57. General Data Protection Regulation (GDPR) art. 22

58. General Data Protection Regulation (GDPR) arts. 13–14

59. European Commission: Report on the safety and liability implications of Artificial Intelligence, the Internet of Things and robotics, COM (2020), vol. 64, , p. 15, 19 February 2020. https://ec.europa.eu/info/files/commission-report-safety-and-liability-implications-ai-internet-thingsand-robotics_en. Accessed 9 June 2020

60. Australian Human Rights Commission: Discussion Paper on Human Rights and Technology, p. 104 (2019). https://humanrights.gov.au/our-work/rights-and-freedoms/publications/human-rights-and-technology-discussion-paper-2019. Accessed 20 June 2020; For a US perspective, refer to Flicker, K.: The prison of convenience, the need for national regulation of biometric technology in sports venues. 30 Fordham Intell. Prop. Media Ent. L. J. **985**, 1015 (2020). https://ir.lawnet.fordham.edu/iplj/vol30/iss3/7/. Accessed 20 June 2020

The Ethics of Artificial Intelligence

Chris Rees[(✉)]

British Computer Society – The Chartered Institute for IT in the UK, 3 Newbridge.Square,
Swindon SNl.18Y, UK
`chris.rees@ficino.org`

Abstract. This chapter focuses on the ethics of narrow, as opposed to general
AI. It makes the practical as well as the philosophical case for discussion of AI
ethics. It considers ethical charters, then discusses the principal ethical issues: bias,
explainability, liability for failure, harmlessness, the ethical use of data, whether
AIs should have legal personality, the effects on employment and society, and AIs
impersonating humans. A case study is presented of AI in personal insurance.
It makes the case for regulation of AI and discusses the challenges of enacting
regulation. It draws conclusions, that the benefits of AI are so valuable that the
ethical risks must be managed, or the benefits may be lost because of the loss of
public trust. There are grounds for optimism, notably the public consciousness of
the issues, the engagement of governments and the amount of private and public
investment in ethical research.

Keywords: Ethics · Charters · Bias · Explainability · Liability · Harmlessness ·
Data-ethics · Legal-personality · Employment · Regulation

1 Introduction

Artificial intelligence theories and technologies are not new. The concepts were first
elaborated by Alan Turing [1] in 1950. Since then AI has gone through periods of hope,
when new developments appeared to offer exciting new possibilities, followed by so-
called "winters", when those hopes faded, together with the investment and much of the
research.

However the technology has exploded in popularity in the last 20 years, for three main
reasons: first, dramatic increases in computing power and storage and corresponding
reductions in cost, particularly cloud computing and storage, secondly the growth in
the internet, providing access to the huge datasets which AI requires, and thirdly the
development of new AI techniques, particularly artificial neural networks and machine
learning.

Until recently, few considered that AI posed particular ethical challenges beyond
those posed by any other computing technique. However that has changed radically. Not
only in academic and professional circles but in the quality press and even the popular
press, articles appear frequently, even on the front pages, raising ethical issues in the
application of AI. The concerns commonly centre on the ethical risks and the threats to

© IFIP International Federation for Information Processing 2020
Published by Springer Nature Switzerland AG 2020
L. Strous et al. (Eds.): Unimagined Futures, IFIP AICT 555, pp. 55–69, 2020.
https://doi.org/10.1007/978-3-030-64246-4_5

privacy posed by AI systems, even where they are developed and applied for entirely laudable ends.

In this chapter 1 shall focus on the ethics of narrow AI, not Artificial General Intelligence (AGI). All current implementations of AI are narrow, in the sense that they are applied to a narrowly focused domain, such as diagnosing cancer or playing chess. They can often do that better than any human, but they cannot then turn their attention to stacking pallets in a warehouse or translating from French to English.

There is much discussion in the literature of AGI, that is AI capable of doing what humans do, turning its hand, as it were, to any task, and far exceeding human capability, with the flexibility of the human mind and using common sense. The concept leads to the notion of "singularity", the point at which, when an AI is implanted in the brain, it is impossible to tell where the AI stops and the brain starts. Gurus like Ray Kurzweil, Elon Musk, and the late Stephen Hawking all predict it is coming, in 20 or 50 years, estimates vary. The alternative position is that it is never going to happen, or at least not for a very long time. Certainly, it is not today's problem. Undoubtedly AI will become smarter, more capable, more effective, but the route to AGI is not a continuum.

In this chapter 1 shall make the case for the discussion of the ethics of narrow AI, consider current ethical charters, discuss the principal risks which arise in relation to the ethics of AI, illustrate some of them through a short case study in the insurance industry, and consider the case for regulation. Finally I shall draw some overall conclusions.

2   Why Discuss the Ethics of AI?

AIs are artefacts, things. They have no ethics, or put another way, they are ethically neutral. It is important that we do not attribute agency to artefacts, a topic that will be further discussed in Sect. 4.6 below in relation to the question of giving AIs legal personality. When we talk about ethics, we are talking about human ethics, the ethics of those who design, develop, deploy and use AI systems. Ethics has been a subject of philosophical debate at least since Aristotle's *Nicomachean Ethics* in 350 BCE, and of course it was the subject of extensive discourse in the much older Hebrew Bible, the Upanishads and other ancient scriptures. There is nothing new about identifying ethical issues in society or in relation to IT in particular.

So why should we consider the ethics of artificial intelligence specifically? There are not only good philosophical reasons to discuss it, but at a practical level we should consider it because of the overarching risk that if AI comes to be seen by the public as unethical, they may lose trust in it and the benefits would be lost. There are precedents. There is no scientific evidence that there is anything wrong with genetically modified foods, but the European and particularly the British public lost trust in them [2] in 2003–4 and rejected them. In the UK this was despite a statement in 2004 by Margaret Beckett MP, then Secretary of State for Environment, Food and Rural Affairs, in the House of Commons saying *inter alia* that "There was no scientific case for ruling out all GM crops or products". And after the fraudulent linking of the MMR vaccine with autism [3] by the disgraced former medical doctor, Andrew Wakefield, vaccination rates for measles, mumps and rubella have dropped in most countries, dangerously so in some, leading to a rise in deaths from measles, particularly among children.

To quote the EU AI High Level Expert Group [4], "Trustworthiness is a prerequisite for people and societies to develop, deploy and use AI systems. Without AI systems – and the human beings behind them – being demonstrably worthy of trust, unwanted consequences may ensue and their uptake might be hindered, preventing the realisation of the potentially vast social and economic benefits that they can bring."

3   Current Ethical Charters

One way to demonstrate ethical principles and earn trust is by publishing an ethical charter. There are many ethical charters for AI in the market. Indeed there is a risk of corporations "charter shopping" until they find a set that suits their purpose. However the basis for regulation and the safe, proper development of AI has been formulated and published by the OECD as The Principles of AI [5]. 44 governments have signed up to these principles, including all the G20, and including some countries which are not members of the OECD. They don't have the force of law, but they are influential. They are set out below.

AI should be:

1. **Human-centred:** AI should benefit people and the planet by driving inclusive growth, sustainable development and well-being.
2. **Fair:** AI systems should be designed in a way that respects the rule of law, human rights, democratic values and diversity, and they should include appropriate safeguards – for example, enabling human intervention where necessary – to ensure a fair and just society.
3. **Transparent:** There should be transparency and responsible disclosure around AI systems to ensure that people understand AI-based outcomes and can challenge them.
4. **Safe:** AI systems must function in a robust, secure and safe way throughout their life cycles and potential risks should be continually assessed and managed.
5. **Accountable:** Organisations and individuals developing, deploying or operating AI systems should be held accountable for their proper functioning in line with the above principles.

These are fine principles, which should inform regulation and be at the heart of those engaged in AI, whether as developers or users. However it is not always so.

4   Principal Risks Which Arise in Relation to the Ethics of AI

The principal ethical issues and potentially associated risks which I shall discuss are these:

1. Bias
2. Explainability
3. Liability for failure
4. Harmlessness

5. The ethical use of data
6. Should AIs have legal personality?
7. The effects on employment and society
8. AIs impersonating humans

4.1 Bias

Why are AI systems biased? Because we are biased, all of us. We are aware of some biases, not others. Not all are bad. We tend to read newspapers whose views reflect our own. We like people who are like us. Many people are biased against people unlike themselves, foreigners, immigrants, people of different colours or religions. There are many other examples.

Bias gets embedded in AI systems in different ways. For example, the vast majority of AI engineers are young, white males. They may not perceive that the systems they build have a bias and, for example, work better for white males than black females. AI's learn bias from biased data in the training dataset. To the extent that the data reflects the biases in the population, or a segment of the population, the data is biased and so the AI systems will learn that bias and carry it through into live operation. Because of their speed and ubiquity, the bias is spread far and fast.

Does this matter? Not always. In machine translation, you are interested in the quality of translation into the target language. Gender bias can creep in here too. Turkish has genderless pronouns. Some automatic translation engines [6] translate

"o bir mühendis" as "**he** is an engineer"

"o bir doktor" as "**he** is a doctor"

"o bir hemşire" as "**she** is a nurse"

"o bir aşçı" as "**she** is a cook"

This is perhaps offensive rather than critical.

Yet gender and racial bias does matter in all sorts of ways. Facial recognition technology (FRT) is one application where it often arises. FRT has been widely used by police forces, in the UK for instance by the Metropolitan Police and the South Wales Police. However it is controversial, because of current inaccuracy, particularly with certain racial groups, as well as raising concerns over privacy. By way of example, its use by South Wales Police was challenged in the High Court [7] of England by Ed Bridges. He lost the case, the court finding inter alia that the current legal regime is adequate to ensure the appropriate and non-arbitrary use of FRT. However this was disputed by the Information Commissioner who expressed reservations about the adequacy of the legal framework. And recently Lord Clement-Jones, Chairman of the Lords Select Committee which produced the report on "AI in the UK: Ready, Willing and Able?" [8] (HL Paper 100), has introduced a Private Member's Bill in the House of Lords which seeks to make it a criminal offence to use FRT for overt surveillance in public places and to require the government to review its use within a year. Such bills seldom become law, but the bill may put pressure on the government to act.

In the USA, IBM's and Microsoft's facial recognition technologies confused dark-skinned people with gorillas. In 2018 Joy Buolamwini, a researcher in AI at the M.I.T.

Media Lab, was not recognised as a human being by the algorithm until she put on a white mask. She conducted an experiment [9] in which she ran the Microsoft AI on 385 photos of light-skinned males, and comparable sets of light-skinned females, darker-skinned males and darker-skinned females. The algorithm got 99% of the light-skinned males right, 93% of the light-skinned females right, 88% of the darker-skinned males and only 65% of the darker-skinned females. When she published her paper, IBM and Microsoft quickly changed their algorithms.

There are many other examples of gender and racial bias. In 2019, Amazon shut down an AI-driven human resources system project [10] because it was perpetuating its male gender bias, by being trained on its recruitment records.

Judges in several American states use an AI system called the Correctional Offender Management Profiling for Alternative Sanctions tool (Compas) [11] to determine whether to grant bail to alleged offenders and in Wisconsin to help the judge decide the length of a sentence. The system relies on a number of indicators, which do not include race. However it does take into account where the alleged offender lives, and given the racial distribution of populations in American cities, geography becomes a proxy for race. So a black accused who may well not re-offend, given his record, is more likely to be denied bail than a white man with a comparable record [12]. Compas is proprietary and Equivant, the company that markets it, will not divulge how it works, asserting that it is a trade secret. Perhaps they cannot divulge how it reaches its conclusions because they do not know.

Perhaps the most conspicuous application of FRT is its use by the Chinese Communist Party in Xinjiang in Western China, to identify and confine some 1.8 million Uighur people in so-called re-education camps. The technology does not need to be very accurate as Uighurs are Turkic people, with features quite unlike those of the Han Chinese. This policy has been widely reported in the Western press [13], and has led to American sanctions [14] on the companies supplying the FRT, but with no apparent effect on the policy to date.

4.2 Explainability

Unlike traditional software programs, AIs based on neural networks cannot explain how they reach their conclusions. Nor can their developers. If a bank is using AI to determine whether to grant you a loan and they decline, but cannot explain why, that is unfair and unethical. You would not know what you had to do to qualify. Similarly with insurance if the insurer declines the risk without explanation. Explainability is the one ethical issue that is unique to AI – discussion of other ethical issues typically goes back to Aristotle.

To return to Compas, in Loomis v. Wisconsin the trial judge gave Eric Loomis a six year sentence for his role in a drive-by shooting, partially because of the "high risk" score the defendant received from Compas [15]. Loomis appealed against his sentence, on the grounds that he was not allowed to assess the algorithm. The state Supreme Court ruled against Loomis [16], reasoning that knowledge of the algorithm's output was a sufficient level of transparency. This is surely unethical. It is a principle of the Common Law that a judge must explain her/his decision.

There is a lot of work going on to solve this problem. The most likely route appears to be an external audit approach, comparable to financial audit. But right now, there is no general solution available.

4.3 Liability for Failure

What happens when things go wrong? The question most frequently arises in relation to automated vehicles (AVs) – self-driving cars and commercial vehicles. But the question does not only apply to them.

As far as automated vehicles are concerned, should it be the AV or the 'driver'? In fact in the UK there is an answer. Under the Automated & Electrical Vehicles Act 2018, (AEVA) [17], the insurer (or the owner, if the vehicle is not insured) is liable if the AV causes damage, death or injury. The insurer then has right of recourse against the manufacturer of the vehicle or the developer of the faulty component. The injured party typically needs recompense quickly. The insurers can afford to wait to recover their costs where appropriate until the post-crash investigation has revealed the root cause.

Cover can be voided if the owner has tampered with the system or failed to update safety-critical software. But what if the vehicle's software has been hacked? And if there is a fleet of vehicles, who is responsible for the software updates? If the insurer escapes cover, who is liable? The individual 'driver'? There are unresolved problems in this field, and as yet no case law to resolve them.

There are many other applications of AI where the same issue arises – who is liable when things go wrong? For instance, what if an AI-controlled medical device implanted in the human body fails? Is the surgeon who implanted it liable, or the hospital, or the manufacturer? What about off-road vehicles like tractors? The list goes on. All of these issues of liability exhibit both ethical and legal concerns. There is no case law. In human resource situations in the UK, the Equality Act 2010 [18] will bite, there are similar laws in other countries. Otherwise it is likely that suppliers will seek to decline the consequences of failure by contract, though normally they cannot do so for death or injury.

Two aspects of such risks which can scarcely be overemphasised are the importance of protecting such AIs from failures in cybersecurity, and from inadequate testing. For instance, if a number of automated vehicles were hacked, they could be turned into a potent weapon – cars, buses and trucks have all been already used as weapons in many cities, when driven by human terrorists.

Testing is a particularly difficult task with AI. In simple terms, this is first because they are typically agglomerations of large numbers of software components, which may never have been tested together, even if the individual components have been tested. Secondly, because they often use publicly available open source code, whose testing status may not be clear. Thirdly, the range of use cases for which test scenarios need to be constructed may be vast, for instance for AVs. When manufacturers claim that an automated vehicle has been driven for several million miles, it says nothing about the effectiveness of the testing regime. If the testing of an AI system is inadequate or defective, then its implementation would be unethical.

4.4 Harmlessness

AIs should be harmless. In *I Robot* [19] in 1942, long before Turing's work, Isaac Asimov formulated his Three Laws of Robotics. The first was "A robot may not injure a human being or, through inaction, allow a human being to come to harm". He later added a fourth: "A robot may not harm humanity, or, by inaction, allow humanity to come to harm."

Today there are two ways in which these laws are being breached. First, through the malicious use of AI. AI, like any tool, is ethically neutral and dual use. A knife can be used to cut cake and stab someone. It can be used for good and ill. Why take the risk of burgling a house if you can use technology to steal "from the comfort of your own home", to quote that hackneyed marketing phrase. AI can maximise the effectiveness of such theft, by reducing the cost and increasing the volume of spear phishing attacks, in which detailed information about the victim, harvested from a number of sources, is used to gain his confidence, so that he imports a virus or trojan. Gathering the information is expensive and laborious. AI reduces the cost and effort.

A wide range of such threats were analysed in a report published in 2018, on the malicious use of artificial intelligence [20]. The report highlighted the potential for AI systems to attack other AI systems, for AI to enable higher speed, lower cost and higher frequency attacks on a wide variety of systems including automated vehicles and utilities, and the need to plan and prepare counter-measures. Today AI is being widely used both to attack and defend systems, including AI systems.

The second way is through Lethal Autonomous Weapons Systems (LAWS). Drones are useful tools. They can be used for crop inspection, distributing aid to disaster victims, searching for crashed planes under water and so on. However they can also be weaponised, and if configured in swarms, become an even more effective offensive weapon system. The use of autonomous, i.e. AI-guided drones constitutes a significant ethical issue and, in terms of international law, a legal issue. It is expressly prohibited by the Geneva Convention [21]. A human operator can react to changing circumstances in the target – if he has moved into a hospital or among a group of children for instance, and abort the mission. Could an AI make such a sophisticated judgment?

The British Government has decided not to develop or deploy LAWS [22], even if the enemy does. That policy could change

What if, for instance, the American, Russian, Chinese and perhaps Israeli militaries are developing them, and may be willing to deploy them? And when human-guided drones are already being deployed to great effect, not just by the USAF in Pakistan and Afghanistan but by rival militias in the Libyan and Syrian civil wars, can LAWS be far behind?

4.5 The Ethical Use of Data

All AI applications depend on large datasets. That gives rise to privacy issues. There is a tension and a trade-off, for instance, between the use of medical data for the public good and the protection of personal data. You can readily anonymise data in a dataset, for instance removing name, address and other identifying characteristics. However it has been shown [23] that if you have two datasets of similar type, then an overlap of less than 20% enables you to de-anonymise them.

Netflix discovered this as long ago as 2009, when it released anonymised movie reviews penned by subscribers [24]. By crossmatching those snippets with reviews on another website, data sleuths revealed they could identify individual subscribers and what they had been watching. A gay customer sued for breach of privacy; Netflix settled.

Ways are being found around these problems. Synthetic data is artificially generated, usually by funnelling real-world data through an algorithm which adds noise to construct a new data set without personal information. The resulting data set captures the statistical features of the original information without being a giveaway replica. This dataset can then be used to train the AI, or provide the data on which it is to operate.

There are other concerns too, of companies misusing the data in unethical ways. For instance using Crispr technology the 23andMe company [25] sells kits with which users can send off samples of their spit for genetic analysis to companies, either to discover more about their ancestry or their ancestry and their future health. This raises concerns that we could lose control of profoundly personal data or unearth unwelcome family secrets. The science of genetics has a long history of abuse by eugenicists, obsessed with the idea of breeding out "inferior" intelligence or ensuring racial "purity". As new Crispr technology opens up a world where embryos might be edited, genetic data needs to be handled more carefully than ever. 23andMe has never suggested it could detect intelligence in people's genes. However, companies such as GenePlaza allow users to upload their genetic data and claim to show how comparatively intelligent they are. Meanwhile, members of the alt-right in the USA have shared their 23andMe results on social media and boasted about their white European ancestry.

From a societal point of view, there is a further risk in this situation, that the benefits of AI will accrue disproportionately to a few, technically capable, wealthy individuals while the mass of the population loses out. Prof. Shoshana Zuboff has pointed out in her book, *The Age of Surveillance Capitalism* [26] that Google and the other huge IT companies use AI to create a new form of capitalism, which she termed 'Surveillance Capitalism', which they dominate and in which individuals willingly if unknowingly surrender their rights to their personal data. She argues that people are very willing to give up their private information in return for perceived benefits such as ease of use, navigation and access to friends and information. The agency we can actively assert over our own futures is fundamentally usurped by predictive, data-driven AI systems. Engaging with the system of surveillance capitalism, and acquiescing to its demands for ever deeper incursions into everyday life, involves much more than the surrender of information: it is to place the entire track of one's life, the determination of one's path, under the purview and control of the market, just as Pokémon Go players are walked, lit by their glowing screens, straight through the doors of shops they didn't even know they wanted to visit, after the company sold virtual locations to the highest bidders, including McDonalds and Starbucks.

4.6 Should AI's Have Legal Personality?

I discussed, in Sect. 4.3 above, AIs that let people down or cause accidents. The question of liability for failure leads on to the question whether AIs should have legal personality.

In 2017 Saudi Arabia granted Sophia, a "female" robot, legal personality [27]. No other jurisdiction has followed this example.

The law in Common Law and Roman Law jurisdictions, and many others, recognises natural persons – real people, and corporate persons – limited companies, partnerships and government entities. The latter have legal personality, they can sue and be sued. Essentially the concept is that these legal persons are controlled by natural persons. Should machines, robots, AIs have legal personality?

The case of animals has useful parallels. The issue of the legal personhood of chimpanzees was considered by a New York court in 2015 in Nonhuman Rights Project, Inc. v. Stanley [28], where a writ of habeas corpus was filed by Nonhuman Rights Project, an NGO, seeking the release of Hercules and Leo, two chimpanzees confined in a laboratory at Stony Brook University.

The NGO argued that for the institution of habeas corpus, the law does not define the notion of a person. Given the lack of any precedent concerning the application of habeas corpus to anyone other than a human, the court decided to consider the issue of its application to a chimpanzee. An *amicus curiae* brief was filed in the case by the Center for the Study of The Great Ideas, arguing that under New York law, legal personality is held by humans and certain public and private entities, but the legal personality vested in such non-human entities is justified because they are composed of humans. Thus personhood should not be extended to cover animals.

In its judgment, the court refused to recognise the personhood of chimpanzees because they are neither capable of bearing legal responsibility for their actions, and also are not capable of performing obligations. The court also pointed out that it is the capacity to assume rights and obligations, and not the physical resemblance to humans, that is decisive for recognising the legal personality of a being.

On exactly the same grounds, one cannot argue that a robot equipped with AI has a free will which could lead to commission of prohibited acts with the aim of achieving its own ends. Thus it cannot be ascribed a degree of fault, such as negligence or recklessness. Nor is it possible to hold it liable for damages for its errors, for example as in the case of an accident caused by an autonomous car or malpractice by surgical robots.

The European Patent Office has refused to grant a patent to an AI invented by Dabus, an AI [29]. They said that AI systems or machines do not have any legal personality comparable to natural or legal persons. They can neither be employed nor can they transfer any rights to a successor in title. "Since an AI system or a machine cannot have rights, it cannot be considered to own its output or own any alleged invention and it cannot transfer any rights thereto."

In summary, granting legal personhood would be a bad idea: "My AI just caused you damage. Oh dear, go ahead and sue it." Companies have capital and therefore can pay damages if they lose a case. If a company has little capital, you take care before you contract with it. Robots do not have financial resources.

4.7 AIs Impersonating Humans

Famously Alan Turing devised the Imitation Game, now commonly known as the Turing Test, whether a machine (then a teletype) could convince a human being on the other side of an opaque screen that it is another human being. Arguably no machine has comprehensively passed the test. However at the Google developer conference in 2018, Sundar Pichai, the CEO, demonstrated Duplex [30], an AI that convincingly called a beauty parlour and a restaurant to make a hair appointment and a table booking respectively. The AI successfully negotiated quite complex conversations, including saying "Ah ha" at appropriate points and correcting a misunderstanding by one of its interlocutors. Neither receptionist realised that they were talking to a machine; it was so realistic. This technology is now live and available from Google. Although the audience at the conference applauded the demonstration, the reaction on social media was that this was unethical. Not to identify that the machine is a machine is unethical. The EU High Level Expert Group has stated that such behaviour contravenes one of their Principles [31], namely transparency. It also contravenes the OECD Principles discussed above.

4.8   The Effects on Employment and Society

Is AI going to replace us all and abolish work and jobs by doing what we do more efficiently and at lower cost? The answer is no, but it will replace many job functions, and not just repetitive tasks. That will lead to some existing roles becoming redundant. New roles will be created. The difference this time is that it is not just the physical functions that are being replaced but the mental ones. Very few professions and occupations are immune: maybe philosophers and priests, not lawyers or software developers. As noted previously, some medical functions but not yet the role of doctor.

There are two fallacies in this discussion, as Daniel Susskind has pointed out in his book, *A World Without Work: Technology, Automation and How We Should Respond* [32]. First is the "Lump of Work" fallacy. It is not the case nowadays that there is a given lump of work and if AI does some of it there is correspondingly less for humans to do. The amount of work to be done has grown year by year at least since the industrial revolution, even if in the agricultural Middle Ages it was pretty static. Job functions and indeed jobs have been continually destroyed and created, e.g. domestic servants (other than for the super-rich) and punch card operators have gone but there were no data scientists or web designers 50 years ago.

AI will create new work functions that we cannot even envisage now. However what Susskind calls the "Lump of Work Fallacy Fallacy" is important too. We cannot assume that the work that AI will create will be best done by humans. It may be work for AIs. Almost certainly some of it will be. We have no way of predicting the speed with which these changes will take place. It is likely that the destructive force of new technology will precede the constructive phase. It usually does.

What is to be done? The key is retraining. There are functions that AI will struggle to touch such as user interface design, and jobs requiring empathy and physical care like nursing. Who will fund such training? It will need to be some combination of government, companies and individuals.

A good example of how it can be done is AT&T's Workforce 2020 project [33]. AT&T recognised in 2013 that the company was not going to need the thousands of technicians they had, who could repair wires up poles and down holes, as it would all be fibre. But they would need an army of software engineers that would cost a fortune to hire and train. So they instituted a major retraining programme for the technicians they already had, which has been fully supported by top management and the workforce themselves, working with universities and training companies. It has been very successful. The project saved the company a huge amount of money in redundancy and recruitment costs and wound up with a happier, more productive and secure workforce.

There will be those who are unable or unwilling to learn the necessary skills to thrive in the new environment. What is to happen to them? Unless we address these ethical issues as a society, the resulting unemployment and inequality could lead to societal unrest.

5 AI in Personal Insurance – A Case Study

The insurance industry is exploring and slowly taking up AI [34] – in most cases slowly because of the technical challenge of grafting new technology onto legacy systems. This has both benefits and risks for the public and constitutes an interesting case study in the ethical implications of AI.
Benefits include:

- More precise risk assessments, enabling previously uninsurable customers to obtain cover, e.g. because of age or location.
- Greater efficiency in a variety of labour-intensive processes, such as onboarding a new customer. Such efficiencies should lead to lower premiums.
- Better claims management, e.g. detecting fraud – by identifying from social media that a claimant was not where they said they were when the incident occurred, again reducing costs.
- It could enable them to offer novel advisory services, like suggesting safer driving routes or healthier exercise regimes (known as 'nudging').

On the other hand, there are ethical risks:

- Hyper-personal risk assessments could leave some individuals uninsurable, e.g. identifying the potential for cancer by analysing sources which could indicate such a propensity, of which the individual is unaware. The principle underlying the insurance business model has always been the spreading of individual risk among a large population. Such risk assessments go against that principle.
- The use of large datasets may affect privacy.
- Insurers could use AI to model the minimum benefit it would take for customers to renew.
- New forms of advisory service, such as 'nudging' could be intrusive.

Clearly there are ethical as well as legal concerns here.

6 The Case for Regulation

Given the risks I have described, is there a need for regulation? Yes, even the industry is recognising that. Some say that the big companies are trying to mould potential regulation to their business models.

Regulation is difficult to formulate in a fast-developing field like AI. There is always a risk that government will introduce regulations based on a view of the technology which goes rapidly out of date. For instance in the UK, many of the strictures on the use of emails for marketing are caught, not by GPDR but by the Privacy and Electronic Communications Regulations (PECR) [35] which sits alongside GPDR. PECR were promulgated in 2003, but modified after lobbying by the mail order industry based on their then model of postal marketing. In the age of email, the constraint on an email to a customer being classed as marketing and therefore illegal unless consent has been given, even if the purpose of the email is to seek consent, is out of date but still in force.

The British and other governments, the EU, and the OECD (see Sect. 3 above) as well as the Nolan Committee on Standards in Public Life in the UK have all recognised the need for regulation. In its report on Artificial Intelligence and Public Standards [36], published in February 2020, the Nolan Committee concluded that the UK does not need a new regulator for AI but noted that: "Honesty, integrity, objectivity, openness, leadership, selflessness and accountability were first outlined by Lord Nolan as the standards expected of all those who act on the public's behalf. Artificial intelligence – and in particular, machine learning – will transform the way public sector organisations make decisions and deliver public services. Demonstrating high standards will help realise the huge potential benefits of AI in public service delivery. However, it is clear that the public need greater reassurance about the use of AI in the public sector." They highlighted explainability and data bias as two key ethical concerns in relation to the use of AI in the public sector. I would argue that these principles should apply equally to AI in the private and third sectors.

The challenge is to regulate the development and deployment of AI in such a way as to protect the public and the individual without inhibiting innovation, to enact regulations quickly enough to have an impact in the near term and to avoid the regulations being hijacked by the giant corporations.

There are questions too as to how to go about it:

- Principle-based or Rule-based
- Vertical (e.g. cars, pharmaceuticals, medicine) or horizontal (Facial Recognition Technology)
- Local vs international (UK/EU/USA/Australia/Japan/China, etc.)

There are no easy answers, but increasing public pressure.

7 Conclusions

At the outset, a contrast was drawn between the benefits of ethical AI and the risks of unethical AI. The benefits are huge and growing for the individual and for society at large. This chapter is being written during the 2020 Coronavirus outbreak. AI is being widely deployed in the search for medicines and vaccines which may counter the scourge. For instance, in China doctors use AI tools provided by Huawei Technologies to detect signs of Covid-19 in CT scans. In Israel, Tyto Care Ltd. offers in-home medical examinations, using AI to deliver clinical-grade data to remote doctors for diagnosis. Chinese tech giant Baidu Inc. devised an algorithm that can analyse the biological structure of the new coronavirus and made it available to scientists working on a vaccine. AI is also behind biometric identification systems being rolled out by governments to track the virus and enforce lockdown efforts, including temperature screening systems deployed throughout Beijing and CCTV cameras hooked up to facial-recognition software in Moscow. "AI is being used to fight the virus on all fronts, from screening and diagnosis to containment and drug development," says Andy Chun, an adjunct professor at City University of Hong Kong and AI adviser at the Hong Kong Computer Science Society [37]. It is critical that these benefits not be lost. But the risks – and they are risks rather than threats – must be addressed.

Despite the ethical challenges set out in this chapter, which may sound doom-laden, there are grounds for optimism. There are several reasons for this. The weight of public opinion concerned about the ethics of AI, stimulated by articles and television programmes about the issues, may move governments to act. The engagement of governments in the issues is serious. In the UK alone there are a number of government and quasi-government organisations with proper funding, devoted to defining, articulating and addressing the ethical issues. All Masters programmes in AI at British universities have to include a course on ethics. And serious money is being committed to research on the ethics of AI. For instance Steven Schwarzman, Chairman and CEO of Blackstone, has committed $350 M to MIT, to be matched by the university, for the creation of the MIT Schwarzman College of Computing [38], focused on the Ethics of AI. He has also given £150 M to the University of Oxford [39] for a similar purpose. There is an international consensus (at least in the West) that action is needed.
To summarise the key points,

- There are huge benefits to be derived from AI but also significant concerns, which, if not addressed, could damage public trust in the technology and put the benefits at risk.
- AI is never responsible. Its makers, owners and operators are.
- Human centring is the only coherent basis for AI ethics.
- There is increasing public and government awareness of the importance of the ethics of AI.
- Regulation is needed and there is widespread support for it, difficult as it will be to draft.

What should we do about it? As IT practitioners, we have a duty both as professionals and as members of society to engage in the debate, and to seek to inform it, concerned but not frightened.

References

1. Turing, A.: Computing machinery and intelligence. Mind **59**, 433–460 (1950). https://tinyurl. com/y8c2juyl. Accessed 16–17 Apr 2020
2. GM food and crops: what went wrong in the UK? US National Library of Medicine, National Institutes of Health EMBO report, May 2004. https://tinyurl.com/ycvg4p8t. Accessed 16–17 Apr 2020

3. Wakefield's article linking MMR vaccine and autism was fraudulent. BMJ (2011). https://tin yurl.com/ybntmdzd. Accessed 16–17 Apr 2020

4. Ethics guidelines for trustworthy AI. Eur. Comm. (2018). https://tinyurl.com/y37czxtc. Accessed 16–17 Apr 2020

5. The OECD AI Principles, May 2019. https://www.oecd.org/going-digital/ai/principles/. Accessed 16–17 Apr 2020

6. e.g. Bing Translator. https://www.bing.com/translator. Accessed 16–17 Apr 2020

7. Haddon-Cave, L.J., Swift, J.: Judgment of the High Court citation no [2019] EWHC 2341 (Admin). https://tinyurl.com/yb3g2btl. Accessed 16–17 Apr 2020

8. AI in the UK: Ready, Willing and Able? House of Lords Select Committee on Artificial Intelligence Report of Session 2017–19, 16 April 2018. https://tinyurl.com/y8yelom9Accessed 16–17 Apr 2020

9. Gender shades: intersectional phenotypic and demographic evaluation of face datasets and gender classifiers. PhD thesis. MIT. https://tinyurl.com/y3xxuye9. Accessed 16–17 Apr 2020

10. Amazon scraps secret AI recruiting tool that showed bias against women, Reuters, October 2018. https://tinyurl.com/y8eelatr. Accessed 16–17 Apr 2020

11. https://www.equivant.com/practitioners-guide-to-compas-core/. Accessed 16–17 Apr 2020

12. The accuracy, fairness, and limits of predicting recidivism. Sci. Adv. (2018). https://tinyurl. com/u2saony. Accessed 16–17 Apr 2020

13. For instance: Absolutely No Mercy': leaked files expose how china organized mass detentions of muslims. New York Times (2019). https://tinyurl.com/vavm8d3. What happens when China's Uighurs are released from re-education camps. Economist (2020). https://tinyurl.com/ tcqyvz9. Accessed 16–17 Apr 2020

14. China's 'Abusive' Facial Recognition Machine Targeted By New U.S. Sanctions, Zak Doffman, Forbes, 8 October 2019. https://tinyurl.com/yays44th. Accessed 16–17 Apr 2020

15. A popular algorithm is no better at predicting crimes than random people. Atlantic (2018). https://tinyurl.com/ycef9mqv. Accessed 16–17 Apr 2020

16. STATE of Wisconsin, Plaintiff–Respondent, v. Eric L. LOOMIS, Defendant–Appellant. FindLaw, July 2016. https://tinyurl.com/y6wgq8x5. Accessed 16–17 Apr 2020

17. Automated and Electric Vehicles Act 2018. legislation.gov.uk, https://tinyurl.com/y99d8dpg. Accessed 16–17 Apr 2020

18. Equality Act 2010. legislation.gov.uk, https://tinyurl.com/3y6kuja. Accessed 16–17 Apr 2020

19. I, Robot, Isaac Asimov, originally published as a series of short stories between 1940 and 1950. Compiled into a book by Gnome Press, September 1950. https://tinyurl.com/ybzxpeur. Accessed 16–17 Apr 2020

20. The Malicious Use of Artificial Intelligence: Forecasting, Prevention, and Mitigation, Arxiv, February 2018. https://tinyurl.com/y9cvemk7. Accessed 16–17 Apr 2020

21. Amidst new challenges, Geneva Conventions mark 70 years of 'limiting brutality' during war, UN News, August 2019. https://tinyurl.com/y7akhqev. Accessed 16–17 Apr 2020

22. The United Kingdom and lethal autonomous weapons systems, Article 36, April 2018. https:// tinyurl.com/yb8bauz5. Accessed 16–17 Apr 2020

23. Archie, M., Gershon, S., Katcoff, A., Zeng, A.: Who's Watching? De-anonymization of Netflix Reviews using Amazon Reviews. MIT, Cambridge (2018). https://tinyurl.com/yau6d57m. Accessed 16–17 Apr 2020

24. Financial Times: The promise of synthetic data. Anjana Ahuja (2020). https://tinyurl.com/ y88flar4. Accessed 16–17 Apr 2020

25. Financial Times: Anne Wojcicki: 'This is the way the world is going' (2020). https://tinyurl. com/ybuw7yzq. Accessed 16–17 Apr 2020

26. Zuboff, S.: The Age of Surveillance Capitalism. Profile Books Ltd. (2019). https://tinyurl. com/ya9bdf8r. Accessed 16–17 Apr 2020

27. Everything You Need to Know About Sophia, The World's First Robot Citizen, Zara Stone, Forbes, 7 November 2017. https://tinyurl.com/y7zo2na9. Accessed 16–17 Apr 2020
28. Matter of Nonhuman Rights Project, Inc. v Stanley, New York State Law Reporting Bureau, 29 July 2015. https://tinyurl.com/ycqk2ztz. Accessed 16–17 Apr 2020
29. EPO refuses DABUS patent applications designating a machine inventor. European Patent Office, 20 December 2019. https://tinyurl.com/wshmc9u. Accessed 16–17 Apr 2020
30. Google Duplex: An AI System for Accomplishing Real-World Tasks Over the Phone Google AI Blog, 8 May 2018. https://tinyurl.com/yasguzo5. Accessed 16–17 Apr 2020
31. Ethics Guidelines for Trustworthy AI. High-Level Expert Group on Artificial Intelligence (AI HLEG), 8 April 2019. https://tinyurl.com/y37czxtc. Accessed 16–17 Apr 2020
32. Susskind, D.: A World Without Work: Technology, Automation and How We Should Respond. Allen Lane, 14 January 2020. https://tinyurl.com/y8sk28xr. Accessed 16–17 Apr 2020
33. Donovan, J., Benko, C.: AT&T's talent overhaul. Harvard Bus. Rev. (2016). https://hbr.org/2016/10/atts-talent-overhaul. Accessed 16–17 Apr 2020
34. Snapshot Paper – AI and Personal Insurance. Centre for Data Ethics and Innovation, 12 September 2019. https://tinyurl.com/y8f69qvu. Accessed 16–17 Apr 2020
35. Guide to Privacy and Electronic Communications Regulations. Information Commissioner's Office. https://tinyurl.com/jpkw4kr. Accessed 16–17 Apr 2020
36. Artificial Intelligence and Public Standards. The Committee on Standards in Public Life (The Nolan Committee), February 2020. https://tinyurl.com/ya5o5ysk. Accessed 16–17 Apr 2020
37. The Virus Gives AI a Chance to Prove It Can Be a Force for Good. Bloomberg Businessweek, 7 April 2020. https://tinyurl.com/ybm45b62. Accessed 16–17 Apr 2020
38. The MIT Stephen A. Schwarzman College of Computing aims to address the opportunities and challenges presented by the ubiquity of computing—across industries and academic disciplines—perhaps most notably illustrated by the rise of artificial intelligence. MIT, October 2018. https://computing.mit.edu/. Accessed 16–17 Apr 2020
39. University announces unprecedented investment in the Humanities. University of Oxford, 19 June 2019. https://tinyurl.com/ydbbam7j. Accessed 16–17 Apr 2020

Imagining the Future of Quantum Computing

Erik P. DeBenedictis$^{(\boxtimes)}$

Zettaflops, LLC, Albuquerque, NM 87112, USA
erikdebenedictis@zettaflops.org

Abstract. The world embarked on an information revolution almost a century ago and has been driven ever since by the well-known evolution of mainframes into Smartphones. While the exponential performance improvements due to Moore's law have slowed, quantum information concepts will drive the information revolution still further. Although the ultimate structure of a quantum computer is evolving, it seems destined to fit into the familiar program-based paradigm while solving some problems at vastly greater scale and speed than previously possible. Imagine a future "general" computer combining both bits and qubits operating at multiple temperatures yet based on familiar principles in electronics and computer architecture. Also imagine a future where some quantum information principles are taught to children and then become a part of society's thinking, much as place value numbers became a part of everyday life over the last two millennia.

Keywords: Quantum computer · Microprocessor · Architecture · Software · Programming · Qubit

1 From the History of Computing to Its Unimagined Future

Computing changed the world over the last century through a combination of faster hardware, more memory, and software that automated an increasing range of activities. The shrinkage of microelectronics and the accompanying increase in energy efficiency made computers ever more capable. The rate of improvement has slowed as technology approached the physical limits of the underlying computing devices. Yet roadmaps [1] still project improvements going forward of an order of magnitude for hardware and somewhat more for architectures and software.

However, quantum computing offers additional orders of magnitude improvement based on a different technical principle. The original type of computer, henceforth called a classical computer, can answer a question by scanning input data very quickly and then computing an answer. In contrast, a quantum computer can answer some types of questions without looking at every item in the input data, or at least not looking at the input data in the way humans' non-quantum eyes look at things. This has obvious speed advantages for large data sets, but it comes at the price of the answer being based on probabilities. We will discuss this new type of information later in this chapter through an analogy to Powerball (lottery) tickets.

© IFIP International Federation for Information Processing 2020
Published by Springer Nature Switzerland AG 2020
L. Strous et al. (Eds.): Unimagined Futures, IFIP AICT 555, pp. 70–83, 2020.
https://doi.org/10.1007/978-3-030-64246-4_6

1.1   A General Computer, Where General Is Classical Plus Quantum

Figure 1 imagines the future of what I call a general computer, or one with a seamless merging of classical and quantum concepts. I am imagining society will move past the accelerator model in Fig. 1a where a traditional computer has sub modules connected to it, such as a floating-point and quantum accelerators, and to the view in Fig. 1b where the general computer uses either bits or qubits as needed. While the new quantum technology may be transparent to end users, specialists may spend the next century refining it.

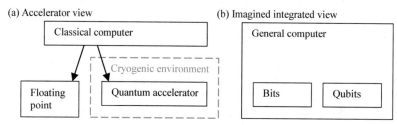

Fig. 1. Floating point and quantum (a) as accelerators vs. (b) integrated. Floating point moved from accelerators to a basic data type in microprocessors long ago, just as in the unimagined future bits and qubits will coexist in the same computer.

A recent quantum computer demonstration [2] pitted what was essentially a one-chip quantum accelerator against the world's largest supercomputer and found a significant speed and energy efficiency advantage for the quantum chip. The demonstration was controversial because the example problem was a natural fit for the quantum computer but was extremely hard for the supercomputer. Yet the demonstration showed the quantum chip had an asymptotic advantage as the problem scaled up, so there is the possibility of the advantage becoming astronomical over time.

Imagining the future of quantum computing will require identifying how far the new methods push out the boundary of what is computable. For example, we have a fairly good idea of the maximum size of a number that can be factored using a classical computer, but we do not know the equivalent size limit for a quantum computer.

Likewise, a classical computer can simulate quantum chemistry using a variety of heuristic algorithms, the results of which enhance our lives through new or improved products based on chemistry. We are sure quantum computers will be better at simulating chemistry, but we do not know how much better or the nature of the future advances that will result.

2   Quantum Information and Place Value Numbers

A lot of attention has been devoted to making a computer outperform the previous generation of itself on benchmarks, but quantum computers may change society in a more fundamental way.

Computers are essential to today's definition of success both directly and indirectly. Design and simulation of aircraft and motion pictures containing computer graphics are examples of products that directly use large amounts of floating-point arithmetic. Yet we use spreadsheets to indirectly assess the profitability of businesses.

2.1 Place Value Numbers

Industry was not always assessed this way. Our current place value number system is only two millennia old. Before then, arithmetic was performed on unary numbers comprising piles of stones, written marks, and so forth. A hunter might draw five deer on a cave wall to document the fact that they obtained five deer for food. If we could go back in time and ask hunters if they would prefer to use Excel spreadsheets instead of cave walls because a spreadsheet could represent up to 10^{38} objects, I am sure they would not understand what we are talking about because it was not known at the time that numbers could be that big.

However, the larger range of place value numbers allowed society to understand the relationship between the number of people needing to eat and the total amount of food available, including meat and other foods. This ultimately led the deer hunter to become part of a food industry, which, along with other industries, changed civilization. Yet with only a unary number system, the deer hunter did not have the mathematical background to understand the concept of industry, and without the concept of industry the hunter would not recognize the value of place value numbers.

2.2 Bits to Qubits

Switching from bits to qubits will present similar issues. Qubits have a bit value, making them backwards compatible with bits, but qubits may also exist in probabilistic states such as zero half of the time and one the other half of the time. While these would be considered errors in today's computers, we now know that some problems can be solved much more efficiently by appropriately using the quantum properties of qubits.

Computers perform a lot of stock trades nowadays, making money for the quantitative trader, but also increasing the efficiency by which society allocates capital.

So, imagine that a quantitative trader learns to use a quantum algorithm to predict the future price of a food industry stock with 90% certainty, where the best classical algorithm is only 51% certain. The quantum-enabled trader would then make more money with less working capital than competing traders, possibly starting an "arms race" where all traders would switch to quantum computers. Yet, the fact that quantum computers would be optimizing the distribution of capital to the food industry would make that industry more efficient over time and thus benefit society.

Neither profit and loss spreadsheets nor quantum computers improve upon deer, but the ancient deer hunters' descendants may end up competing based on quantum computers optimizing the way they do business.

2.3 Simulations

People designed just about everything with pencil and paper until computers became powerful enough to make computer-aided design practical. Computers can assist in designing an aircraft, for example, not only by automating steps previously performed by humans, but by adding new steps, such as putting computer simulation into a loop that optimizes the shape of the wing.

However, many physical simulations in chemistry and biology are too hard for classical computers, ultimately preventing computers from assisting technological development in those fields. This is due to exponential run time for classical algorithms simulating some complex chemicals. There is a theoretical basis for quantum computers having an advantage, but the advantage relies on leaving place value numbers behind and using probabilistic qubits.

Yet unlike the deer hunter, biology provides us with a tantalizing example of what is possible. Biological evolution has explored the possibilities of a carbon-based set of chemical elements, DNA as a storage media, codons as an alphabet, and so forth. We know that chemistry can lead to life and intelligence. Yet due to the limitations of classical computers, we cannot modify life very much or develop alternative approaches. However, quantum computers could be instrumental in creating new products on top of existing life, such as new medicines.

We could also use quantum computers to simulate and design new products from inorganic chemicals, such as better batteries. This would not be building on top of what life has already created but rather using life as inspiration for developing chemistry based on different assumptions.

2.4 New Thinking

While a quantum computer is an improved classical computer, it is also a computer for quantum information. The biggest opportunity is if society starts thinking in new ways due to quantum information. This does not mean people will think like a quantum computer, but rather that people will understand what a quantum computer can do and make sense of its results for other purposes.

Perhaps instead of doing profit and loss statements at the end of a quarter, businesses would also do profit and loss statements for the next quarter based on quantum computer optimizations. Perhaps experimental science will become more like aircraft design, where scientific discoveries will be "designed" on a quantum computer and checked with experiments.

This could change society in unimaginable ways, but our descendants might thank us anyway.

3 Education

We teach our children mathematical concepts that eluded even the greatest adult minds two millennia ago, such as place value number systems. Can we imagine a future where children are taught enough about quantum information to apply it to everyday tasks?

Just as most users of spreadsheets cannot write a spreadsheet application in, say, C++, it will not be necessary for most users of quantum computer applications to know how to build or program a quantum computer.

There are many ways to visualize quantum information, yet children will need a form that does not have extensive mathematical prerequisites. I've used a popular lottery in the United States called Powerball as proof that many people can appreciate correlated probabilities [3], which is all that is necessary to apply the results of quantum computing.

3.1 Powerball and Quantum Computing

The buyer of a Powerball ticket picks five numbers between 1 and 69, as illustrated in Fig. 2a. At a designated time, the Powerball operator conducts a random drawing of five numbers between 1 and 69, with no duplicates. Powerball has multiple games rolled into one ticket, but in one game the ticket wins if three numbers are common to both sets, as shown in Fig. 2b.

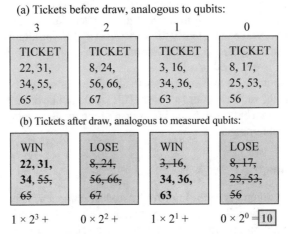

(a) Tickets before draw, analogous to qubits:

3	2	1	0
TICKET 22, 31, 34, 55, 65	TICKET 8, 24, 56, 66, 67	TICKET 3, 16, 34, 36, 63	TICKET 8, 17, 25, 53, 56

(b) Tickets after draw, analogous to measured qubits:

WIN 22, 31, 34, 55, 65	LOSE 8, 24, 56, 66, 67	WIN 3, 16, 34, 36, 63	LOSE 8, 17, 25, 53, 56
$1 \times 2^3 +$	$0 \times 2^2 +$	$1 \times 2^1 +$	$0 \times 2^0 = \boxed{10}$

Fig. 2. User view of quantum program computing 10. (a) Qubits are like lottery tickets with pick numbers that are only of interest to programmers. (b) The drawing picks 22, 31, 34, 36, 63 and the pattern of winning tickets reveals the number 10 when viewed as a binary number.

Powerball tickets and qubits both have two phases in their lives. A ticket is characterized by "pick" numbers during the first phase of its life. The second phase starts with the drawing, after which the pick numbers become irrelevant and all that matters is whether a ticket won or lost. Figure 2b shows the winning/losing tickets with corresponding binary values 1/0 creating the multi-bit binary number 10.

A ticket viewed in isolation either wins or loses at random, yet tickets with identical pick numbers will win or lose at the same time. If two tickets share fewer than five numbers, their probabilities of winning or losing will become correlated.

Qubits have a similar life cycle. Quantum computers create qubits in a standard form, which the physicists call |0>. To create a custom ticket, or qubit, single-qubit quantum gates effectively modify the pick numbers. To enable computation, two-qubit quantum gates can mix up the pick numbers, although some of these gates increase the size of the pick number space multiplicatively, such as a ticket with 4 pick numbers and another with 8 yielding two tickets with 32 each. The drawing, which physicists call qubit measurement, yields a result that has a lot of randomness but also has correlations due to the past application of quantum gates. A quantum computer does not use the specific Powerball rules, such as numbers between 1 and 69, nor can a lottery compute, but Powerball tickets represent the probabilistic nature of quantum information.

It may not have occurred to a deer hunter that putting a deer symbol (digit) to the left of another one would make it represent ten deer, but today's children easily learn that concept.

The Powerball example incidentally addresses a broad concern that place value numbers tend to be interpreted too precisely. Say you fill your car with 38.2 L of gasoline and note from your odometer that you drove 426 km. After a division, you say your car gets 11.15183246 km/l, which overstates precision. The Powerball number system analogy has uncertainty built into it.

Can we teach children to be comfortable with quantum computers spitting out random bits or numbers, yet accepting that the computers' output is the solution to an important problem?

4   Unimagined Products from Quantum Linear Algebra

Let me use linear algebra to illustrate the progression of a technology from scientific discovery to products, for both classical and quantum computing. Table 1 (adapted from [4, fig. 3]) illustrates the progression for the purposes of this chapter.

Table 1. Levels of classical and quantum technology development

Job title	Function
A. Hardware engineer	Creates quantum devices and a classical control system
B. Physicist	Designs pulse sequences to drive a quantum circuit
C. Information scientist	Creates a quantum circuit to create desired output
D. Software developer	Uses a quantum system to run an application and find a solution
E. Domain expert	Uses applications to create value in areas outside of computation

The ability of a computer so solve matrix equations, called linear algebra, is an enabler for many higher-level applications, so classical and quantum linear algebra should be of interest to IFIP readership. I will explain the progression based my personal experience with a microwave simulator called the High Frequency Structure Simulator (HFSS) [5].

4.1   HHL Quantum Algorithm

Harrow, Hassidim, and Lloyd (HHL) [6] discovered a quantum algorithm, or circuit, in 2009 that gives exponential speedup on linear algebra problems. The HHL algorithm solves $Ax = b$, where A is an $N \times N$ matrix, b is an N-element input vector, and x is an N-element output vector. The algorithm runs in O(log N) time.

I owe the reader an explanation because the algorithm counterintuitively runs in less time than it takes to write down the answer. The algorithm computes x as a quantum superposition of all the elements in the output vector x. The superposition can be thought of as a group of $\lceil log_2 N \rceil$ Powerball tickets, as illustrated in Fig. 2. The win/lose pattern after the drawing reveals an index i. If the algorithm is run many times, the probability of i appearing is the vector value x_i.

Skipping forward to 2020 when this chapter was written, the HHL algorithm is mentioned in textbooks and source code is available [7] for both classical simulators and quantum hardware. Students can run HHL on quantum computers available on the Internet up to size $N = 2$.

While quantum simulators should be able to solve larger problems, one textbook included the explanation "[i]n fact, the overheads required by [the eigenvalue inversion] step are a contributing factor to why the full code sample of even the simplest HHL implementation currently falls outside the scope (and capabilities!) of what we can reasonably present here" [7, 8].

While students can experiment with HHL, current quantum code has many limitations, which ref. [8] describes as "the fine print." This phrase refers to the fine print in contracts, where contracts that look like a good deal on the surface have fine print at the bottom of the page that makes it difficult for a person to actually get the value they expect from them.

An example of the fine print for the HHL algorithm is the fact that it does not compute the entire vector x, but instead requires the user to embed HHL into a larger problem that can make use of probabilistic samples of index i. If expanded to 53 qubits, this sampling is exactly what happened in the quantum supremacy experiment [2].

4.2   Sparse Matrices

I recall taking a class on sparse matrix algorithms as a master's student in 1980. The sparse matrix algorithm for solving $Ax = b$ was about as mature as HHL is now, although there are significant differences. The sparse matrix methods in that era involved storing matrix elements efficiently, such as linked lists of rows. The sparse matrix algorithm suppressed multiplications by zero but otherwise performed the same arithmetic operations as dense matrix algebra. Students could experiment with sparse matrix algorithms in homework assignments about as easily as they can with HHL today.

After improvements to HHL in 2010 [9] and 2013 [10], in 2016 the U. S. government funded an assessment of the resources required for a quantum linear algebra solution to a radar scattering problem [11]. The assessment counted the number of quantum gates as a function of the size of the problem N, concluding that the number of quantum gates would be less than the number of classical gates for problems above the size $N = 332,020,680$ (which is huge). At that size, the circuit would include 3.34×10^{25} gates applied to 340 qubits (exclusive of Oracles, which are beyond the scope of this chapter).

Setting aside parallelism, an Exascale supercomputer executes 10^{18} floating point operations per second and each floating-point operation involves about 10^5 gate operations, so an Exascale supercomputer performs 3.34×10^{25} classical gate operations in about 5 min.

The assessment pointed out that an algorithm developed in 2015 [12], which was apparently not ready to be used for resource estimation, should allow a "reduction of circuit depth and overall gate count by order of magnitude $\sim 10^5$"—or potentially cutting run time to about 3 ms based on our loose analogy to an Exascale supercomputer.

So, the limitations of HHL, or the fine print [8], made radar scattering computations on a quantum computer impractical. Yet, the degree of impracticality dropped by algorithmic improvements in 2010 [9], 2013 [10], 2015 [12], and others not mentioned. If improvements continue to reduce gate count in steps of 10^5, quantum linear algebra will be practical before long.

4.3 Finite Elements and Solid Modelers

Getting back to my personal experience, I learned about the finite element method in my class in 1980, but I could not use it because it was too complicated for a student to code in a homework assignment. Yet over several decades, finite elements went from 2D to 3D and became adaptive, meaning that the elements were dynamically resized for higher accuracy near features where a lot of physics was in play. Solid modeling front ends were developed once graphical user interfaces became effective on personal workstations around 1990. This led to the HFSS product where a student or an engineer could design a 3D structure on a workstation and simulate its microwave response. HFSS is in use today for many things, including simulating transmon quantum computer systems.

However, finite elements and solid modelers are not linear algebra algorithms; they are technologies further down Table 1. Classical and quantum linear algebra algorithms correspond to row C of Table 1. Once the technical community was confident with sparse matrix algorithms, new research went to finite element methods, at row D of Table 1, which solves differential equations, and so forth.

Many quantum algorithms have limitations like HHL [8], but classical algorithms have limitations as well. Even though bits are different than qubits, I'm suggesting that the process of computer technology maturing is the same in both cases.

I cannot imagine what specific quantum applications will be discovered, but quantum machine learning looks like a promising candidate. Instead of the finite elements in row C of Table 1, there is a framework for a neural network.

The process of working down the list at the top of the section applies to other quantum algorithm classes as well, such as period finding (Shor's algorithm for factoring), simulation of quantum physics, and optimization.

Readers seeking more insight may find [8] helpful. I have tried to illustrate solutions to the issues Scott Aaronson found in the fine print.

5 Integrating Bits and Qubits

This section assumes the physics of quantum computing will be further refined and then engineered into computers. The physicists' view of quantum computing has always presumed a close coupling of the quantum hardware with a classical computer, yet this section views qubits and quantum gates as second computational technology that will be integrated with Complementary Metal Oxide Semiconductor (CMOS) gates to create a "general" computer as shown in Fig. 1b.

This section treats qubits like Dynamic Random-Access Memory (DRAM) cells. DRAM cells are distinct from CMOS gates in function, structure, and electrical interfaces, but are often collocated on the same chip.

5.1   Qubits vs. Transistors

Qubits are different than transistors but are on a similar evolutionary trajectory.

The transmon superconducting qubit [13] is perhaps the quantum analogy to Transistor-Transistor Logic (TTL), a semiconductor logic family from the 1970s.

Over time, the TTL logic family spawned variants such as low power Schottky TTL (LS TTL), which could be analogous to superconducting qubits with a name other than transmon, like capacitively shunted flux qubits [13]. TTL's silicon bipolar transistor was ultimately replaced by a different type, although it was not known in advance whether the successor would be Gallium Arsenide or CMOS.

Superconducting and spin qubits must be cooled to 10–20 mK for operation today whereas ion traps work best when cooled to around 4 K. There are ideas for room temperature qubits, but qubits seem more sensitive to thermal noise than transistors, so we cannot count on room temperature qubits just because they would be convenient.

It seems inevitable that transmons will be improved and the improvement will have a different name. However, trapped ions, spin qubits, or a room-temperature qubit could replace superconducting qubits in general, yet nobody knows which will be analogous to Gallium Arsenide (which was never successful in computers) or CMOS (which is preeminent).

5.2   The Chandelier and Physical Structure

The physical structure of a superconducting quantum computing accelerator is very different from standard computer packaging. The quantum computing structure is called a chandelier due to physical appearance and is shown diagrammatically in Fig. 3.

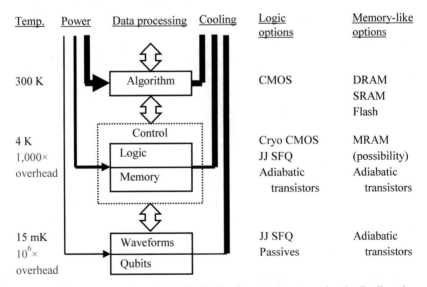

Fig. 3. Chandelier structure. (vertical) Classical and quantum processing is distributed across temperature stages, exposing issues of (left) cooling overhead, (center) power generated by control electronics and leaked on cables crossing temperature gradients. (right) Options for logic and memory vary by temperature. Acronyms: JJ = Josephson junction, SFQ = Single Flux Quantum, SRAM = Static Random Access Memory.

Qubits are in a 10–20 mK temperature stage due to physical requirements. The classical control system is distributed across progressively warmer stages, such as 4 K, until reaching room temperature (300 K) where there is a computer of conventional design. Design issues unique to qubits are listed in Fig. 3, such as cooling overhead, heat and noise flow between stages, and the device options available at each temperature stage.

The current structure evolved cryogenic apparatus for physics experiments yet is moving towards a scalable computer architecture. For example, a recent paper adapts Rent's rule to quantum computers [14].

5.3 Minimum Dissipation of Classical Computation

People who are familiar with microprocessors will recall that their clock rate and performance rose over time until the early 2000s, at which point top-of-the-line microprocessors had a 4 GHz clock and were dissipating ~200 W per chip. While laptop and supercomputer system performance continues to rise over time, a close look reveals that the additional performance is from the graphical processing units (GPUs). Since the microprocessor is essentially mature, it will be used as the base classical technology for the imagined future computer.

The physics of computation includes concepts and tools for understanding classical computers. At the low level, Landauer [15] made a physics-based argument that the heat generated by AND or OR gates must be on the order of kT per (irreversible) operation. Engineers know that the practical minimum is hundreds of times larger due to wire losses, variances in device manufacturing, noise, and so forth. Yet it is a good approximation to say that a microprocessor's heat dissipation is the product of the dissipation of a single gate operation multiplied by the number of gate operations used by an algorithm.

5.4 Mixed Classical-Quantum Circuitry

Future computer engineering will need to extend the reasoning in the last paragraph to include qubits. The straightforward extension of Landauer's minimum energy to quantum computers would conclude that qubits do not create any heat. Without debating the previous point, we will see below that many qubits will need to be partnered with classical logic, leading to much the same effect as if there were a minimum energy per qubit, or qubit gate. There are several cases:

1. Data must be converted between quantum and classical forms at the input and output of quantum algorithms. Translating bits to qubits requires applying electrical waveforms (or sometimes laser signals) to the qubits. The reverse translation is called quantum measurement. Both involve classical electronics on one side.
2. Large-scale quantum computers will require continuous quantum error correction of all qubits, not just the ones used for I/O. Errors in qubits are revealed by a quantum measurement that must change the state of a classical state machine so that it knows to correct the error.
3. Some quantum algorithms can be performed more efficiently if they include a measurement step and possibly a loop, which will be explained below.

All the cases above lead to a mixed classical and quantum sub circuit, where the classical portion is governed by Landauer's minimum dissipation. For example, Fig. 4 illustrates a circuit to rotate a qubit $|\Psi>$ by a small angle of about θ^2. The method is to execute the quantum circuit in Fig. 4a repetitively until the measurement returns a 1 [16].

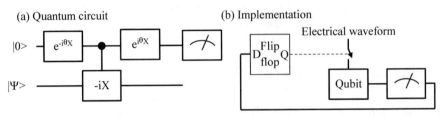

Fig. 4. (a) If 1 is measured, the circuit will have rotated $|\Psi>$ by a small angle of about θ^2, otherwise a correction must be applied to $|\Psi>$ and the process repeated. (b) The implementation requires a flip flop, qubit, an electrical switch, and measurement circuit in the cold environment. See [16] or https://www.youtube.com/watch?v=zwBdwCoVmSw @5:56 for more information.

Imagine applying the rotation in Fig. 4b to many qubits at once. The electrical waveform can be created at room temperature and routed to many qubits in parallel with near zero heat dissipation. Yet each instance of the circuit performs a measurement that is latched into a per-qubit classical flip flop. When the measurement returns a 1, the flip flop blocks the electrical waveform for that qubit only. The flip flop is governed by Landauer's minimum heat dissipation, and that heat will be multiplied by the overhead factor of the cooling system.

If the classical electronics were not collocated with the qubit, a separate microwave cable to room temperature would be needed for each qubit, leading to heat backflow and other issues that would limit scalability.

While there is an argument that qubits do not create any heat, many qubits will be associated with a classical circuit that must dissipate heat. This leads to a minimum dissipation per quantum operation that is somewhat analogous to Landauer's minimum dissipation per classical operation.

The thermodynamics of the "general" computer in Fig. 1b has not been fully developed, but we can imagine a time when we will be able to say how many joules will be required to solve a problem, such as solving a linear algebra problem or performing a quantum simulation.

6   New Issues in Computer Architecture

While CMOS is being proposed for classical control systems, its requirements are different from a microprocessor and should lead to different tradeoffs in device optimization and architecture. Table 2 contains simple models of classical and quantum computer throughput and cost.

Table 2. Energy efficiency and throughput tradeoffs

	Classical	Classical control system	Quantum
Throughput	$N_G f_{Clk}$	$N_q\, S(N_q) f_{Clk}$	
Cost of ownership	$N_G\, (\$_G + \$_e)$	$N_q\, k\, (\$_G + \$_e\, 300\,K/T_q)$	$+ N_q\, \$_q$
N_G, N_q $\$_G, \$_q$ $\$_e, \$_R$	= number of gates, qubits = cost of gate, qubit = lifetime cost of energy, refrigerator	$S(N_q)$ T_q f_{Clk}	= quantum speedup = qubit temp = clock rate

Let us first look at the throughput row in Table 2. Classical computer throughput, such as a microprocessor, is proportional to the number of gates N_G times the clock rate f_{Clk}. This motivates engineers to clock microprocessors as fast as possible.

However, a quantum computer's throughput $N_q\, S(N_q)\, f_{Clk}$ also depends on the quantum speedup, $S(N_q)$, which can vary between 1 and 2^{N_q}. With a little thought it's clear that the engineer has a lot more to gain by raising speedup. Doubling a quantum computer's clock rate doubles the throughput but doubling the number of qubits or quantum gates can create as much as an exponential increase in throughput. Of course, the quantum speedup is dependent on the algorithm.

Now let us look at the cost of ownership row in Table 2. The cost of ownership for a classical computer contains the term $(\$_G + \$_e)$, the cost of buying the computer in the first place plus the lifetime cost of energy. While it is socially appropriate to save energy, the cost of energy is well under the original purchase price of most computers. This creates an economic disincentive to employ energy savings technologies particularly if throughput decreases. So, auto-sleep mode on laptops is acceptable but not reversible logic, because the latter requires reducing the clock rate during computation.

However, a cryogenic classical control system contains the term sum $(\$_G + \$_e\, 300\,K/T_q)$. This multiplies the effective cost of energy by $300\,K/T_q$, a factor in the range $10^3 \ldots 10^9$. This makes energy saving technologies that were uneconomical at room temperatures into huge winners at cryogenic temperatures. Reversible logic is such a technology.

The microprocessor has been one of the biggest economic drivers of all time, essentially imposing its requirements on both the computer and software industries. Some computer design principles carry over from classical to quantum computing, yet design principles related to energy efficiency and throughput will change. These decisions are fundamental in classical computer design, so changing the decisions for quantum computer design will require rethinking many aspects of computer engineering.

6.1 Quantum Error Correction and Computer Aided Quantum Computer Design

Current quantum computer technology is called Noisy Intermediate Scale Quantum (NISQ) [17], which is defined as raw physical qubits without quantum error correction.

Raw qubits are analog devices that naturally accumulate error over time. While decoherence time, essentially the average time before an error, varies between qubit types, the leading quantum computer demonstration to date [2] can only perform about 40 gate operations before the result becomes meaningless due to noise. Quantum error correction will create logical qubits from multiple physical qubits, allowing an essentially unlimited number of gate operations.

We have discussed qubits as though they were a non-CMOS classical device, such as DRAM bit or a sensor element. The engineering processes for generating control signals for DRAM have been built into tools like CACTI [18], allowing a DRAM block to be integrated into a higher-level design through the same interfaces as a digital circuit.

It seems inevitable that somebody will write a CACTI-like program for mixed classical-quantum circuits, ultimately becoming a computer aided design tool for what I call "general" computers. Writing such as tool will be quite a challenge—particularly considering the need to cope with multiple temperatures—but this section should at least give an idea of where to start.

7   Conclusions

Until a year ago, skeptics postulated that progress in quantum computing might be blocked by unanticipated challenges in the physics. The recent demonstration by Google [2] pitting a single quantum computer chip against the world's largest supercomputer alleviated this concern significantly.

With well-studied potential quantum chemistry simulations, cryptographic, and some other applications, it is likely that multiple parties worldwide will make the investment to at least evaluate the engineering challenges in building a large-scale quantum computer.

I suggest that such a system should be called a "general" computer, as it must contain novel classical, quantum, and integrated classical-quantum technology.

Qubits may evolve much as transistors evolved in the history of computing. However, the physical architecture would have some novel properties, including spanning a temperature gradient and two technologies for computation (classical gates and qubits).

If such a computer can be built, its application to physics simulation is likely to lead to new materials, biotechnology advances, as well as advances in other areas. The potential advantage of quantum computers in optimization and machine learning is tantalizing and could develop into other important application areas.

The result could change the way society thinks more broadly. Society already knows how to think precisely using place value numbers, but place value numbers may be augmented by the probabilistic data that emerges from a quantum computer.

References

1. International Roadmap for Devices and Systems. https://irds.ieee.org. Accessed July 2020
2. Arute, F., et al.: Quantum supremacy using a programmable superconducting processor. Nature **574**(7779), 505–510 (2019)
3. DeBenedictis, E.P.: Powerball and quantum supremacy. Computer **52**(10), 110–112 (2019)

4. Córcoles, A.D., et al.: Challenges and opportunities of near-term quantum computing systems. Proc. IEEE (2019)
5. Ansys HFSS. http://www.ansys.com. Accessed July 2020
6. Harrow, A.W., Hassidim, A., Lloyd, S.: Quantum algorithm for linear systems of equations. Phys. Rev. Lett. **103**(15), 150502 (2009)
7. Johnson, E.R., Harrigan, N., Gimeno-Segovia, M.: Programming Quantum Computers: Essential Algorithms and Code Samples. O'Reilly Media, Incorporated., Newton (2019)
8. Aaronson, S.: Read the fine print. Nat. Phys. **11**(4), 291–293 (2015)
9. Ambainis, A.: Variable time amplitude amplification and a faster quantum algorithm for solving systems of linear equations. arXiv preprint arXiv:1010.4458 (2010)
10. Clader, B.D., Jacobs, B.C., Sprouse, C.R.: Preconditioned quantum linear system algorithm. Phys. Rev. Lett. **110**(25), 250504 (2013)
11. Scherer, A., et al.: Concrete resource analysis of the quantum linear-system algorithm used to compute the electromagnetic scattering cross section of a 2D target. Quant. Inf. Process. **16**(3), 60 (2017)
12. Berry, D.W., Childs, A.M., Kothari, R.: Hamiltonian simulation with nearly optimal dependence on all parameters. In: 2015 IEEE 56th Annual Symposium on Foundations of Computer Science. IEEE (2015)
13. Kjaergaard, M., et al.: Superconducting qubits: current state of play. Annu. Rev. Condens. Matter Phys. **11**, 369–395 (2020)
14. Franke, D.P., et al.: Rent's rule and extensibility in quantum computing. Microprocess. Microsyst. **67**, 1–7 (2019)
15. Landauer, R.: Irreversibility and heat generation in the computing process. IBM J. Res. Dev. **5**(3), 183–191 (1961)
16. Wiebe, N., Kliuchnikov, V.: Floating point representations in quantum circuit synthesis. New J. Phys. **15**(9), 093041 (2013)
17. Preskill, J.: Quantum computing in the NISQ era and beyond. Quantum **2**, 79 (2018)
18. Wilton, S.J.E., Jouppi, N.P.: CACTI: an enhanced cache access and cycle time model. IEEE J. Solid-State Circ. **31**(5), 677–688 (1996)

The Internet of Things: Opportunities, Challenges, and Social Implications of an Emerging Paradigm

Ulrika H. Westergren$^{(\boxtimes)}$ (iD)

Department of Informatics, Umeå University, Umeå, Sweden
`ulrika.westergren@umu.se`

Abstract. The Internet of Things (IoT) is an ongoing technological revolution where ordinary objects are fitted with sensing capability and connected to the Internet. The number of smart and connected devices is increasing exponentially, creating an arena for both product and service innovation. Research on the IoT has to date focused mainly on the technology itself, with less attention being directed toward the potential for value creation and the social implications of this phenomenon. This essay examines that gap and takes a look at the emergence of IoT from a social perspective. Addressing both the private and public sectors, it takes a look at opportunities and challenges associated with IoT implementation and use and discusses implications for a number of different actors. In addition, it shows how IoT is connected to a strong discourse on security, privacy and ethical use of technology and offers suggestions for future research directions grounded in IoT as being a current example of the ongoing digital transformation of society.

Keywords: Internet of Things · Digital transformation · Value creation · Social implications

1 Introduction

Over the past 20 years we have witnessed the dawning of a new digital era, where information technology has become smarter, faster, smaller and cheaper and, as a result, an integral part of our daily lives. The exponential growth of the Internet of Things (IoT), where ordinary objects are embedded with sensors and Internet connectivity, has moved the frontlines for what ICT is, does, and facilitates, and serves as a key enabler of the digitalization of society (Krotov 2017). Encompassing everything from smart homes with intelligent lighting, remote-controlled thermostats and advanced home security systems, to health care applications, personal monitoring devices and fitness trackers, as well as solutions for smart agriculture, connected vehicles, and industrial applications where product and process data are collected and analyzed for logistical, strategic, and product-development purposes, the IoT creates vast opportunities for both product and service innovation. These opportunities are based on the availability of real-time, context-aware data. For example, a smart object can transmit information about its exact location,

© IFIP International Federation for Information Processing 2020
Published by Springer Nature Switzerland AG 2020
L. Strous et al. (Eds.): Unimagined Futures, IFIP AICT 555, pp. 84–93, 2020.
https://doi.org/10.1007/978-3-030-64246-4_7

usage, and condition, and programmed to send alerts if values deviate from a set norm. This means that maintenance needs and product failures can be addressed as soon as they arise. However, the collected data can also be analyzed to find patterns and behaviors over time, and if combined with data from other connected products, IoT data can be used to make data-driven strategic decisions about whether a product should be updated, service performed, or a process optimized. In fact, this type of analysis makes it possible to make predictions about future behavior and foresee an incident before it actually occurs. In addition, real-time data can be collected and analyzed and used in the development of new products and services; during the procurement of services; or as input to ecosystems of IoT-suppliers that cooperate and jointly create value for their customers. The IoT thus enables situation-specific and efficient handling of both products and processes, based on data and actual needs instead of pre-defined variables, such as specified time intervals. It comes as no surprise then, that the public and private sectors alike are scrambling to take advantage of the opportunities enabled by this new technological paradigm.

In order to do that, one needs a clear understanding of what the IoT is, what types of value it is likely to produce in different contexts, as well as a thorough consideration of the opportunities and challenges associated with sensor-based systems. The previous forecasted growth figures of 20 billion connected objects by the year 2020 have already been surpassed and new measures mention numbers of up to 75 billion connected objects in 2025 (Statista.com 2020). This chapter takes a deeper look at the implications of the IoT and its effects on public- and private sector value creation, privacy and security. It draws on current research on IoT and highlights the social aspects of the technology. As both people and devices continue to move online, markets are predicted to transform and grow, creating an increase in innovations, productivity gains and economic growth. In addition, public organizations may take advantage of IoT to create value for citizens and make efficient use of public funding. The combination of technological advancements and new business logic makes the IoT a powerful and transformational force to be reckoned with for the private and public sector alike.

2 IoT Architecture

A fundamental building block of IoT is of course the technological components. Smart technology in itself is no novelty, and for example RFID-tags have been used for decades to identify and track specific objects (Gubbi et al. 2013). However, miniaturization has made it possible to embed technology within a diverse range of objects and with the cost of technology going down, and the capacity going up, the number of smart objects is increasing exponentially. A smart object is defined as "an autonomous, physical digital object augmented with sensing/actuating, processing, storing, and networking capabilities" (Fortino and Trunfio 2014). These smart objects form the basis of the IoT.

A simple conceptualization of IoT architecture is the three-layer architecture described by Lin et al. (2017). At the bottom we find the perception layer with smart objects, where there are sensors and actuators that capture context-aware data from physical objects. This is followed by the network layer, which consists of both connectivity devices, protocols, and communication- and network technologies. Wireless networks that are short-range (such as Bluetooth, RFID, and Zigbee), medium-range (such as Wi-Fi and zWave), and long-range (such as LPWAN and VSAT) are being actively developed for IoT connectivity. Low power wide area networks (LPWAN) provide low cost, low-rate, long-range radio communication and leading technologies are Sigfox, LoRa, and NB-IoT (Mekki et al. 2019). The network layer receives data from the perception layer and transmits it further to or from devices and IoT applications. At the top, we find the application layer, which receives data transmitted from the network layer and uses it to perform operations or services. This basic architecture contains complex operations and some researchers have therefore suggested adding additional layers, for example a service/middleware layer between the network and application layers (Lin et al. 2017), and a business layer on top of the application layer, responsible for the management of the overall IoT system (Khan et al. 2012), to the architecture to better capture its complexity.

Once up and running, IoT devices are dependent on efficient power consumption in the form of reliable, long lasting batteries. As organizations start to implement IoT strategies at the core of their processes, systems must be able to deliver a continuous stream of real-time data. Unreliable devices could be detrimental to business, and the cost of constantly changing batteries would deplete the potential savings made by using IoT. Many IoT devices have batteries that last between three and ten years, but battery life remains a crucial question and there is ongoing research, both on battery technology development, but also on alternatives such as energy harvesting technology and remotely charging batteries, through for example Wireless Power Transfer (Torun et al. 2018).

IoT technology must meet high performance needs and ensure scalability and flexibility. The rapid rate of innovation has led to a multitude of different IoT solutions being simultaneously developed by different providers. However, due to a lack of common standards, each solution being developed is connected to its own set of various choices made in regard to architecture, APIs, devices, data formats, etcetera, which in turn causes interoperability problems (Noura et al. 2019). Such interoperability issues may push businesses into vendor lock-ins and make it difficult to develop cross-platform IoT or to connect different systems to each other. The lack of agreed upon industry standards creates an uncertainty regarding "making the correct choices" and creating sustainable and interoperable IoT systems that will be able to function with other IoT systems. This ultimately prevents large-scale IoT where all smart objects can potentially be connected to each other and is seen, together with efficient energy consumption, as one of the big questions that has to be resolved in order for IoT to continue to grow and create value.

3   Creating Value with IoT

The digitization of the physical world holds much untapped business potential (Brynjolfsson and McAfee 2014). Previous research has shown that as technology is coming to permeate almost every aspect of our lives, firms must form strategies that make use of the ongoing technical developments and combine them with new business logic in order to stay relevant to their customers (Saarikko et al. 2017). In light of the rapid technological development, it has been suggested that managers need to develop the capacity to *sense*, *assess*, and *respond to* change (Haeckel 2010). Strategically working with IoT thus incorporates asking questions about 1) How to create knowledge about technological developments, the research frontier and value creation potential? (sensing), 2) How to identify and evaluate IoT-value? (assessing), and 3) How to use and incorporate this knowledge into business processes? (responding). In addition, the speed of technological progress not only drives change, but also increases complexity and places high demands on finding staff with appropriate skills (Bullen et al. 2007). Many firms are not able to deliver all competence in-house and therefore find it beneficial to participate in networks, forming ecosystems of firms, where mutual efforts reduce complexity and increase benefits for all participating actors (Teece 2010). When entering into such arrangements, firms must reflect upon their role in the ecosystem and how the firm's identity is related to that role. There will be firms who supply the technology needed to implement IoT solutions, those who embed IoT into their products and services and offer new forms of value creation, and those who create entirely new services based on what the technology affords (Burkitt 2014; Westergren et al. 2018).

As these different types of firms come together, new and innovative IoT solutions and applications will be developed. Indeed, IoT solutions are used to enable the intelligent home, that is receptive to its residents' preferences and habits and offers a personalized smart living experience. IoT home automation solutions include controls for, lighting, entertainment, appliances and security. Furthermore, one sees the opportunity to use IoT to create data-driven insurance services for the safe home, where premiums and offers are linked to individuals' behavioral patterns and use nudging tactics to push for behaviors that are advantageous. Another area for IoT ecosystem innovation is the automotive industry, where IoT solutions may bring together such disparate actors as car manufacturers, insurance firms, and entertainment hubs. The possibility of incorporating IoT in cars and measuring a large amount of data points (Bian et al. 2018; Husnjak et al. 2015), makes it possible to relay vehicle data back to the manufacturer, download updates, and schedule repairs and maintenance as needed, as well as enables so-called usage-based insurance (UBI) where the insurance premium is based directly on the driver's behavior. The same data can also be fed back to the driver for the purpose of promoting eco-friendly and safe driving (Soleymanian et al. 2019). In addition, IoT can be used to provide Wi-Fi onboard and entertainment services for passengers. A third example is the connected workplace where steady access to context-aware data can serve as the basis for climate control, efficient cleaning services, and intelligent lighting, providing the individual worker with a customized indoor climate and a more efficient workday (Mähler and Westergren 2019). Being part of such an ecosystem comes with challenges of its own, as firms must collaborate with others in order to create business value and are thereby also subjected to others' time schedules, expectations and processes. A key to succeeding in ecosystems is thus creating organizational strategies that explicitly account for challenges associated with collaborative networks (Adner 2006). This includes ideas on how to build trust among network partners and create a context that allows for both alignment of interests and adaptation to emerging conditions (Westergren et al. 2019).

The data that is captured, stored, and transmitted through IoT is at the heart of IoT value creation. In the private sector, service business firms mainly motivated by the possibility to increase process efficiency and to create efficient, customized services based on data analysis. They also see the potential in using accumulated data to better understand their customers and thus gain a competitive advantage when negotiating new contracts (Westergren et al. 2018). Manufacturing firms that incorporate IoT into their existing products see an opportunity to use data to reduce machine downtime, improve product quality and customer relations, as well as enhance supply chain efficiency (Dai et al. 2019). IoT provides a possibility to efficiently monitor products and offer context-based services after the point of sale (Baines and Lightfoot 2014; Kortuem et al. 2010). A deeper understanding of a product in use can prevent costly unplanned stops and product failure and enable the service organization to adapt its business model to the benefit of both the supplier and customer (Brax and Jonsson 2009). The move toward data-driven services, and the possibility to make informed decisions based on real-time contextual data, paves the way for proactive instead of reactive services and opens up for deeper levels of analyses (Tao et al. 2018). However, although access to data is seen as crucial, many firms lack the skills and analytical capabilities needed to use it for other purposes than quite basic anomaly detection and control. In order for firms to obtain greater value from IoT data and move toward prediction and optimization, they both need to develop analytical skills and resolve technical challenges regarding for example data acquisition, data pre-processing and storage, and data analytics, that need to be overcome (Dai et al. 2019).

The majority of IoT initiatives have thus far been implemented in the private sector, but studies show that IoT adoption is increasing within the public sector as well (Borgia 2014; Neirotti et al. 2014; Saarikko et al. 2020). Under constant pressure to simultaneously lower costs and increase citizen value, the application of IoT in the public sector is mainly motivated by the possibility to improve efficiency, increase transparency and enhance public services (Saarikko et al. 2020). It is therefore not surprising to see that implemented solutions often focus on areas that are connected with high maintenance costs, such as infrastructure, utilities, transportation, and facility management and on services that are directly addressing citizen needs, such as various applications for health- and self-care. IoT enables in-home health care, where outpatients can continuously monitor their own condition, while staying connected to their health care provider (Delmastro 2012; Pang et al. 2015) In addition, IoT may also support elderly or disabled citizens with assisted living solutions, where connected pressure pads can detect falls, and smart pill boxes can assist with medication adherence (Abbey et al. 2012). Public sector use of IoT also entails many smart city solutions, such as smart buildings with sensor-controlled ventilation and efficient power consumption, smart waste management, intelligent street lighting, smart parking solutions and more. Furthermore, there are IoT solutions that focus on citizen safety and continuously monitor urban environments as an aid to police in their work. Indeed, the incorporation of IoT into the public sphere can provide more efficient and effective public services as well as encourage citizen participation. A challenge for this sector, however, is to find the economic space for innovation in a context often characterized by cost savings, which shows the importance of building a solid business case.

4 IoT Challenges

We have seen how IoT enables innovation in both the private and the public sector and that there are many different ways in which IoT can create value. However, there are also a number of challenges that must be overcome in order for IoT to deliver on its promises. Some have already been mentioned, like the lack of common standards, battery life, problems of interoperability, scalability issues and other technological considerations. IoT data is often messy and comes from a range of heterogeneous sources which brings forth questions of data integration, reducing data redundancy and cleaning data, as well as data transmission and analysis (Dai et al. 2019). This creates a complex landscape for organizations looking to incorporate IoT into their processes and sets expectations concerning technical know-how. However, decisions about IoT investments are often made by managers who, while extensively trained to make business assessments, are not usually equipped to make decisions that require extensive and deep knowledge of emerging technologies. Poor understanding of the technological dimension may lead to investment in narrow, proprietary solutions and enhance the interoperability problem, as isolated solutions create challenges in accessing, sharing, and reusing data in different services and contexts. In order to avoid vendor lock-ins or being stuck with ill-fitting solutions, many therefore choose to partner with firms that can provide both private and public sector organizations with the technological expertise needed to make choices about sensors, connectivity, application- and IoT platforms, and IoT standards (Saarikko et al. 2017). By teaming up with trusted partners in IoT ecosystems, organizations can thus make use of network competence and overcome challenges related to a lack of technological competence.

The decision to invest in IoT is not only about making technology choices, it is about building a proper business case, that clearly states *what* problems IoT is expected to solve, *how* the application of IoT will provide value, and *for whom*. By identifying IoT application areas, it is also easier to map out what potential value might be created and where the pitfalls are. The implementation of IoT within the public sector differs from IoT usage within the private sector in a number of ways. A challenge for any public organization is to create economic spaces for innovation when daily activities most often are characterized by cost savings. Public sector IoT value creation thus often focuses on improving efficiency, increasing transparency, developing public services, and enhancing the quality of life for citizens- actions that directly or indirectly cater to citizens' needs. Private sector use of IoT, on the other hand, is about increasing profit, capturing market shares, and creating value for customers. Furthermore, firms in the private sector normally have a well-defined customer base as opposed to the public sector where needs of citizens of all ages, capabilities and interests must be included and addressed. This creates a complex and dynamic innovation landscape, which should be acknowledged and accounted for in each new IoT project. Despite the growing number of IoT ecosystems and partnerships, many IoT solutions are being developed in-house, and in the public organizations, often in projects financed by external funds. A challenge for project based IoT innovation is to move from short term project activities to long term sustainable solutions that become an integrated part in daily operations.

Another major challenge is ensuring IoT security. IoT devices are easily accessible and often have limited built-in security features. The possibility of data leakage and node compromising is high (Jing et al. 2014) and the more IoT is incorporated into products, services and processes, the more one opens up for the possibility of malicious attacks and malware. Distributed denial-of-service attacks may use botnets to infiltrate ordinary smart home objects, causing networks to overflow and services to crash (Bertino and Islam 2017). Hackers may take control over self-driving cars or disrupt critical IoT healthcare solutions (Yang et al. 2017), and ransomware attacks can be used to interrupt industrial IoT applications causing standstills or production failure. Ultimately human safety could be at risk. Making security a priority should thus be essential for any IoT project. Due to the heterogeneous nature of IoT systems and their inherent design that encourages flexibility and scalability, traditional security measures are often insufficient. Since IoT systems are too dynamic and too complex to benefit from a "one solution fits all"-package (Sicari et al. 2015), there is a call for customizable IoT security architectures, that are carefully tailored to meet specific application needs, while at the same time ensuring a systematic and grounded approach to IoT security (Jing et al. 2014). Previous research shows how issues such as authentication and authorization, privacy and confidentiality, and secure communication and computation must be addressed before, during and after IoT implementation (Alaba et al. 2017; Li et al. 2018). By defining needs and balancing the potential for value creation with the prospect of putting themselves and their customers at risk, organizations can prepare to use IoT in a safe and secure way. This includes asking questions regarding what needs to be protected and for how long, who has access to data, how will data be communicated, what standards will be used, and how accessible and simple to use should the IoT system be? In order to make sure all parts of the system are protected secure solutions must then be implemented at all layers of the IoT architecture (Sicari et al. 2015). IoT system failure can be detrimental to business and poorly developed IoT security can deplete not only company assets but also customer trust. Finding ways to ensure IoT security thus remains one of the major challenges with IoT

Smart solutions affect their surroundings. By constantly capturing, collecting and communicating data, IoT can be used to customize environments and offer services based on individual preferences. However, as more and more objects become connected to each other and to the Internet, there is also a potent risk of privacy infringements for example through identification, localization, tracking, and profiling (Ziegeldorf et al. 2014). Ensuring privacy and an ethical use of data is thus a central concern for IoT adopters, making sure personal and potentially sensitive data do not end up in the wrong hands (Perera et al. 2020), or are wrongly interpreted and misused. Context-aware data can be used to track, monitor, and map out individual behaviors and patterns not only of objects, but of humans in proximity to smart objects, without them even being aware of this happening. For example, the use of room occupancy sensors to control indoor climate can be an efficient solution that saves energy and provides individuals with optimized working conditions. However, the same sensors could be used to discern who stays in their office at their desk, and who spends a lot of time by the coffee machine, effectively transforming climate control into a surveillance tool. In such a scenario, it is of the utmost importance to reflect not only on what IoT can do and what patterns can become visible through the analysis of real-time contextual data, but also on what is desirable, necessary, and ethically justifiable. This requires being able to balance the perceived benefits of transparency (from the perspective of the observer) with the risks of privacy infringements (from the perspective of the observed) enabled by smart technology (Bernstein, 2017). As IoT continues to grow in scope and pervade all aspects of human life, new privacy threats such as privacy-violating interactions and presentations, lifecycle transitions, inventory attacks, and information linkages will surface, and the need for privacy-aware IoT applications will increase (Ziegeldorf et al. 2014; Perera et al. 2020). A successful implementation of IoT technology whether it be in the private or public domain, must therefore consider the privacy implications and possible ethical consequences of IoT use.

5 Summary and Conclusions

The IoT is only in its infancy. The growth thus far has been exponential and shows no signs of waning. As our world gets connected the potential for innovation is immense, and future IoT developments are projected to have an even more transformational impact on society. The research community has largely focused on the technological implications of IoT. This essay positions IoT as a socio-technical phenomenon and presents a number of opportunities and challenges that both private and public organizations face when engaging with IoT. By tracing the progress trajectory of IoT we can see certain patterns that emerge. First, **technological knowledge** is becoming a central concern for all types of organizations. In order to keep up with the rapid rate of digital innovation, organizations must develop an ability to sense, assess, and respond to technological change, either by developing skills in-house or by teaming with partners that can provide them with new competence. Second, a clear idea of **value creation** should be at the heart of all IoT investments. By building a business case and considering not only what IoT can do, but what value it will create and for whom, IoT moves from being just another technological phenomenon to a transformational power with the potential to cause long lasting change. Third, **security issues** threaten to hamper IoT development. Due to the complex and dynamic nature of IoT, security solutions need to be customized to the specific context, and many organizations find it hard to gain an overview of all potential risks and threats. Ranging from annoying (as in someone remotely turning lights on and off) to potentially life threatening (if said lights are traffic lights and unauthorized remote access may cause lethal accidents), IoT security issues must be swiftly identified and dealt with, to ensure safety and to build trust. Fourth, IoT enables unprecedented amounts of data to be generated, collected and analysed. While data can be used to increase transparency, improve efficiency, and enhance efficacy, the apparent risk of misuse, for example, unwarranted tracking and profiling means **privacy and ethics** must be on the agenda. A secure, responsible, and ethical use of IoT has the potential to transform society and provide value far beyond that found in ordinary technological innovation. Further research should therefore address IoT as an integral part of the ongoing digital transformation of society and take a deeper look at implications for both individuals and organizations. By conceiving of IoT as a technological, social, and cultural phenomenon, we can begin to understand its full potential and create strategies to account for both opportunities and challenges, as well as social implications, of this emerging paradigm.

References

Abbey, B., et al.: A remotely programmable smart pillbox for enhancing medication adherence. In: 2012 25th IEEE International Symposium on Computer-Based Medical Systems (CBMS), pp. 1–4. IEEE, June 2012

Adner, R.: Match your innovation strategy to your innovation ecosystem. Harvard Bus. Rev. **84**(4), 98–107 (2006)

Alaba, F.A., Othman, M., Hashem, I.A.T., Alotaibi, F.: Internet of things security: a survey. J. Netw. Comput. Appl. **88**, 10–28 (2017)

Baines, T., Lightfoot, H.W.: Servitization of the manufacturing firm: exploring the operations practices and technologies that deliver advanced services. Int. J. Oper. Prod. Manag. **34**(1), 2–35 (2014)

Bernstein, E.S.: Making transparency transparent: the evolution of observation in management theory. Acad. Manag. Ann. **11**(1), 217–266 (2017)

Bertino, E., Islam, N.: Botnets and internet of things security. Computer **50**(2), 76–79 (2017)

Bian, Y., Yang, C., Zhao, J.L., Liang, L.: Good drivers pay less: a study of usage-based vehicle insurance models. Transp. Res. Part A: Policy Pract. **107**, 20–34 (2018)

Borgia, E.: The internet of things vision: key features, applications and open issues. Comput. Commun. **54**, 1–31 (2014)

Brax, S.A., Jonsson, K.: Developing integrated solution offerings for remote diagnostics: a comparative case study of two manufacturers. Int. J. Oper. Prod. Manag. **29**(5), 539–560 (2009)

Brynjolfsson, E., McAfee, A.: The Second Machine Age: Work, Progress, and Prosperity in a Time of Brilliant Technologies. WW Norton & Company, New York (2014)

Bullen, C., Abraham, T., Galup, S.D.: IT workforce trends: implications for curriculum and hiring. Commun. Assoc. Inf. Syst. **20**(1), 34 (2007)

Burkitt, F.: A strategist's guide to the Internet of Things. Strateg. Bus. **4**(77), 2–12 (2014)

Dai, H.N., Wang, H., Xu, G., Wan, J., Imran, M.: Big data analytics for manufacturing internet of things: opportunities, challenges and enabling technologies. Enterp. Inf. Syst. 1–25 (2019)

Delmastro, F.: Pervasive communications in healthcare. Comput. Commun. **35**(11), 1284–1295 (2012)

Fortino, G., Trunfio, P. (eds.): Internet of Things Based on Smart Objects: Technology. Middleware and Applications. Springer, Cham (2014)

Gubbi, J., Buyya, R., Marusic, S., Palaniswami, M.: Internet of things (IoT): a vision, architectural elements, and future directions. Future Gener. Comput. Syst. **29**(7), 1645–1660 (2013)

Haeckel, S.: The post-industrial manager. Mark. Manag. Mag. 24–32 (2010)

Husnjak, S., Peraković, D., Forenbacher, I., Mumdziev, M.: Telematics system in usage based motor insurance. Procedia Eng. **100**, 816–825 (2015)

Jing, Q., Vasilakos, A.V., Wan, J., Lu, J., Qiu, D.: Security of the Internet of things: perspectives and challenges. Wirel. Netw. **20**(8), 2481–2501 (2014)

Khan, R., Khan, S.U., Zaheer, R., Khan, S.: Future internet: the internet of things architecture, possible applications and key challenges. In: 2012 10th International Conference on Frontiers of Information Technology, pp. 257–260. IEEE, December 2012

Kortuem, G., Kawsar, F., Fitton, D., Sundramoorthy, V.: Smart objects as building blocks for the internet of things. Internet Comput. IEEE **14**(1), 44–51 (2010)

Krotov, V.: The internet of things and new business opportunities. Bus. Horiz. **60**(6), 831–841 (2017)

Li, J., Yan, Q., Chang, V.: Internet of things: security and privacy in a connected world. Future Gener. Comput. Syst. **78**(3), 931–932 (2018)

Lin, J., Yu, W., Zhang, N., Yang, X., Zhang, H., Zhao, W.: A survey on internet of things: architecture, enabling technologies, security and privacy, and applications. IEEE Internet Things J. **4**(5), 1125–1142 (2017)

Mähler, V., Westergren, U.H.: Working with IoT – a case study detailing workplace digitalization through IoT system adoption. In: Strous, L., Cerf, V.G. (eds.) IFIPIoT 2018. IAICT, vol. 548, pp. 178–193. Springer, Cham (2019). https://doi.org/10.1007/978-3-030-15651-0_15

Mekki, K., Bajic, E., Chaxel, F., Meyer, F.: A comparative study of LPWAN technologies for large-scale IoT deployment. ICT Express 5(1), 1–7 (2019)

Neirotti, P., De Marco, A., Cagliano, A.C., Mangano, G., Scorrano, F.: Current trends in smart city initiatives: some stylised facts. Cities **38**, 25–36 (2014)

Noura, M., Atiquzzaman, M., Gaedke, M.: Interoperability in internet of things: taxonomies and open challenges. Mob. Netw. Appl. **24**(3), 796–809 (2019)

Pang, Z., Zheng, L., Tian, J., Kao-Walter, S., Dubrova, E., Chen, Q.: Design of a terminal solution for integration of in-home health care devices and services towards the Internet-of-Things. Enterp. Inf. Syst. **9**(1), 86–116 (2015)

Perera, C., Barhamgi, M., Bandara, A.K., Ajmal, M., Price, B., Nuseibeh, B.: Designing privacy-aware internet of things applications. Inf. Sci. **512**, 238–257 (2020)

Saarikko, T., Westergren, U.H., Blomquist, T.: The internet of things: are you ready for what's coming? Bus. Horiz. **60**(5), 667–676 (2017)

Saarikko, T., Westergren, U., Jonsson, K.: Here, there, but not everywhere: adoption and diffusion of IoT in Swedish municipalities. In: Proceedings of the 53rd Hawaii International Conference on System Sciences, January 2020

Sicari, S., Rizzardi, A., Grieco, L.A., Coen-Porisini, A.: Security, privacy and trust in internet of things: the road ahead. Comput. Netw. **76**, 146–164 (2015)

Soleymanian, M., Weinberg, C.B., Zhu, T.: Sensor data and behavioral tracking: does usage-based auto insurance benefit drivers? Mark. Sci. **38**(1), 21–43 (2019)

Tao, F., Qi, Q., Liu, A., Kusiak, A.: Data-driven smart manufacturing. J. Manuf. Syst. **48**, 157–169 (2018)

Statista.com: Internet of Things (IoT) connected devices installed base worldwide from 2015 to 2025 (2020) https://www.statista.com/statistics/471264/iot-number-of-connected-devices-worldwide/. Accessed 20 Mar 2020

Teece, D.J.: Business models, business strategy and innovation. Long Range Plan. **43**(2), 172–194 (2010)

Torun, H.M., Pardue, C., Belleradj, M.L., Davis, A.K., Swaminathan, M.: Machine learning driven advanced packaging and miniaturization of IoT for wireless power transfer solutions. In: 2018 IEEE 68th Electronic Components and Technology Conference (ECTC), pp. 2374–2381. IEEE, May 2018

Westergren, U.H., Saarikko, T., Blomquist, T: Initiating the internet of things: early adopters' expectations for changing business practices and implications for working life. In: The Internet of People, Things and Services, pp. 111–131. Routledge, Abingdon (2018)

Westergren, U.H., Holmström, J., Mathiassen, L.: Developing inter-firm collaboration to create IT-based value: a contextual ambidexterity approach. Inf. Org. **29**(4) (2019)

Yang, Y., Wu, L., Yin, G., Li, L., Zhao, H.: A survey on security and privacy issues in internet-of-things. IEEE Internet Things J. **4**(5), 1250–1258 (2017)

Ziegeldorf, J.H., Morchon, O.G., Wehrle, K.: Privacy in the internet of things: threats and challenges. Secur. Commun. Netw. **7**(12), 2728–2742 (2014)

Software Engineering, Across Two Centuries

Bertrand Meyer[1,2,3](✉) iD

[1] Schaffhausen Institute of Technology, Schaffhausen, Switzerland
Bertrand.Meyer@inf.ethz.ch
[2] Innopolis University, Innopolis, Russia
[3] Eiffel Software, Goleta, USA

Abstract. A survey of fundamental software engineering concepts, and their evolution since the time of IFIP's creation in 1960.

Keywords: Software engineering · Software quality

1 Introduction

The extraordinary development of information technology since the end of World War II has left almost no area of human activity untouched. It has been driven by the astounding (one runs out of superlatives, but how can it be otherwise with improvements by factors in the tens of billions since 1970 alone?) progress of hardware technology; but what lies at the core of the IT revolution is software. Software powers the world's devices and the world's processes.

Professional software construction is only possible through the systematic principles, methods, practices, techniques, notations and tools of software engineering, the art and craft of constructing quality software systems (a more precise definition appears below). Software engineering as a discipline was born in the late 1960s[1], not long after IFIP itself. In the decades since then, many of the basic concepts have remained the same, but the challenges that the field faces have grown enormously, and so has the sophistication of software engineering.

This short survey, devised for the sixtieth anniversary of IFIP, summarizes both parts: the constants of the discipline, and how it has changed.

2 Definitions

There exist lengthy and fancy definitions of "software engineering", but in truth the term defines itself: software engineering is the application of engineering to the production of software. As to the constituent terms:

---

[1] An often repeated piece of supposed trivia states that the name was coined on the occasion of a 1968 conference, but the term was in use before, as attested by a 1967 reference found by the author.

L. Strous et al. (Eds.): Unimagined Futures, IFIP AICT 555, pp. 94–104, 2020.
https://doi.org/10.1007/978-3-030-64246-4_8

- "Software" denotes the specification of systems that require computers for their operation, where "computers" are automatic devices for information processing (involving computing, storage and communication). The term "specification" is broad enough to cover, under "software", not only programs (source- or machine-level) but also auxiliary products such as requirements, designs and test suites.
- Since software distinguishes itself from other engineering products by its changeability (hence "soft") and more generally by its virtual rather than physical nature, the term "production" should be taken in a broad sense as well, to include not only initial development but also deployment and updates.
- "Engineering" denotes (per its standard definition) the application of scientific methods to the construction of systems. Here one may quibble that not all people having "software engineer" as their job title apply scientific methods in their daily work. A scientific approach implies the use of mathematics: electrical and mechanical engineers routinely specify problems through equations then solve them. Mathematics does not directly play such a central role for most software development; while some areas such as life-critical systems increasingly rely on "formal methods" (mathematics-based approaches requiring proofs of correctness of the programs under construction), most software production remains largely informal. Even there, however, mathematics is indirectly present: the basic tools and concepts of software construction are defined with mathematical-like rigor. Programming languages are akin to mathematical notation, with the same need for precision in their definitions. Algorithms, the basis for programs, must also be expressed with as much rigor as a mathematical presentation requires.

While not strictly part of the definition, two features are essential to characterize software engineering as going beyond mere "software development" and requiring a true engineering approach: size and quality.

Size: modern software systems can be large in several respects; not just the sheer length of the programs (in source or object form), but the number and complexity of requirements to be satisfied, the number and diversity of users, the project's duration (months, years, sometimes decades), the number of people involved in development, the variety of deployment situations, the number of bugs uncovered, the number of changes and extensions requested after an initial delivery... Without software engineering methods and tools, it would be impossible to master that complexity.

Quality: successful software must satisfy requirements of ease of use and learning, correctness (doing the job right), robustness (handling abnormal situations), security (handling hostile situations), efficiency (running fast and tight), extendibility (accommodating change of functionality and environment), timeliness (staying within schedule), cost-effectiveness (staying within budget), reusability (letting different developments benefit from each other's products) and others. Achieving these goals is difficult, in particular because of the inevitable tradeoffs, for example between ease of use and security.

To complement these definitions, we note that software engineering can seldom limit itself to the engineering of software only. Software systems typically exist in either a human context (for enterprise systems) or a material-world context (for embedded and "cyber-physical" systems, of which smart phones are a typical example). Although the present discussion limits itself to software concerns, they are often part of a more general systems engineering effort that must also encompass human and physical aspects.

3   Some Universals of Software Engineering

Whether in 1960 or in 2020, software engineering is characterized by a number of fundamental concepts, some of which we now explore.

3.1   Tasks

All methods of software construction, in spite of their diversity, involve the following tasks. Tasks, not necessarily steps; how to order the tasks in time is a separate question, reviewed in the next subsection.

Any reasonable project must perform a **feasibility study**, meant to decide whether it is worthwhile to build a system. Not all problems have a solution in software (sometimes, for example, it is preferable just to change the human processes); and for those that do call for a software solution, it may be suitable to reuse an existing software system, or to purchase one from the market. The following tasks assume that a decision has been made either to build a new system ("greenfield" project) or to adapt an existing one ("brownfield").

Any development project needs **requirements**. In 1960 and still in 1980, anyone in the field would have defined requirements as *"specifying what the system will do"*. The modern view can be expressed by the "4 PEGS" acronym (devised by the author but reflecting, we believe, a general understanding): Project, Environment, Goals and System. The requirements set the parameters of the project; they express the properties of the environment (in the sense of the business or natural-world features that bind the future system, and which the development team has no power to change); they reflect business goals for the commissioning organization; and they specify the behavior of the future system (the old *"what the system will do"*). Requirements engineering is a core part of software engineering, critical in particular because the best program is of little value if it does not address the right problem as perceived by project stakeholders, or addresses it in a way that is not acceptable to them.

Software construction requires *design*. This task consists of defining a high-level structure, or "architecture", for the system. "Decomposing systems into modules", the title of a classic article from the 1970s, is a particularly important task for the large systems developed today (think for example of modern operating systems with tens or even hundreds of millions of line of code). A good architecture is, among other qualities, one that clearly delimitates modules, protecting each from errors and security attacks originating in the others and making it possible to develop and later modify each independently of the others.

There will always be a task of **implementation** (or "coding"). With modern programming languages, coding is not radically different from design in its spirit, methods, languages and tools, but focuses less on structure and more on the description of algorithms and data structures.

Software development is a human activity and as a result constantly faces the problem of human error. A fundamental task of software development is "**V&V**", which stands for "verification and validation"[2]. The difference between the two tasks is that verification is internal, devoted to assessing that the software is of good quality, and validation is external, devoted to assessing that it meets its specification (in particular, that implementation meets requirements). That difference is often expressed more vividly as "checking that the system does things right" versus "checking that it does the right things". V&V is applicable to all software products, including requirements and design, but its most visible application is to code (program texts), for which it uses two classes of techniques: *dynamic*, requiring execution of the program, and *static*, working on the sole basis of the program text. Dynamic V&V is also called testing and consists of running the program on example inputs and checking the effect against expected outcomes (defined in advance). Static techniques include:

- Static analysis, which analyzes the program text—or (in "model checking" and "abstract interpretation") an automatically simplified version of it—to spot potential violations of specified correctness rules, for example, arithmetic overflow or null-pointer dereferencing.
- Program proving, which mathematically ascertains the conformance of the program to a full specification, using special theorem-proving software tools.

Testing is by far the most widely used V&V technique for programs, but can only exercise a minuscule subset of cases and hence is mostly useful to find errors (rather than to guarantee the absence of errors). Program proving is far more ambitious, but still difficult to apply to mainstream program development, in particular because it requires writing a mathematical specification of the intent of very program element. Static analysis does not demand such a specification effort and is increasingly used as a more systematic alternative (or complement) to testing.

The next major task is **deployment**, which consists of making the system available for operational use. For a traditional program, deployment can be trivial (compile and link the code to produce an executable version), but for complex systems it is an engineering effort of its own, as in the case of an automatic-teller-machine system which must be deployed in many different locations with many different versions and under strict security requirements. In some cases, deployment does not even involve transferring any executable program to customers: software is increasingly being deployed "on the cloud", meaning installed on Web servers and made available to its users through their Web browsers.

Finally, **maintenance** denotes all activities that occur after construction and deployment. The main components of maintenance are:

- Late V&V: finding and correcting errors that were not found and corrected prior to deployment, but come to light during operation of the system.
- Extensions: updating the software to account for users' criticism and suggestions, new user goals, and changes in the environment.

---

[2] Often called just "verification", but this discussion uses the more general and accurate term.

3.2 Lifecycle

Traditional software engineering presentations typically described and prescribed software development in terms of "lifecycle models", which define specific orderings of the tasks discussed in the preceding subsection, or some close variants.

The starting point for such discussions is generally the "waterfall model", a strictly sequential ordering: feasibility study, then requirements, then design and so on. Since this model is too rigid to be applicable in practice, its main use is as both a foil (an easy target for criticism, serving as a prelude for advocacy of other models) and as a pedagogical device to present the above tasks.

A variant of the waterfall model is the "V-model", which emphasizes the symmetry between construction activities (first branch of the V) and V&V activities (second branch) at different levels: unit testing corresponds to implementation, integration testing corresponds to design, and acceptance testing corresponds to requirements. Another variant is the "spiral model", which makes the waterfall more flexible by applying a simplified version of it to successive *prototypes* of the system, each more refined than the previous one and building on the lessons learned from it; the first one of these prototypes to be judged good enough will be the one deployed. The author has used and described the "cluster model", which applies a mini-waterfall to successive layers of the system, beginning with the most fundamental ones.

Agile methods, which have increasingly permeated the software industry since the early 2000s, use a lifecycle model divided not into tasks but into successive time slots or "sprints", typically of a few weeks. In these approaches, the emphasis is on deadlines at the expense (if one has to choose) of functionality: if at the end of a sprint some of the planned functions have not been implemented, the sprint's deadline never gets extended but, after suitable discussion, the functions get either moved to the next sprint or altogether removed from the project's goals. Agile methods also characterize themselves by emphasizing two kinds of project deliverables, code and tests, and the associated tasks, implementation and V&V, over others such as requirements (typically handled through simple "user stories" describing units of interaction with the system) and design.

3.3 Modularization Techniques

The presentation of design in Subsect. 3.1 pointed out the challenge of "decomposing systems into modules". Given the size of some of the programs it produces, software engineering has had to develop unique techniques for multi-level structuring of complex systems. They include (among others):

- **Data abstraction**, also known as abstract data types and *object-oriented* decomposition: the idea of decomposing systems not around their functions (operations) but around the types of objects they manipulate, also known as *classes*, each function becoming attached to the class to which it most directly relates. The notion of class unifies the dynamic concept of *type* (of objects) with the static notion of *module* (of a system).
- **Information hiding**, which directs the designer of any module (for example a class) to distinguish drastically and explicitly between properties that are relevant inside the

class only, and properties made available, or *exported*, to other classes. This technique, also known as *encapsulation*, is critical to supporting the goal of module separation mentioned earlier, avoiding the "chain reactions" of changes in many modules that would otherwise occur whenever a module needs to be changed as part of the normal process of system evolution.

- **Inheritance**, which supports the organization of classes (or other kinds of modules) into taxonomies, grouping common elements at higher levels of a taxonomy so that the inheriting classes can use them without having to repeat their description. Inheritance is applicable to programs, for which it enables supplementary modularization techniques of *polymorphism* and *dynamic binding*, but also to other artifacts such as designs and requirements.
- **Genericity**, which allows classes to be parameterized and hence to lend themselves to different variants.

While originally invented for software and more particularly for programs, these mechanisms are general techniques for describing and building complex systems of any kind. They are an example of software-originated concepts that have a potential epistemological application to many other disciplines.

3.4 Size and Exactness

A unique characteristic of software is its combined requirement for complexity and precision.

Human systems, such as a city, are *complex*, but tolerate many imperfections. (While you are reading this paragraph, many things in the closest large city are not right, such as traffic lights going out of order, accidents happening, people engaging in prohibited actions; but the city as a system is still functioning acceptably.)

Mathematical theories are *precise*, and so are non-software engineering systems, built on the basis of mathematical analysis; but their complexity typically remains far below that of ambitious software systems.

The complexity of such software systems is in a league with that of large human systems. Unlike them, however, software systems have very little tolerance for imprecision. Replacing a "+" by a "—" in one instruction (among millions) of an operating system's source code, or just one bit (among billions) of its executable version, may result in nothing functioning any more. Software construction is a harsh endeavor in which every detail must be right and the slightest error can cause havoc.

Everything in software engineering—all the techniques of requirements, design, implementation, V&V and other challenges of the discipline—is part of this attempt to reconcile the goals of complexity and precision.

4   Across Two Centuries: Some Fundamental Advances

Software engineering 2020 differs from software engineering 1960 as a result both of changes in the environment in which it operates, particularly hardware and networks, and of its own intrinsic developments. Section 4.1 briefly summarizes changes in the context; the following subsections cover important evolutions in software engineering itself (development techniques in Sect. 4.2, management techniques in Sect. 4.3, and software engineering research in Sect. 4.4, with some forays into the future of the field in Sect. 4.5).

4.1   The Evolution of Software Engineering's External Context

The external factors are clear:

- The exponential growth of *computing power* mentioned at the beginning of this article, and the resulting growing ambition of software systems.
- The *"marriage of computing and telecommunications"* explained in a 1977 French report (Nora-Minc). Early software engineering treated computers as the name implies: computing devices, with some input and output. Today's computers are nodes in a network, and their computing functions are inseparable from their communication functions.
- As crucial examples of this evolution, the ubiquity of *the Internet, the World-Wide Web and cloud computing*. These developments, game changers for society, have raised the stakes for software development, in particular by making *information security* one of the dominant concerns. They brought in a new slate of technologies, from blockchain (for distributed trust) to containers (for application isolation).

4.2   Key Developments in Software Construction

Here are some of the key concepts that took hold in the last half-century in techniques for designing and implementing programs.

Structured programming started in the late sixties and brought in the realization that programming is a demanding intellectual activity demanding discipline and reliance on mathematical reasoning. Some of the basic ideas, particularly the shunning of direct "goto" instructions, have become widely accepted (although the "goto" is not far away from the "break" and "return" instructions of many modern languages). The more ambitious goals of the creators of structured programming, particularly the use of mathematical correctness arguments, have still not become mainstream.

Programming languages have become more sophisticated, in particular through their abstraction and modularization mechanisms sketched earlier, but also through the growing reliance on the notion of *type* to frame the semantics of programs. (It should be noted that the recent popularity of the Python programming languages departs from this multi-decade trend, favoring instead the comfort of non-expert developers through "quick and dirty" techniques. But such forms of development do not really qualify as software engineering.)

Object-oriented programming, mentioned in Sect. 3.3, rapidly conquered much of the software development field starting in the late eighties, providing the engine that enabled software development routinely to tackle much more ambitious developments than ever before (which would not have been possible without the structuring mechanisms of OO technology, particularly classes and inheritance).

The **design pattern** movement, coming out in the nineties and building on the basic concepts of object orientation, brought software design to a new level of professionalism by identifying a number of fundamental architectural schemes that proved at the same time widely applicable, efficient, better than naïve solutions to the underlying problems, and eminently teachable.

Formal methods are the application of mathematical techniques to the specification and V&V of systems. They underlie, for example, the discipline of *program proving* mentioned in Sect. 3.1. As noted in Sect. 1, formal methods give software engineering the justification for the "engineering" part of its name, which, in other engineering disciplines, implies the use of mathematics. Formal methods are still a minority phenomenon in software development, but play an important role in certain areas where correctness and security are essential. Many of the basic concepts have been known since a few years after IFIP's creation, but patient work over the following decades made them step-by-step more practical, leading in particular to the construction of program-proving tools that can handle ever more ambitious practical systems.

4.3 Key Developments in Software Management

Many changes have also occurred in the way we organize software projects.

The **open-source software** movement, initially a militant initiative to counter the dominance of commercial software, has become less controversial in recent years and contributed enormously (along with its nemesis) to the progress of the field. While the details of open-source legal licenses vary, the general idea is that the resulting software can easily be incorporated into new developments. This philosophy has spurred countless developers to provide the world with open-source products, repeatedly building on each other and providing for example a large part of today's Internet and Web infrastructure, as well as an operating system (Linux) that runs many of the world's computers and (in adapted form) phones and other devices, and prompted the development of a profitable industry of its own. Open-source development is often collaborative and distributed, leading from a software engineering perspective to the development of many new techniques, tools and repositories (such as the wildly popular GitHub) for multiple-person, multiple-site, multiple-target software construction.

Agile methods, already mentioned in Sect. 3.2, have had a profound effect on the practice of software construction by departing from the rigid project management schemes propounded by textbooks of yore and offering instead a flexible development model based on the primacy of code and tests (over requirements and design), the dominant role of the development team, the downplaying of traditional manager roles, a close relationship with stakeholders and business needs, and the reliance on short development iterations (sprints) observing strict time limits. Not all the consequences have been good (the agile rejection of upfront requirements and design documents, in particular, can have a detrimental effect on project success), but overall agile methods have brought a new level of excitement to software development and made teams far more reactive to true user needs.

Configuration management has developed as a fundamental management technique for software projects large and small. The complexity of software development has several dimensions; in "space", projects include myriad *components*; in time, each of these components can undergo many *transformations* during the life of a project; in a third dimension, many developers may independently perform *changes* to the components. Configuration management errors (such as combining versions of two modules at incompatible stages of their respective evolution) can cause disaster. Modern configuration management tools enable teams to avoid these mistakes and keep the evolution of systems and their components under control. Here too the complexity to be handled lies beyond what one encounters in other fields of engineering.

DevOps is a new paradigm of software development made necessary in particular by the frantic growth of Web and cloud applications. The discussion of software tasks in Subsect. 3.1 presented *deployment* as separate from *development* tasks (requirements, design, implementation). If a system is deployed on the Web—think for example of a search engine—the classical paradigm of working on new versions to be delivered every few months or years no longer applies; it would be unthinkable to force users to stop the previous version, install the new one and start again. Instead, usage never stops, and new versions must be deployed while this usage is proceeding, with most users not even noticing at that time (they might only notice, over time, that the service progressively improves). The term "DevOps" covers this scheme of interwoven development ("Dev"), deployment and operation ("Ops"), and raises fascinating new challenges for software engineering.

4.4   Key Developments in Software Engineering Research

Software engineering is not only an important applied activity but also a vibrant research field, with numerous journals, conferences (the most famous one, held yearly, goes back to 1975), PhD theses, prestigious IFIP working groups, and all the other trappings of an independent scientific discipline.

Software engineering research falls into four broad categories:

- **Conceptual:** propose new ideas or methods.
- **Constructive:** develop new tools, languages and other artifacts.
- **Analytical:** develop mechanisms for assessing artifacts and their quality.
- **Empirical:** process software artifacts using quantitative methods to derive general results.

In considering the evolution in recent decades, the most remarkable phenomenon has been the spectacular growth of the last category.

Empirical software engineering has come of age as a result of the growth of available subject material, starting with large software repositories (mentioned earlier in the context of open-source software, but also including commercial projects). Projects such as Linux have associated development databases going back many decades and containing (in addition, of course, to large amounts of source code, tests and other artifacts) the record of hundreds of thousands or even millions of individual code contributions and changes, as well as bug[3] reports and bug fixes. This material provides researchers with

---

[3] "Bug" being, of course, the colloquial term for a software error.

a fascinating basis to study the process of programming and all the technical and human factors that can affect a project.

In other words, empirical software engineering treats software artifacts the way natural sciences treat the targets of their study (be they from the inanimate or living world): as objects worthy of systematic quantitative study, nowadays using the most advanced techniques of "big-data" analysis, in particular data science and machine learning.

This form of research (so successful that it has come to dominate the field at the sometimes-regrettable expense of other kinds of research mentioned above) has led to many insights on software processes. It makes the majority of software engineering research publications in 2020 very different from what one finds in conference proceedings of 1980, 1990 or even 2000.

One of the consequences of this new focus has been a change of the kind of *mathematics* used for software engineering. Aside from the numerical techniques needed in the early days, math for computer science has traditionally involved logic and combinatorics ("discrete mathematics"). Big data and machine learning imply a shift to linear algebra and statistics as the main mathematical tools.

4.5   What Next?

Aside from the obvious predictions, such as the ever increasing influence of machine-learning techniques, one may venture that software engineering will probably become *less* mainstream than today.

In the early days, even after the personal computing revolution started, software engineering occupied a special niche, reserved for large projects, mostly in the government and aerospace areas. It did not affect much the practices of developers in more mundane application domains. (At the 1987 main international conference in the field, the author suggested, in the closing program committee meeting, that the next conference should invite some of the famous leaders of the PC software industry as keynote speakers. The reaction was that the community had nothing to learn from such amateur bit-players.) The situation then changed drastically: from the nineties on, many of the key software engineering ideas gained influence in the software development community at large, in the same way that techniques first tried out in Formula-1 racing find their place, a technology generation or two later, in the design of mass-market cars.

The chasm is coming back. Perhaps as a consequence of the democratization of programming (the basics of which are increasingly taught nowadays in secondary or even primary school), there has been a regression of the influence of software engineering principles on the mainstream development. The spread of programming languages for quick-and-dirty coding, mentioned in Sect. 4.2, is an example of this regression. The impression here is that as long as your program produces any results at all, no one is going to look into the sausage-making. Clearly, such an approach does not transpose to mission-critical developments. But it is increasingly the dominant one today in most software development: "anything goes". Software engineering proper gets confined to the advanced professional developments, the ones that we cannot afford to get wrong.

While regrettable, this trend of separating mainstream development from professional software engineering is probably going to continue. Being able to program a computer is no longer the mark of a sought-after expert. The true difference is between casual developers, who can somehow put together ("hack") some code, with little guarantee of quality, and actual software engineers, who know and apply the principles and practices of software engineering characterized—as defined in this article—by a fundamental focus on quality.

While professional software engineers may lament the lack of quality concerns in much of today's developments, they can take pride in noticing that it is, for a part, a sign of the very success of their field. A sloppy programmer in 1960 would have produced lamentable, unusable programs. Because of the tremendous development of software engineering languages and tools since then, even a sloppy programmer today can produce acceptable code. The reason is that so much of the work actually gets done by the underlying layers (operating system, libraries of reusable components to take care of numerous aspects from user interfaces to numerical computation, compilers, development environments, debugging tools, configuration management tools, repositories…) that you can produce a decently working system by just throwing in a few elements of your own, whether properly software-engineered or not, on the top of that mighty technology stack. This ability to let non-professionals benefit from the hard work of the professionals is a sign of the field's growing maturity.

5   Conclusion

Modern software systems are among the most complex and ambitious systems of any sort that humankind has ever attempted to build. Software engineering, some of whose concepts and techniques have been sketched in the preceding sections, provides a way to achieve these ambitions and produce systems that will work to the satisfaction of their intended beneficiaries—people and organizations. These concepts and techniques, patiently developed over six decades, provide the closest the human mind has ever produced to a science and engineering of complexity.

The very success of the discipline puts an ever-heavier burden on the shoulders of software engineering professionals, who must constantly bear in mind that their programs are not just elegant intellectual exercises using the best algorithms, data structures and software engineering techniques, but tools to address society's goals. Society relies ever more heavily on software to achieve these goals, forcing software engineers to confront numerous ethical issues (exacerbated, in particular, by the growing use of machine learning, which reproduces existing patterns rather than renewing them) and making ever more central the role of quality, in all its facets, in the pursuit of true software engineering.

Meeting these challenges is hard, but as anyone who has genuinely tried to tackle them can testify, there does not on earth exist a more fascinating pursuit.

To Centralize or Decentralize: What is the Question? An Application to Digital Payments

Ron Berndsen[1,2]([⊠]) [iD] and Ruth Wandhöfer[3]

[1] Tilburg University, Tilburg, The Netherlands
ron.berndsen@tilburguniversity.edu
[2] LCH Ltd and LCH SA, London, UK
[3] CASS Business School, London, UK
ruth.wandhofer@cass.city.ac.uk

Abstract. Computing in the general sense of the word has been centralized in the early days of IFIP (1960s) with mainframe computers and became distributed in later decades (1980s) with stand-alone personal computers. Then distributed ledger technology was introduced and the arrival of Bitcoin emphasized the intention in addition to distribution to also decentralize the system as much as possible. In this article we focus on the meaning of centralized versus decentralized computing and apply this to the world of digital payments.

Keywords: Distributed ledger technology · Bitcoin · Centralized computing · Decentralized computing · Digital payments

1 Introduction

Computing in the general sense of the word has been centralized in the early days of IFIP (1960s) with mainframe computers and became distributed in later decades (1980s) with stand-alone personal computers. Subsequently, the internet connected those personal computers and computing became mobile. In 2009 the Bitcoin network started to mine the first bitcoins. The intention of bitcoin is to decentralize the system as much as possible out of a lack of any trust in intermediaries. Initially, because of the Lehman crisis financial institutions were the target to disintermediate but within a couple of years distributed ledger technology became a hype, trying to cut out intermediaries in almost any sector of the economy. The next major development in payments will probably be the introduction of central bank digital currency (CBDC). This means opening up the possibility of consumer (retail) payments in central bank money in a digital form where the trend seems to be to move back to centralized but distributed systems.

The views expressed in this paper do not necessarily reflect the views of our affiliations. All remaining errors are ours.

L. Strous et al. (Eds.): Unimagined Futures, IFIP AICT 555, pp. 105–118, 2020.
https://doi.org/10.1007/978-3-030-64246-4_9

There is still substantial confusion about what decentralization in the above-mentioned trends entails [15]. In this article we focus on the meaning of centralized versus decentralized computing in terms of governance and geographical location. To illustrate and make the difference more concrete, those concepts are applied to the world of digital payments or in general the transfer of monetary or financial value. In Sect. 2 we provide a working definition of (de)centralization. In Sect. 3 we present the centralized world of financial market infrastructures. Section 4 provides examples of decentralized means of payment such as bitcoin. Section 5 discusses central bank digital currencies in two prominent cases: Sweden and China. Section 6 concludes briefly.

2   Working Definition of Decentralization of Governance

In order to set the scene, we will begin this section by explaining the core differences between centralized and decentralized systems. From the literature, e.g. [8], it appears that it is difficult to arrive at an all-purpose definition of centralization and decentralization as it depends very much on the domain of application as well as the aspect under consideration.

The domain we will be examining is that of computer systems, which are the underlying operating systems for the transfer of value in digital format, i.e. in a broad sense the exchange of fiat currency (the official currency of a country) as well as cryptocurrency or crypto assets. For simplicity we will refer to such systems as 'payment systems'. In general, a payment system consists of a network of one or more nodes where nodes can have the same function or different functions. If all nodes have exactly the same function, we will call such nodes 'peers'.

Governance in Centralized Systems
The first question to ask in order to establish as to whether a system is centralized is the following: 'Is there a single decision maker?' With a single decision maker or central authority, the well-known advantages of a centralized system become immediately clear: those systems are simple to administer and reaching 'consensus' is cheaper and faster compared to truly decentralized computing. The underlying reason for centralization in the system context, including computer systems, is the network effect. The positive utility of the network effect increases with more participants joining – a reinforcing cycle. The drawbacks of centralized systems are of course the single point of failure at the governance level, the lack of controllability of the user vis-a-vis the single decision maker and the possibility of censorship.

Governance in Decentralized Systems
In contrast to the centralized system, the question we ask here is 'Are there several decision makers, which ensure that no single individual or entity is in control?' If the answer is affirmative, we are dealing with a decentralized system: there is no single entity representing authority. Instead we encounter a plethora of authoritative nodes, which are in charge of serving a group of end users. Full decentralization would denote that decision-making would be dispersed across all participants. Full decentralization would therefore imply the absence of any form of influence, power, or control over developers or contributors.

The advantage of a decentralized system is its resiliency and redundancy, which however tends to also make it more costly in terms of computing and more complex to manage. In the early days the Internet was an example of a decentralized system, which however has evolved into a much more centralized system when we think about the controls that governments have established within it.

There is one overarching type of governance architecture when creating decentralized systems in the space of distributed ledger technology: public/un-permissioned ledgers. A public blockchain typically aims at providing anonymity or pseudonymity, the governance structure is cooperative, and the association or network is aimed at being democratically controlled based on the consensus mechanism employed.

In practice there are many hybrid versions that may be public but still permissioned and are therefore not completely decentralized given that a gatekeeper function is established in order to limit participation in the decision making of the system. Examples include the Ripple ledger and Hedera Hashgraph among others. In terms of permissioned blockchains there are state run distributed ledgers (DLs), e.g. for land registries or identity management systems (Estonia) where stakeholders elect board members that provide a certain level of know-how and direction and where a broad audience may be able to view the ledger but only select entities can validate and process transactions. There are also private blockchains where the aim is the creation of applications for the business and where the management board are the primary stakeholders or owners and they ultimately govern the direction of the system. And we have seen consortium-run permissioned DLs which are managed by a group of organizations such as financial institutions (for example R3 Corda) where a process is followed to elect or remove members that hold seats on collective boards as part of the network.

It is important to note that the openness of the system, i.e. unpermissioned versus permissioned or hybrid, as well as the consensus mechanism which governs the transaction validation process all have a direct impact on the degree of decentralization in terms of governing the underlying system. So, (de)centralization is not a binary concept. The major consensus mechanisms, which we want to mention here as a manifestation of governance, are Proof of Work and Proof of Stake.

Proof of Work is commonly seen as the first type of consensus mechanism that was used in a public blockchain, specifically the Bitcoin Blockchain [13]. Proof of Work uses a process of mining where the nodes, which keep the network operational, solve complex mathematical problems through the use of computing power. The more computational power used, the faster the asymmetric mathematical problems that need to be solved in order to calculate the hash of a new block [17]. For solving these problems, miners are then rewarded with coins in return. In order for the miners to make a successful attempt at identifying the winning block they randomly vary what is termed a nonce, the timestamp of the previous block. Node operators are incentivized in the Proof-of-Work model by rewards of transaction fees and block rewards if and only if the block they have identified is included in the chain [14]. Due to this architecture, it is often assumed that it is difficult for any one party or entity to control the majority of total computational power and thus prevent a Sybil attack from occurring [6].

Proof of Stake utilizes a randomized process to identify who or what will determine the consecutive block. In order to be considered by the process a certain number of tokens must be staked/locked up for a particular duration. Once this is done, the entity will become a validator on the network whereby they are able to discover new blocks of data and receive a reward if the transaction is included in the chain. This is the protocol that is aimed to be used in Ethereum, which will undergo a shift from the Proof of Work mechanism to a Proof of Stake one, planned to occur by 2021. Proof-of-Stake is considered to be more energy efficient than Proof-of-Work [12]. The central tenet to the various Proof-of-Stake mechanisms is that the node, which is allowed to propose a consecutive block, is determined by the proportion of a particular digital asset being staked. This assumes that the more an entity, individual, or group stakes, the less likely they will attempt to sabotage the decision-making process because they have 'skin in the game' [17].

Furthermore, there are a variety of hybrid solutions that have emerged or are beginning to emerge, which include private databases on public blockchains, or off-chain storage units with a public blockchain, alternatively open consensus but permissioned governance (e.g. Hedera Hashgraph with their 39 multination corporates serving as their Global Governing Council and their main node operators) but also Ripple. Although these hybrid models do not allow any individual or entity to participate, they are partially permissioned environments. Due to this there have been implementations of Proof of Authority where the consensus itself is determined by selecting or randomly selecting an authority and it is assumed that these authorities are trustworthy to determine the most recent version of the database [1]. There are many other consensus mechanisms that exist and that are being researched, tried, and tested including proof-of-existence, proof-of-burn, proof-of-elapsed time.

In terms of practical application of these three key definitions we see that systems can either operate on a pure basis, e.g. a fully centralized system, or they can combine features of two types of systems, e.g. a centralized and at the same time distributed system. In the paragraphs below we depict the definitions reflecting this.

Distributed Systems
In order to find out if a system is distributed, the question to ask is 'Are all actors (or nodes in computer system terms) in the same geographical location?' A negative answer means that the system is distributed. Distribution therefore refers to the geographic location of the 'nodes' and the storage of the recorded data, as well as the location of the requisite computational power being utilized. Control by one or more entities has no bearing on whether a system is distributed. The most important difference between a decentralized and a distributed system is that in the latter every node is in communication with every other node such that they all behave as a single unit. Whereas the processing in the system is distributed in the sense of being shared across the nodes, decisions are centralized as the nodes behave in a collective decision-making process. In a fully distributed system, there are no end users and only individual nodes. The database is distributed to all participants and viewable in real time. When we compare this to the way Bitcoin operates today, we can see that a tiering of participants took place and we have many end users that are not running a node themselves but relying on other nodes (e.g. a crypto wallet provider or crypto exchange). This also means that they do not see

the full Bitcoin blockchain but instead are being presented with a recent snapshot in relation to their transaction [16].

Overview of the Four Dimensions

To conclude this section, within the domain of payment systems, we present the three different system characteristics discussed above applied to digital payments in Table 1.

Table 1. The four dimensions of (de)centralization and distribution/concentration

		Governance	
		Centralized	Decentralized
Geographical location	Concentrated	Classical mainframes	–
	Distributed	Multiple sites Cloud computing	Pure Bitcoin system

First aspect: in terms of governance, centralization means the presence of a central authority, which controls the payment system and is responsible for its operational services to its users. The central authority has complete control and up-to-date information about the state of the system [3]. A central authority may be a single person or a small group – in terms of the ledger, which is also relevant for our purpose – which has the exclusive power to write and update the ledger. We also distinguish IT-wise between 'run' and 'change'. In a governance-centralized system the single authority also decides how to change the system i.e. on the content and timing of new software releases.

A fully decentralized system from a governance perspective is a system where there is no central control and responsibility only exists at the level of peers i.e. individual nodes which all have full autonomy, e.g. each node can decide to join or leave the network by itself. The way to achieve a uniquely defined state in a decentralized environment is by consensus.

Looking at the issue of running versus changing the software, it is an intriguing question whether full decentralization in terms of changing the software is really possible. This only seems to be the case if every peer is in principle able to propose and effect a new software release. Consensus is then reached if other peers adopt that release and reach a majority over time. Peers, which keep running an old version or are in a minority using the new version would then represent the outcome of decentralization.

Second aspect: As far as the location is concerned, payment systems will to some extent have a geographically dispersed structure nowadays. The obvious reason is adequate business continuity: in order to be resilient against all kinds of natural hazards the system needs to have nodes that have a distinct geographical risk profile (see the principle on Operational Risk in [5]) such that a single incident (e.g. flooding, fire, earthquake, gas explosion) will not impact all nodes of the system. Hence, a fully concentrated payment system – i.e. in terms of location - will not exist anymore [5]. Every payment system will be distributed in terms of location. Applied to the concept of ledger, this implies that ledgers will be decentralized to some extent. The term distributed ledger or distributed ledger technology does therefore not refer to decentralization in terms of geographical location. In that sense all ledgers of payment systems are distributed nowadays.

For the remainder of this article, we will take as a working definition for the term decentralization to mean decentralization in terms of governance. Furthermore, (de)centralization is not a binary concept; we will allow for a certain degree of decentralization as some functions or actions can be delegated.

3   Centralized Systems: Financial Market Infrastructures

Building on the concepts of decentralization and distribution of the previous section, we will discuss a prominent class of centralized but distributed systems in this section: Financial Market Infrastructures (FMIs). These infrastructures take care of the fundamental task of providing the function of transfer of value (monetary and financial) to an economy. There are four main types of FMI: Automated Clearing House (ACH), Systemically Important Payment System (SIPS), Central Securities Depository (CSD) and Central Counterparty (CCP). Additionally, there is fifth type of FMI, the Trade Repository. However, that type does not play a role in the payment, clearing and settlement processes. Instead it provides ex-post transparency on over-the-counter derivative transactions. Every FMI performs a specific function for its participants (Ps) which can vary from a few dozen to several thousands. Given the various types of FMIs it may be insightful to use a stylized network structure for visualization. In Fig. 1 the different FMIs are depicted in a multiplex consisting of three layers [4].

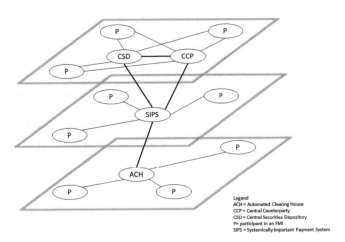

Fig. 1. FMI multiplex

The bottom layer represents the network of retail payments with the Automated Clearing House in the center. The ACH acts as a concentrator: the millions of individual payments (part of which may be in batches) are collected, aggregated per participant and multilaterally netted (this process is called clearing). The resulting long or short position of each participant is then sent by the ACH to a Systemically Important Payment System.

Located in the middle layer of the multiplex, the SIPS perform the actual transfer of value (settlement) by debiting the account of all 'short' participants and crediting the account of all 'long' participants. If this is all successful, the SIPS send the positive result back to the ACH. In general, the SIPS will be operated by the central bank and uses the Real-Time Gross Settlement mode where every transaction is settled individually (gross settlement) and processed as soon as possible after receipt (real-time). In addition to acting as the settlement agent for the ACH, the SIPS also perform settlement among its participants for various purposes such as large-value payments, monetary policy and settlement of securities transactions (payment side).

The top layer contains two FMIs: the central securities depository settles securities transactions (settlement of the delivery side); the central counterparty clears (comparable to clearing by the ACH) and in addition mitigates pre-settlement risk. The latter means that if a participant would default prior to settlement, the CCP would take over the portfolio of the defaulter thereby guaranteeing that all obligations and rights of that portfolio are maintained.

All FMIs are centralized in the sense of their governance: the Board of the FMI is the central authority which controls the system and is responsible for its operational services to its users. The day-to-day operations are delegated to operational departments within the organization of the FMI. The transactions that are sent in by the participants are validated by the FMI, subsequently processed by the FMI, and the results are sent back to the participants, hence the FMI has complete control and up-to-date information about the state of its system. The underlying reasons for centralization are straightforward. First, as the Board is responsible and accountable, it wants to ensure that the FMI is performing as it should, which supposes ultimate control. Second, regulation and supervision apply to each FMI, given that these are usually systemically important: the multiplex of the euro area transfers a total amount of value every working day of € 6,700 bn., roughly half of the annual Gross Domestic Product (GDP) of the euro area. Third, FMIs need to process many transactions and/or complex transactions in short timespans, which in industrial applications so far is only possible using traditional databases and client-server configuration.

The fact that in the multiplex governance is centralized per FMI does not mean that FMIs are geographically concentrated. In reality, FMIs are distributed in order to be operationally resilient (business continuity) as well as cyber resilient. FMI's operate a two (or more) data center configuration, which are geographically distinct so as to minimize the risk that all data centers are affected by a single incident, yet close enough to allow for synchronous communication. In this regard, the increasing use of cloud services for computing, storage and backup by FMIs implies a potential further dispersion of location but also provides for an extra layer of defense against cyber risks. In case one datacenter suffers from a cyber-attack, the other datacenter will be infected immediately as well because of the synchronous communication between the two. A disaster recovery or datacenter in the cloud may then provide a cyber-resilient option in the form of an earlier known-to-be-good state of the system with minimal data-loss. All in all, at the time of writing centralized processing is still superior in terms of performance compared to the decentralized techniques discussed in the next section.

4 Decentralized Systems

A good example of a decentralized and distributed system is the Bitcoin blockchain, which we will discuss in this section which is largely based on [16]. In practice, blockchain is considered a type of DLT that utilizes cryptographically-linked blocks to store data through hashes in a distributed data architecture, whereas distributed ledger technology is any form of ledger-based technology whether using hashes and linked blocks or not but which does utilize ledgers in a distributed data architecture environment replicated across the network as part of the system. The ultimate benefit of any such system is to effectively transfer value directly to another party or entity.

In addition, we will also explain the emerging Libra project, a form of e-money that is aiming at providing domestic and cross-border retail payment services over the coming years.

The Bitcoin System

In 2008 Nakamoto postulated a protocol and network for exchanging value that would not rely on financial institutions as centralized trusted third parties but instead be based on cryptographic proof. As such it is aimed at functioning in a completely trust-less world. The problem of creating a workable system in a trust-less environment is a difficult one, which previous attempts to create electronic cash systems such as e-gold, Liberty Reserve etc. could not solve. In essence, it relates to two important challenges in distributed computing:

1. the Byzantine Generals Problem [10] which describes the difficulty of ensuring the secure exchange of messages in a network of unknown participants that cannot be trusted; and
2. the Double Spending Problem [7], which occurs when electronic cash can be spent twice or more times by broadcasting malicious transactions to the network, which has no central authority to check and track transactions and thus cannot validate the correct sequence of transactions.

The solution to these two problems provided in [13] builds on a particular combination of well-known algorithms for asymmetric cryptography such as SHA-256 (Secure Hash Algorithm) and Proof of Work consensus algorithm Hashcash developed in [2]. The key differences and similarities between Bitcoin and traditional payment systems are summarized in Table 2 below.

Table 2. Comparison of Bitcoin and payment systems

Payment systems	Bitcoin blockchain
• Network with a central operating node	• Distributed network
• Account Based	• Cryptographic Keys

(continued)

Table 2. (*continued*)

Payment systems	Bitcoin blockchain
• Fiat currency (backed by or in central bank money)	• Private cryptocurrency (not backed)
• System and currency are separate	• System and currency are integrated
• Highly regulated and supervised	• Not regulated and in parts almost impossible to supervise
• Full information/transparency on sender and receiver by central operator	• Pseudonymity, with option to separately combine data to identify individuals
• Batch or single transaction processing	• Batch processing
• Within ledger transfers	• Within ledger transfers
• Multitude of ledgers with no common view and associated complexity, significant reconciliation costs for participants	• One immutable ledger or transaction log, that is shared with all participants and updates automatically

Blockchain technology is a type of distributed database, which is shared across a computing network. Within the blockchain network, each computer node maintains a full copy of the database. Nodes are the hardware or software that broadcasts or transmits information to begin the transaction process which, if validated will result in a new appended block. Nodes also contain full copies of the total transaction history of the network.

In the Bitcoin system specific algorithms plus the use of cryptography enable the creation of consensus over transactions in the system, which result in a chain of verifiable transactions on the DL, thus removing the need for a central authority, e.g. a bank. The ledger is distributed to all users of Bitcoin and the system is decentralized, i.e. administered by multiple authoritative nodes. The key is the underlying decision-making governance and the way information is shared through the control nodes in the system. A miner, responsible for the validation of transaction blocks, must necessarily always be operating a node in the Bitcoin blockchain. Every new piece of information added to the data base is added as a block of data along the historic data chain, which records information in the database. The aim of the Bitcoin blockchain is to allow parties who do not necessarily trust one another to agree on information and to engage in a series of different activities directly in an encrypted and pseudo-anonymous way through the use of public and private cryptographic keys. A public key is the identification of the storage of an individual's or entity's digital assets, and a private key provides access to their unique storage facility.

In practice the Bitcoin system however has been displaying increasing signs of control and at this stage it appears that only a few coders maintain and evolve the ledger's core algorithm (and for those that do not agree these code changes can result in a 'hard fork').

With regard to our classification the Bitcoin system can be considered as decentralized and distributed, with the level of decentralization having decreased over time.

Decentralization still therefore makes it impossible to be regulated from within, which is why all applicable regulations at this stage, such as Anti-Money-Laundering and Know-Your-Customer (KYC) rules, only apply to entities and processes at the nexus between the Bitcoin system and fiat currencies, administered in most cases by cryptocurrency exchanges and crypto wallet providers.

Libra 1.0 and 2.0

In June 2019 the "Libra Association", founded initially by Facebook, announced its plan to launch a new global digital currency. Referred to as "Libra", the cryptocurrency would be supported on the "Libra Blockchain" and governed by the Libra Association. On the Libra Blockchain, users can utilize Libra as a lower-cost means of payment, providing efficiency, cross-border capability and financial inclusion. Initially scheduled to launch in the first half of 2020, since its announcement, Libra has been the subject of significant attention from governments and regulators alongside interest from the emerging and incumbent financial services ecosystem.

Libra is being widely described as a cryptocurrency, but while it has similarities to existing cryptocurrencies such as Bitcoin, it also has key differences.

Libra will be a "StableCoin" – that is, its value will be pegged to a pool of stable and liquid assets, which the Libra Association has called the "Libra Reserve". The goal of the Libra Association is for Libra to be used as a transactional currency, rather than exploited for speculative or investment purposes. The Libra Reserve will therefore be structured with capital preservation and liquidity in mind. The Libra Reserve is planned to only hold fiat currencies and government securities from stable and reputable central banks. The aim of this is for Libra to be far less volatile than Bitcoin and other cryptocurrencies, which will make it easier to use for transactional purposes.

In addition, unlike Bitcoin, Libra will be a permissioned currency. Only "Validators" – the Libra Association's founding members – will have the power to verify and validate transactions on the Libra Blockchain, earning transaction fees denominated in Libra. These Validators will be granted voting rights based on the number of coins they hold. Due to the size of the network, it should be sufficiently wide to prevent single bad actors from causing disruption. Validators will be selected for their ability, in aggregate to keep costs low and to smooth capacity.

In response to significant challenge by policy makers and central banks around the world a refreshed version, the "Libra White Paper 2.0" [11] was published on 16 April 2020. This second version sets out four key changes:

1. Extension from the global multi-currency Libra coin to include selected single currency StableCoins.
2. Reinforced Anti-Money Laundering (AML) and sanctions approach, including a compliance framework, moving away from the initially envisaged outsourcing of KYC checks to wallet providers.
3. Abandoned plan to move from a permissioned network to a permissionless system over time.
4. Development of a capital framework (including a buffer) for the Libra Reserve to increase operational resilience.

When applying our criteria on centralization and distribution, the Libra proposition can be described as centralized and distributed, with initial plans of moving towards more decentralization – via the ambition to potentially move from a permissioned to a permissionless DL – being abandoned as a consequence of regulator demands. In addition to the challenges that Libra faced from central banks and policy makers the refocus of Libra is also relevant with a view to becoming a platform to distribute CBDCs as they come to the market, rather than potentially rivalling sovereign currencies.

5 Central Bank Digital Currencies

Beyond centralized payment systems and infrastructures and distributed and decentralized systems in the cryptocurrency space there is third emerging strand, which will impact the payment infrastructure landscape – Central Bank Digital Currencies (CBDC).

Christine Lagarde, at the time Head of the International Monetary Fund (IMF), made a public statement underlining the importance of central banks to reconsider their role as money issuer in the digital age, emphasizing key principles and design considerations [9]. Simply put, where cryptocurrencies allow for zero control, central-bank owned platforms would give regulators control back, making innovation in money issuance a key priority for central banks. No surprise therefore that a number of research and pilot projects have been developing over the last few years with many central banks and supranational bodies including BIS and IMF issuing research papers and results of Proof-of-Concepts (PoCs). It is also interesting to note that the theme of Central Bank Digital Currencies (CBDC) is gaining further momentum in the current COVID-19 crisis with different bodies (e.g. Positive Money) calling for central bank digital cash in order to maintain financial stability and limit the mass-privatization of money.

In the following we will shed light on two particular CBDC initiatives, which are significantly diverging in their underlying policy approach and objectives and thus in their degrees of centralization and distribution.

The first case is Sweden, which has been primarily motivated to work on a form of CBDC because of its significantly low percentage of cash usage, which continues to decline. The project started in 2017 and in February 2020 the Swedish central bank announced a general public technical trial for the e-krona. The CBDC DLT solution that has been developed for this purpose will run separately to the country's central payment system, the latter only used by node operators (primarily banks) to swap part of their central bank deposits into e-krona. Wallets will be activated by participants of the DLT (again mainly banks) and users can make retail, Person to Person (P2P) and transfers between wallets and bank accounts. Different interfaces for smartwatches and cards are also available whilst the option of enabling offline usage is still being explored. The Riksbank emphasizes that this is only a test that is designed to learn about the technology and functioning of the e-krona and that no decision to truly launch a CBDC has been made. The e-krona can be described as a centralized and distributed system. The distributed nature of the DLT solution was a key design factor in terms of resilience, in particular in times of crisis such as cyberattacks. Naturally the DLT system had to be operationally kept separate to the existing centralized and concentrated payment system.

The second case is China, which has been exploring CBDC since 2014 and has recently been in the press announcing the launch of their Digital Yuan in 2020 with trials already in progress in a number of selected provinces. China's CBDC is focusing on replicating cash, in digital form, maintaining the three key pillars of money: transactional/medium of exchange, store of value and unit of account. This means that smart contract deployment will be limited to purely monetary functions. The Digital Yuan is 100% backed by deposits from commercial banks at the Chinese central bank (People's Bank of China, PBoC) and other institutions and operated via a two-tier system as the PBoC has no interest in becoming consumer facing. China's largest banks as well as key conglomerates such as AliPay and Tencent have been identified for secondary issuance of CBDC. For China's government the CBDC is a tool that helps pass on zero or negative interest rates faster than traditional monetary policy mechanisms. However, we are wondering whether reducing the lower bound below zero is really the point here. Since the 2008 financial crisis and certainly in light of the current extraordinary circumstances under Covid-19 it is clear that monetary policy itself needs to be rethought and redefined.

China has been clear that it has no intention to impair the commercial banking sector, hence the two-tier system. The Digital Yuan is also seen as a means to reduce the demand for cryptocurrencies and help consolidate the national currency's sovereignty. A slew of patents for the end-to-end value chain are being issued and implemented, revealing that the solution will operate with "controlled anonymity", where anonymity is maintained between sender and receiver, but transactional information is held by the operator. The national supervisor is able to directly block or restrict wallets that are considered suspicious or in violation of Anti-Money-Laundering (AML), Counter Terrorist Financing (CTF) or tax laws for example. At the same time a selection of different types of Digital Yuan wallets – where the Yuan is depicted in digital bank note format – is being proposed based on users' behavioral data and the identity data provided. Whereas some elements of the solution are building on DLT, for China the need for speedy transactions means that none of the major existing cryptocurrency models, e.g. Bitcoin or Ethereum, are being deployed in terms of consensus and validation algorithms. China's online transaction speeds are up to 92771 transactions per second compared to less than 20 transactions for Bitcoin and Ethereum.

China has also created a National Blockchain Platform, where developers can deploy solutions subject to access permissions – clearly not a decentralized model. It operates on permissioned protocols, which amongst other solutions also leverage Hyperledger Fabric and Baidu's Xuperchain. Cities will operate their own nodes in what is to become a national information highway. China has also recently launched a national blockchain committee with many leading research institutes and organizations in order to facilitate standard setting, the creation and support of their national blockchain infrastructure and the provision of services nation-wide.

In sum, China's approach is significantly centralized. Even the choice of DLT shows that whilst a certain level of 'controlled' distribution is at play, there is no decentralization whatsoever. In particular, the fact that despite secondary issuance full control in terms of monitoring individuals' transactions at all times remains with the central bank shows that the 'bearer' characteristics of physical cash have been all but removed.

6 Concluding Remarks

Centralized but distributed systems (FMIs) for the transfer of digital value still seem superior to decentralized systems (Bitcoin and similar altcoins), in terms of settlement speed, costs and accountability. Therefore, it is not surprising to see that both CBDC approaches discussed in this paper (Sweden and China) are built on a combination of centralization in terms of governance – CBDC is issued by the central bank alone who has the control over its lifecycle – and distribution in relation to the physical location of the data nodes and servers. It is overall highly unlikely that a central bank would opt for a decentralized system of CBDC as this would result in a lack of sovereignty and control over the administration of part of its currency with the same ensuing challenges that we today see in cases where countries, in particular certain emerging markets, show a significant amount of economic activity being transacted in non-sovereign currency, whether that is the USD or Bitcoin. In those situations, monetary policy becomes less effective and transparency around financial flows and trade starts lacking. On that basis it can be safely assumed that we will not see a CBDC model emerging that involves the ingredient of decentralization. Whereas decentralized systems such as Bitcoin and other cryptocurrencies have served as a technology driven inspiration for many actors, from businesses to governments and central banks, it is the element of distribution rather than the decentralized governance that is being more or less embraced.

References

1. Angelis, S.D., Aniello, L., Baldoni, R., Lombardi, F., Margheri, A., Sassone, V.: PBFT vs proof-of-authority: applying the CAP theorem to permissioned blockchain. In: Italian Conference on Cyber Security, pp. 1–11 (2018)
2. Back, A.: Hashcash - a denial of service counter-measure (2002). http://www.hashcash.org/papers/hashcash.pdf
3. Back, R.-J., Kurki-Sounio, R.: Decentralization of process nets with centralized control. Distrib. Comput. **3**, 73–87 (1989)
4. Berndsen, R.J.: Financial Market Infrastructures and Payments: Warehouse Metaphor Textbook (2018). www.warehousemetaphor.com
5. CPMI-IOSCO: Committee on Payment and Settlement Systems and Technical Committee of the International Organization of Securities Commissions: Principles for Financial Market Infrastructures, Bank of International Settlements (2012). www.bis.org/cpmi/publ/d101a.pdf
6. Douceur, J.R.: The sybil attack. In: Druschel, P., Kaashoek, F., Rowstron, A. (eds.) IPTPS 2002. LNCS, vol. 2429, pp. 251–260. Springer, Heidelberg (2002). https://doi.org/10.1007/3-540-45748-8_24
7. Garcia, F.D., Hoepman, J.H.: Off-line karma: a decentralised currency for static peer-to-peer and grid networks. Appl. Cryptogr. Netw. Secur. 364–377 (2005)
8. King, J.L.: Centralized versus decentralized computing: organizational considerations and management options. Comput. Surv. **15**(4) (1983)
9. Lagarde, C.: Winds of change: the case for new digital currency. Speech at the Singapore Fintech Festival, 14 November 2018. IMF (2018)
10. Lamport, L., Shostak, R., Pease, M.: The Byzantine generals problem. ACM Trans. Program. Lang. Syst. **4**(3), 382–401 (1982)
11. Libra White Paper 2.0. https://libra.org/en-US/white-paper/. Accessed 17 May 2020

12. Malone, D., O'Dwyer, K.: Bitcoin mining and its energy footprint. In: 25th IET Irish Signals & Systems Conference 2014 and 2014 China-Ireland International Conference on Information and Communities Technologies (ISSC 2014/CIICT 2014), pp. 280–285 (2014)
13. Nakamoto, S.: Bitcoin: a peer-to-peer electronic cash system (2008). https://bitcoin.org/bitcoin.pdf
14. Narayanan, A., Bonneau, J., Felten, E., Miller, A., Goldfeder, S.: Bitcoin and Cryptocurrency Technologies: A Comprehensive Introduction. Woodstock: Princeton University Press, Oxford (2016)
15. Walch, A.: Deconstructing 'Decentralization': Exploring the Core Claim of Crypto Systems (30 January 2019). Crypto Assets: Legal and Monetary Perspectives (OUP, Forthcoming) (2019). SSRN https://ssrn.com/abstract=3326244
16. Wandhöfer, R.: Technology innovation in financial markets: implications for money, payments and settlement finality. PhD thesis Tilburg University and CASS Business School, June 2019
17. Zheng, Z., Xie, S., Dai, H.-N., Chen, X., Wang, H.: Blockchain challenges and opportunities: a survey. Int. J. Web Grid Serv. **14**(4), 325–375 (2018)

Social Media – A Systemic Change Perspective

Regina Bernhaupt[(✉)] ⓘ

Eindhoven University of Technology, Eindhoven, The Netherlands
r.bernhaupt@tue.nl

Abstract. Social media would not have been possible without the advances in the field of human-computer interaction (HCI). It was laying the basis for interactive systems early on when computers became personal, focused on how humans would not only work collaboratively, but how people could connect and socialize beyond boarders, be it organizational or geographical. Social media has changed society dramatically. From a systemic change perspective, the interplay between people and technology was moving from a single user interacting with a system, to groups of users interacting with a variety of connected systems – impacting companies, organizations, communities and societies. This chapter gives a brief and simplified overview on the history of social media, followed by a systemic change oriented analysis how social media is changing the way people live, how they socialize and make friends. It then focusses on how societies change on national and international level using as an example the recent twitter activities of Kpop fans during the US presidential election campaign showing how new organizations and groups of people start to interact in ways that were unimaginable 15 years ago.

Keywords: Social media · Kpop · Systemic change

1 Introduction

Meet the Dutch couple, Sara Park and Jesse Jansen, and their 12 year old daughter Emma. Sara is communicating with her Korean parents via Kakao [12], she started a trello board [25] to organize the neighborhood activities and spends quite some time on Instagram following her favorite fashion brands.

Jesse is working at an international company for hardware technologies and social media is a central part of his daily work as well as family life. Jesse uses WhatsApp not only to reach out to his co-workers but organizes his cooking club activities and all the sharing of recipes, invites and of course all the joking, in a WhatsApp group for more than three years now.

Emma is not allowed to use Facebook, and her parents are strict on the set age limit of 13 to have a Facebook account. Emma does not mind, her main interest is to watch funny TikToc [24] videos and everything is anyway shared via WhatsApp messages with her friends, typically distributing Twitter and YouTube content and related discussions. When it comes to Emma rambling about Kpop, her parents are just rolling their eyes. For

© IFIP International Federation for Information Processing 2020
Published by Springer Nature Switzerland AG 2020
L. Strous et al. (Eds.): Unimagined Futures, IFIP AICT 555, pp. 119–128, 2020.
https://doi.org/10.1007/978-3-030-64246-4_10

Emma the type of BLINK or ARMY[1] subgroup she ships[2] (and why the pink hair of her favorite idol was so much better than now the blue hair of the leader of the kpop group) are central for her daily communication. But Emma was surprised last week, when she was able to follow the political discussion her parents had with friends over dinner, when she knew more than her parents about the twitter groups that were spamming racist twitter channels and how ARMY had helped to book seats for an event with the US president to influence attendance [20].

As the Park-Jansen family demonstrates, social media has become not only an integral part of business and family life, it is interwoven in local groups and neighborhoods, and now reaches beyond to impacting society on a broader level. There is a plethora of new services, platforms and possibilities to enable users to connect, share, discuss and communicate, allowing everyone to find and use their own personal mix. In this sense we have become even closer to McLuhans "the medium is the message" [15].

In the following a brief overview on the history of social media is presented. Then the POISE-framework is presented, describing how social media can be analyzed and understood based on three relations between people, system and society. The chapter concludes with some recent examples on how social media has been influencing society and gives an outlook on future challenges when it comes to the design, implementation, evaluation, deployment and usage of social media.

2 History of Social Media

2.1 The 1980ies and 1990ies

The foundations for social media come from many fields, with, from a technological viewpoint, human-computer interaction its most central one. In the 1980s HCI focused a lot on how to allow people to interact efficiently and easily with computers, most often for individual users with one machine and followed by the support of users to communicate and interact in groups. Main forms of interaction styles at that time were of course textual, as in command line interfaces, and the first versions of graphical user interfaces like Apple's Lisa [27]. While history typically associates these early years of social communication as business-driven mainly operating on text and direct e-mail communication, there were already large communities using even basic text-based command-line interfaces to play games and develop games as groups. Games like [2].

When it comes to how people communicated and shared information in terms of business as well as entertainment, most available channels were limited in reach (e.g. within an institution or group) and limited access was rather the norm. With the introduction of the world wide web (WWW) and its basic protocols HTML, URL and HTTP it became possible to provide information for a global audience. In 1993 there were about 50 https webservers worldwide, with about 700 websites available, ranging from the

---

[1] BLINK fans following and supporting the Korean Pop group Blackpink [5], ARMY fans following and supporting the Korean Pop Group BTS [7].
[2] Shipping: initially derived from the word relationship, is the desire by fans for two or more people, either real-life people or fictional characters (in film, literature, television, etc.) to be in a romantic relationship [21].

music television channel MTV to local news from the university at MIT. Most websites at that time could be found within universities.[3]

The commercialization of the WWW started in 1996, with an exponential growth in available websites and from 1998 to 2001 the dot.com boost. The main turning point for social media was the introduction of the Web 2.0, with its aim to allow new forms of sharing and exchanging content [10].

2.2 Web 2.0 as the Foundation of Social Media and Its Uptake

As Wikipedia summarizes, [23] most commonly, social media is understood to be interactive computer-mediated technologies that facilitate the creation or sharing of information, ideas, career interests and other forms of expression via virtual communities and networks. The common point for most of them in terms of technology is that they are based on the web 2.0, and use related protocols to distribute, share and display information on a broad variety of devices, including mobile phones.

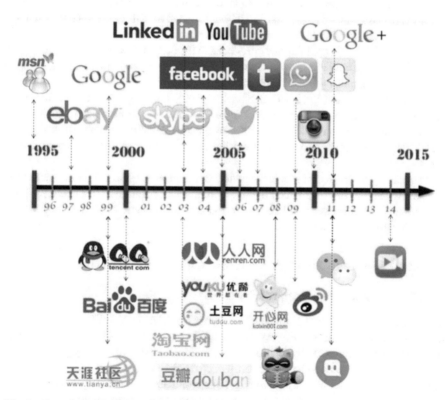

Fig. 1. Overview of social media applications, platforms and services from 1995 onwards [28]

---

[3] Personal note: I would like to take this opportunity to apologize to the course instructor of networks and distributed systems in my computer science education in 1995, asking us to set-up our own personal website. I commented, it was useless time spent having a personal website. He was right, I was wrong.

As Fig. 1 shows, the rise of social media started with the introduction of services like MSN, ebay and google. Similar services started in Asia like Baido or Tencent. With the introduction of Facebook, LinkedIn, YouTube, Twitter and Skype, five key social media channels were established that today are still amongst the top 10 used services. Figure 1 shows the introduction of similar services for Asia. With the addition of Whatsapp, Snapchat and Instagram around 2010, the major social media channels for worldwide usage had been established.

2.3   Social Media Becoming an Integral Part of People's Daily Lives (2010–2020)

In 2010 social media had around 1 billion active users, and within the past 10 years, this tripled to about 3 billion active social media users in 2020 [22]. The major social media companies Facebook, Twitter, LinkedIn and Youtube were accompanied by Snapchat with about 1 million daily active users in 2012. A broad range of other services have since then reached these milestones of more than 1 million active daily users, including Pinterest, Reddit, Tumblr, Medium, Flickr or Twitch. One of the latest social media platforms that was added to the mix is TikToc, founded in 2016, and since then the app was downloaded worldwide more than 2 billion times.

Not all social media applications introduced in the last 10 years have been successful. One of the most prominent ones is Google+ which disappeared most likely due to the privacy issues the platform had experienced.

From a non-US and European perspective there is a range of services that reach millions and billions of people in other parts of the world. For example, in China WeChat reaches about 1.2 billion and Tencent QQ has a user base of more than 650 million. In Korea, platforms like Kakaotalk is currently having more users than Facebook has in Korea.

The prediction for social media usage is that the growth trend will continue at least at the same pace. It has thus become unlikely that social media will disappear [26]. On the contrary, social media will become an integral component when it comes to how society develops in the next 10 years.

3   Social Media in 2020: A Systemic Change Perspective

3.1   The Systemic Change Approach POISE

The POISE systemic change framework describes the relationship of People, Organization, Interactive System and Environment (Fig. 2). The development of social media can be described using three relations (Fig. 2, [13]) analyzing and describing how social media has developed from supporting activities from personal and group related perspective to all activities within organizations, companies and society in general.

In the original model persons (and people) were typically considered to be trained operators with validated qualifications, but today can be seen as individual users or a group of users, performing activities and tasks while interacting with a multitude of interactive systems or the Internet of Things (IoT).

Interactive systems are usually computer-based ones which present a certain level of automation and are supposed to fulfill requirements that enable users to perform

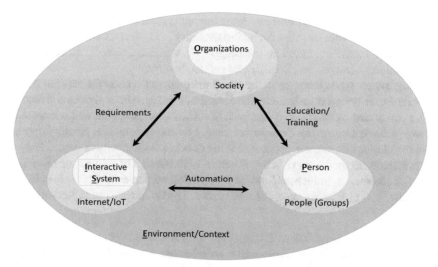

Fig. 2. The POISE research framework for people, organization, interactive system and environment extends a standard socio-technical system model from the 1960ies [6]

activities and tasks. The computer will "disappear" in the future in the sense that it will be invisibly integrated in the physical system with which the human interacts, going even beyond the current IoT related interaction concepts.

The organization is usually a large entity composed of several organizational layers and can be extended to depict society in general. Furthermore, the organization deals with the context and the environment into which it is embedded.

The people node in Fig. 2 includes aspects like the study of the human using and interacting with the system and what activities they perform when interacting with social media. The edge between people and organization/society typically is about learning and training about social media usage, its advantages and limitations. The node on organization/society includes the description of (business) processed and regulations, while the edge interactive system/organization is central for any engineering requirements of the system. The interactive system node includes all technological aspects ranging from network, to system design, and finally the edge of interactive system and people is central for how users can interact with the system and to what degree such systems enable and support users by introducing automation.

3.2 User vs System → Automation

Social media in the first place is an interaction of a user with an (interactive) system. The goal of the social media user is to perform an activity or to accomplish a task, be it to communicate, to inform, to educate or to be entertained. Tasks and activities range from a simple and specific activity like sending a text message to trying to change their mood by being entertained in general during a Sunday afternoon.

The overall experience a user has when interacting with social media is influenced by a range of software qualities including usability [11], user experience with subdimensions like aesthetics, emotion, meaning/value, social connectedness, identification or stimulation [3], or privacy, security and service quality.

A key aspect when it comes to the social media experience is the relation between system and user, and what tasks and activities are automated: what activities and functions can be performed by the user? What type of information is visible and transparent to the user and what things are done automatically by the system, like personalization or recommendations the system proposes? What data is automatically collected and what can be influenced by the user? When it comes to the design of a social media app, the degree of automation influences how the service will be perceived by the user in terms of usability and user experience, but more critically also in terms of privacy or service quality.

Usability and User Experience: Examples of such automation common in real applications are recommendation engines for targeted advertisement used by google or amazon. Once you have been buying a Christmas present for your parents, the system is still recommending similar articles, related to that present, even if you personally would not be interested in them. Another example is the repetition of a product advertisement that you have been buying recently, with the possible downside that the advertisement might indicate the product you have bought at a discounted price. Being offered the product you were buying with a 40% lower price can heavily influence the brand perception you have of a store or company.

Privacy: The perception of the user to what extent their personal data is handled with the specific service (and connected to other services) with regards to automation. As example, Apple's iPhone does not allow a user to deactivate the transfer of location information of the device [1]. This shows how central the automation aspects are for the overall perception of privacy.

Service Quality: The 'filter bubble' originally coined by Pariser [18], describes the phenomenon that algorithms used for personalization of content can lead to an effect that a person only receives content that is similar to previous visited or selected content, thus creating a bubble around a user. This has recently become a central discussion for Facebook and the claim that Facebook is spreading fake news. The role of automation in filter bubbles is based on the algorithm implementation. The way users are interacting with the system can also play a central role [19].

3.3   System vs Organization → Requirements

For social media to be successful a key component is the functionality different services and applications offer. When it comes to the interactive system, it is not only about the user's perspective on what is automated, but how what type of data is presented and used when it comes to different perspectives, like the organizational view. The need of an organization or company for example will be to use social media and the data generated with it, to track with as much detail as possible what and how users are interacting with their system, while on a personal basis the individual users might prefer that less personal relevant information is made available.

Requirements for social media applications are thus key when it comes to the implementation aspects of the different software qualities, and how to balance between them. Will it be more beneficial to enhance the overall user experience by personalizing the service for the user by using location information of the smart phone, or is it more important to ensure the users privacy? Is it more important to have a better word completion prediction using the users movement and holding patterns of a remote control to identify the user, or do we respect the security and privacy concerns of the user, and expect that such data might be mis-used by an insurance company, say, as it allows it to predict early detection of specific diseases [4].

Key aspects when it comes to requirements for social media are transparency and how to enable and ensure transparency [14], and privacy (from a technical perspective), the use, for example, of differential privacy algorithms and aspects like security, reliability or dependability. What will be central in the coming years is not how to solve each of these challenges, but how to address multi-properties and balance them [17]. Is it more important to have a good user experience, or is a focus on privacy more important? Is it necessary or worth it to focus on dependability to ensure social media will not influence ongoing elections?

Or do we allow the users (and society) to handle the balancing? And simply teach and train the users, instead of solving it from a technical perspective?

3.4   People vs Organization → Learning/Training

Computer Supported Collaborative Work (CSCW) is focusing on how to design and develop technologies to support groups of users, and how interactive digital systems affect work. On a more general level, there are entire research fields focusing on how digital media and social media are influencing communication, education, entertainment and business in general.

The third angle of the system change framework is focusing on what aspects we should be focusing on when it comes to learning and training people and how to interact with social media. This can range from simple education on how to use e-banking systems for the elderly to ensure that there will be no digital gap in society, to higher level goals, on how to develop regulations to ensure social media providers are reactive enough when it comes to hate speech, fake news or country-depending un-appropriate content (for example the German NetzDG).

For the next 10 years, recent developments including some country-wide lockdowns will shift the focus even more on the necessity to understand the role of social media when it comes to society in general and how for example to enhance resilience of citizens. Recent events including the Covid 19 pandemic, for example, have already been bringing a considerable shift in the perception of how entertainment like social media entertainment and games can be highly beneficial when it comes to coping strategies, and a deeper understanding will be of profound interest when it comes to societal strategies ranging from architecture (work and life at home vs. office work) to transport (cars currently are considered safer than trains, contrary to goals we might have when it comes to sustainability).

3.5   Using the POISE Framework as Analysis Guideline for Systemic Change

The POISE framework and its three defining edges can be a guiding framework when it comes to the analysis of social media and its societal impact on a systemic change level. The POISE model should be a guide, where the components like learning, requirements, processes or automation aspects are not individual, but they are interwoven and dependent on each other. The balance between these aspects allows to balance between the different software qualities that should be achieved for the social media systems and services. The POISE model has the advantage that it encompasses the micro-mesa-macro approaches of systemic change approaches.

4   Social Media Changing Society: A Twitter Case Study

Twitter, the micro blogging and social media service, started in 2007. Users typically send short text messages called tweets to each other. These tweets initially were maximum 140 letters, and today have up to 280 letters. Twitter is commonly used for information sharing, it is a key medium for companies, businesses and people in politics and entertainment to accompany their social media strategies. There is a number of statistics that can help understand this type of social media. Among the top 50 persons with most followers are former President Obama, Ellen DeGeneres and a number of other people in entertainment like Justin Bieber or Katy Perry. From a content perspective the 20 tweets that were most shared belong to President Obama, with the Korean pop boyband BTS having 10 most shared tweets among these 20. The majority of the 20 most shared tweets is from 2020. The tweet with the most received likes in 24 h is again from BTS (June 2020).

Twitter and twitter activities today are not only related to marketing, information sharing or public complaints. There are groupings within followers structures that are influencing societal events. In June 2020, the followers of the BTS called ARMY have been actively spamming a number of accounts to support the activities of the BlackLives-Matters Campaign [8] by spamming accounts with BTS memes.

This is a central example how political activism and influences have changed from traditional media and geographical influence to social media with international activism in a US election campaign. A possible explanation of the strength of these kpop twitter followers is that their interaction ration compared to number of followers is extremely high [9].

A second example for such activity from June 2020 is the reservation of tickets for Trumps election campaign which was disturbed by Twitter activists and TikToc users [16]. The goal of the campaign was to have (in most cases teenagers) reserve tickets for a campaign event in Tulsa, and then not using them. The strategy was very successful and even acknowledged by the Trump election campaign team.

These examples lead us back to our Dutch couple and Emma, who was surprised that her understanding of politics was better than her parents. Today social media enables very different user groups to access information worldwide, shifting traditional media approaches and campaigns to new ways of outreach and influence for society on a more general basis.

5   Conclusion and Future Challenges

The goal of this chapter was to give a brief overview of social media history, and to show how the impact of social media can be analyzed using the POISE framework. The POISE framework connects traditional computer science-oriented approaches and theories based on socio-technical systems with the potential to address social media influence on the larger societal level. This chapter was written in times of change and, given the current drastic changes in society, it becomes clear that, in the foreseeable future, social media will become an integral part of our daily lives, given the necessity to connect and socialize more digitally and virtually than through personal contact.

Fig. 3. Demonstration of changes in the last 15 years following the Pope with audiences in 2005, 2013 and without audience in 2020

Since the introduction of social media and its rise since 1995 digitalization has changed the world. Figure 3 shows a comparison of the impact of such trends using the Pope as an example. While in 2005 usage of smart phones was very limited, the pictures for 2013 speak a different language, showing the uptake of social media. Today the pope is having the most influential twitter account in the religious world (@Pontifex, @Pontifex_es and @Pontifex_it), and as the picture in Fig. 3 right-side shows, this has become key to reach followers, given the limitations in personal interaction in 2020.

Future challenges will be the design and development of interactive systems and more general social-technical systems and services that allow the integration of different social media channels with existing systems to lay a basis for next generation services based on cross-usages of IoT based infrastructures. ICT professionals, both researchers and practitioners, and professional societies must contribute to a responsible development and implementation of such technologies and services.

References

1. Apples Location Tracking. https://www.inc.com/jason-aten/apple-preaches-privacy-heres-why-your-iphone-is-tracking-your-location-anyway.html. Accessed 16 Aug 2020
2. Bartle, R.: Hearts, clubs, diamonds, spades: players who suit MUDS (1996). https://mud.co.uk/richard/hcds.htm

3. Bernhaupt, R., Pirker, M.: Evaluating user experience for interactive television: towards the development of a domain-specific user experience questionnaire. In: Kotzé, P., Marsden, G., Lindgaard, G., Wesson, J., Winckler, M. (eds.) INTERACT 2013. LNCS, vol. 8118, pp. 642–659. Springer, Heidelberg (2013). https://doi.org/10.1007/978-3-642-40480-1_45
4. Bernhaupt, R., Pottier, G., Pirker, M., Drouet, D., Battut, A.: Authenticating the TV user by biometric continuous measurements. International Broadcasting Convention 2017 (IBC). IBC (2017)
5. Blackpink. https://en.wikipedia.org/wiki/Blackpink
6. Brandt, D., Cernetic, J.: Human-centred approaches to control and information technology: European experiences. AI Soc. **12**(1–2), 2–20 (1998)
7. BTS. https://en.wikipedia.org/wiki/BTS
8. CNN (2020). https://edition.cnn.com/2020/06/04/us/kpop-bts-blackpink-fans-black-lives-matter-trnd/index.html
9. Forbes (2020). https://www.forbes.com/sites/emilyblake1/2018/04/04/k-pop-numbers/#69717b4548ab
10. History of the WWW (2020). https://en.wikipedia.org/wiki/History_of_the_World_Wide_Web]
11. ISO 9241-11:2018(en)
12. Kakaotalk (2020). https://www.kakaocorp.com/service/KakaoTalk?lang=en
13. Ragosta, M., Martinie, C., Palanque, P., Navarre, D., Sujan M.A.: Concept maps for integrating modeling techniques for the analysis and re-design of partly-autonomous interactive systems. In: Proceedings of the 5th International Conference on Application and Theory of Automation in Command and Control Systems (ATACCS 2015), pp. 41–52. Association for Computing Machinery, New York (2015)
14. Matei, S.A., Russell, M.G., Bertino, E.: Transparency in Social Media, pp. 109–123. Springer, Cham (2015). https://doi.org/10.1007/978-3-319-18552-1
15. McLuhan, M.: Medium is the Message. McGraw-Hill Education, New York (1964)
16. NYTimes (2020). https://www.nytimes.com/2020/06/21/style/tiktok-trump-rally-tulsa.html
17. Palanque, P., Basnyat, S., Bernhaupt, R., Boring, R., Johnson, C., Johnson, P.: Beyond usability for safety critical systems: how to be sure (safe, usable, reliable, and evolvable)? In: CHI 2007, Extended Abstracts on Human Factors in Computing Systems, pp. 2133–2136, April 2007
18. Pariser, E.: The Filter Bubble: What the Internet is Hiding from You. Penguin UK, London (2011)
19. Seargeant, P., Tagg, C.: Social media and the future of open debate: a user-oriented approach to Facebook's filter bubble conundrum. Discourse Context Media **27**, 41–48 (2019). ISSN 2211-6958. https://doi.org/10.1016/j.dcm.2018.03.005
20. Presidential Elections 2020, US (2020). https://fortune.com/2020/06/22/kpop-fans-trump-rally-crowd-size/
21. Shipping. https://en.wikipedia.org/wiki/Shipping_(fandom)
22. Social Media Usage Statistics. https://www.statista.com/statistics/272014/global-social-networks-ranked-by-number-of-users/
23. Social Media. https://en.wikipedia.org/wiki/Social_media
24. TikTok (2020). www.tiktok.com
25. Trello (2020). www.trello.com
26. van Dijck, J.: The Culture of Connectivity: A Critical History of Social Media. Oxford Publishers, Oxford (2013)
27. Webdesignerdepot (2020). https://www.webdesignerdepot.com/2009/03/operating-system-interface-design-between-1981-2009/
28. Social Media History (2020). https://postfity.com/history-social-media/

A Resource Perspective on E-Waste: A Global Problem with Local Solutions?

David Kreps[1]([⊠]) [iD] and Per Fors[2] [iD]

[1] National University of Ireland Galway, University Road, Galway H91 TK33, Ireland
david.kreps@nuigalway.ie
[2] Uppsala University Ångströmlaboratoriet, Lägerhyddsvägen 1, 751 21 Uppsala, Sweden
Per.Fors@Angstrom.uu.se

Abstract. ICT is, at least to some extent, material, and different phases of the ICT lifecycle present us with different challenges related to the physical properties of ICT. E-waste is a term used to describe discarded electronic and electrical equipment that is neither reused or repaired, nor refurbished. While it is clear that e-waste is currently mainly a big social and environmental problem, we also see opportunities in re-introducing materials from existing e-waste into the ICT supply chain. Although e-waste is a pressing problem, it can also be seen as, and become a resource. The shift in perspective required is towards a life-cycle perspective on all materials in the production, marketing, and end-of-life processes of ICT artefacts. A combination of Design for Repairability and End-of-life Design can contribute to a set of electronics design guidelines that would meet circular economy principles.

Keywords: E-waste · Green IT · Design for repairability · End-of-life design

1 Introduction

Because of the abstract nature of ICT, many have long assumed that the negative social and environmental side effects of ICT are non-existent, or at least negligible given the immense potential of ICT to create wealth and prosperity and even to promote sustainability [16, 41]. However, in recent decades it has become increasingly apparent that ICT is, at least to some extent, material, and that different phases of the ICT life-cycle present us with different challenges related to the physical properties of ICT. ICT products – such as mobile phones, servers, desktops and laptops – are produced by an increasing number of different materials that need to be extracted from the earth in one way or another, usually with severe environmental, health and safety issues. Components used in ICT products also need to be produced, and these components need to be assembled into the final product. In this phase, we are also presented with different problems related to social and environmental factors. It is in the use phase of ICT products where the social, economic and potentially also environmental benefits are reaped. However, we are also becoming increasingly aware of the energy consumption

L. Strous et al. (Eds.): Unimagined Futures, IFIP AICT 555, pp. 129–141, 2020.
https://doi.org/10.1007/978-3-030-64246-4_11

of these products. Although these products are becoming more energy-efficient by the day, the quantity of ICT products is rapidly increasing, and the total amount of electricity needed for them to function also increases.

While all phases of the ICT lifecycle are intimately connected, this chapter will focus on the disposal phase, or the of end-of-life (EoL) of ICT products, often termed electronic waste or e-waste. E-waste is a term used to describe discarded electronic and electrical equipment that is neither reused or repaired, nor refurbished [30]. According to the Solving the E-Waste Problem initiative, e-waste should be defined as "all types of electrical and electronic equipment (EEE) and its parts that have been discarded by the owner as waste without the intention of re-use" [49]. While we acknowledge the fact that e-waste is not entirely made up of ICT products, we mainly focus on ICT related e-waste in this chapter, both since the majority of the products referred to as e-waste are ICT products and also since this book has a focus on ICT.

There are many reasons materials used in ICT products are not properly recycled. The main reasons include the complex material composition of ICT products, that make them virtually impossible to fully recycle, at least without the use of extremely high-tech facilities. Such facilities can recycle between 70 and 90% of the materials in e-waste, but they only exist in few locations around the world (Sweden, Japan, Canada, Germany and Belgium). A second reason is the lack of incentive for ICT companies to design products for longevity, repairability, upgradeability, disassembly and recycling – rather than for cost-efficiency, performance, aesthetics and a relatively short useful life. A third reason is the lack of proper systems for recovery and recycling of e-waste in many places, and a lack of incentive for consumers of electronic goods to actually use these existing systems and hand back worn-out electronics. There are also other reasons that we have failed to create a circular system for ICT products with the accumulation of e-waste as a result, including the use of virgin materials over recycled materials, short-term profits of exporting waste over long-term profits of keeping them in the cycle, and the overconsumption of new electronic products in the developed world.

However, while it is clear that e-waste is currently mainly a big social and environmental problem, we also see opportunities in re-introducing materials from existing e-waste into the ICT supply chain. There are indications that the linear production system (i.e. take-make-waste) is not only inferior from a sustainability-perspective, but also that many elements (such as copper and gold) are getting increasingly profitable to recycle rather than to extract from virgin ore [25]. Considering the three pillars of sustainability (social, environmental, economic), we argue that with e-waste recycling we have a rare case of "win-win-win" synergies, as solving the e-waste problem will lead to economic, social and environmental benefits.

This chapter will discuss e-waste from a social, environmental and economic standpoint on both the local and global level. The principal areas of concern for this chapter are e-waste, sustainable development and resource use and reuse and these concepts will be briefly touched upon in the next section of the chapter.

2   Background

Sustainable development is a term that was coined in the late 1980s and got its famous definition in the renowned Brundtland report "Our Common Future" [8]. Here, it was concluded that sustainable development should be seen as human development that meets the needs of the present without compromising the ability of future generations to meet their own needs [8]. Since then, sustainable development has become a buzzword with many different interpretations. What unites these interpretations is the fact that sustainable development is an assemblage of complex and interrelated social, environmental and economic aspects that need to be taken into consideration simultaneously. Despite the focus on different sustainability-related goals, in more recent decades, not least the Millennium Development Goals (MDGs) and the Sustainable Development Goals (SDGs), sustainable development should not be seen as an end-goal or something that "can be achieved", but rather as a process of continuous improvements.

It is clear that the e-waste problem presents numerous sustainability-related challenges, as it affects the environment and human societies at both local and global levels. Turning to the SDGs [52], it is clear that the e-waste problem needs to be solved in order to reach some of them, most notably Goal 3, to "Ensure healthy lives and promote well-being for all at all ages", Goal 8, to "Promote sustained, inclusive and sustainable economic growth, full and productive employment and decent work for all", Goal 9, to "Build resilient infrastructure, promote sustainable industrialization and foster innovation," Goal 11, to "Make cities and human settlements inclusive safe resilient and sustainable", and Goal 12, to "Ensure sustainable consumption and production patterns". For a closer scrutinization of how the e-waste problem relates to the targets within each SDG, please see the UN Environmental Management Group (EMG) report "United Nations System-wide Response to Tackling E-waste" [51].

3   Resource Use

As Meadows et al. [38] famously announced in their 1970s report to the Club of Rome, there are Limits to Growth. Economist Hermann Daly pointed out in 1973, moreover, "in a finite world continual growth is impossible. Given finite stomachs, finite lifetimes, and the kind of man who does not live by bread alone, growth becomes undesirable long before it becomes impossible" [12, p. 5]. These warnings, however, went largely unheeded. Instead, faith in technology as "an omnipotent deus ex machina who (sic) will get us out of any growth-induced problems" [ibid. p. 5] continues to guide economists, technologists and politicians to this day. Daly's ultimate and fundamental point nonetheless remains key: "nature really does impose 'an inescapable general scarcity,' and it is a serious delusion to believe otherwise" [ibid. p. 8]. Dutch atmospheric chemist Paul Crutzen, by the turn of the millennium, had concluded that a new stage in Earth's history had begun: the Anthropocene [10]. Defined as a new geological era, the Anthropocene is characterised by the extent of man-made changes – not least to the weather system – our activities have effected upon the planet we share. The Great Acceleration [48] of these changes since 1945, moreover, means that the modern period "deserves to be marked off as different from what came before it in environmental history" [37, p. 208]. The crucial point here is that although the Anthropocene is here to stay, the acceleration must stop, if humans are to be able to continue living on this planet in anything like the manner we have been used to over the last 10,000 years – i.e. in settled, civilised conditions supported by the planet's ecosystems.

Key to an understanding of these changes – and how to remedy them – remains economics. The production cycle of our economic growth model – how we make, use, and then discard things – is extremely inefficient, leading to massive and unsustainable resource depletion, and enormous amounts of polluting waste. As John Bellamy Foster [17] and others have outlined, our systems of production and trade are so divorced from the needs of the natural world - and so efficient at its use - that they are "killing the planet" [17, p. 8]. The core premise of this thinking is that we cannot continue to use natural resources in such flagrant and wasteful a manner as we have become used to, without devastating consequences. According to the Global Footprint Network, "Humans use as much ecological resources as if we lived on 1.75 Earths" [19]. According to 2011 figures, the average American uses seven "global hectares", compared to a global average of 2.7, so if we all lived like US citizens we would need four Earths, not one [36]. New economic thinking, including ideas like the steady-state economy [13], and the more recent 'doughnut' economics of Kate Raworth [42, 43], are complementing the ambitions of supra-national bodies such as the UN and the EU to move toward a "circular economy" [7, 40] fundamentally changing the habits of industrial capitalism.

As is becoming increasingly clear, moreover, "digital's (growing) contribution to the ecological catastrophe unfolding in the 21st century" [29] cannot go unchallenged. The production cycle of digital devices is immensely wasteful. To take just one example, over a billion iPhones have been made since 2007 using some 40 million tons of gold ore. How little of this is recycled is quite shocking, considering that gold was made trillions of years ago in the heart of exploding stars, later to coalesce into the rocks and dust from which planets such as ours were formed around our own, relatively young Sun.

Perhaps the most extraordinary tale, however, concerning the resources used by our everyday technological devices, is that of Rare Earth Elements, or RREs. These are precious resources found in only a very few places on Earth, each fraught with problems. China, which has the greatest sources of these precious materials, has either restricted or blocked their export on a number of occasions. It is perhaps as much - or more - to do with these resources than the relatively cheaper labour that is behind the decisions of Apple and other smartphone manufacturers to base their manufacturing operations in China, rather than elsewhere [15, 26, 31, 57]. In the US, deposits of these materials are to be found, but only with relative difficulty, and thus expense. A Congressional Research Service Report on Rare Earth Minerals [24] pointed out that in 2011 96.9% of all Rare Earth Mineral production took place in China, where some 50% of global reserves are to be found, compared to only some 13% in the US, with the rest spread across the world, notably in Russia.

Resource depletion is a growing problem for many industries. As the global population rises, and the economic model of GDP growth encourages constant innovation, the use of resources is increasing rapidly. This rapaciousness includes the depletion of metals, such as gold and aluminium as well as RREs, [15, 26, 31, 57], which are central to the production of ICTs. The recycling of e-waste, for the recovery of these minerals (urban mining), is thus a central concern for the electronics industry.

4 The "E-Waste Problem"

Having briefly touched upon some of the problems with e-waste, this section of the chapter will focus upon different sustainability-related (social, economic and environmental) problems, both on a local and a global scale.

E-waste, often referred to as the fastest growing waste stream globally, is a global problem with both local and global consequences. According to the Global E-Waste Monitor "the world generated 44.7 million metric tonnes (Mt) of e-waste and only 20% was recycled through appropriate channels" in 2016 [4]. The majority of the other 80% remains with the user [56], is thrown in residual waste (4%), is exported as second-hand goods or illegally exported as e-waste to be informally recycled under inferior circumstances. The Global E-Waste Monitor records that the United States produced 6.3 Mt of e-waste in 2016, of which only 1.4 Mt was collected (22%). Norway produces the most e-waste (28.5 kg per inhabitant), but it has one of the highest collection rates (49.2%). While the West has traditionally been the largest producer of e-waste / China will be the biggest producer of e-waste, with over 28 million tons produced each year. This makes China a bigger producer than all countries in the EU combined [58].

A crucial aspect that has contributed to the e-waste problem is the fact that electronic goods have not and are not designed with longevity and recycling – but instead with attributes such as cost-efficiency, performance and aesthetics – in mind. Planned obsolescence also remains a key problem in the ICT industry [3, 55]. For example, many current smartphones are glued, rather than screwed together, making battery replacement difficult and expensive. Diminished battery capacity is one of the primary drivers for replacement of the whole device [44, 45]. In pursuit of cost-efficiency and performance, the material composition of electronic goods is also becoming increasingly complex. According to [35], a microprocessor used in desktops in the 1980s consisted of 12 different chemical elements. Today, a microprocessor is usually made up of as many as 60, or more than half of all the elements in the periodic table [39]. While high-technological facilities for recycling of e-waste do exist, as previously mentioned, they are few and can currently not keep up with the rapid technological developments within the ICT industry.

While approximately 70 to 90% by weight of each electronic product can be recycled today, very few of these many different elements are actually recycled. For example, most, if not all, of the Rare Earth Elements (REEs) will end up in landfills because of the small amount used in each product [45]. REEs, such as iridium, palladium and gallium, are elements used to give electronic products certain unique properties. The name is used collectively for Group 3 elements of the periodic table, and they are chemically similar and are often found together in the Earth's crust [28]. While these are used in very small amounts, the use of them gives rise to local environmental and social problems as well as global environmental problems. Many of these precious resources are found in only a very few places on Earth, each fraught with problems. [47] have looked into REE extraction in China and conclude that refining REEs is a very energy-intensive process which often causes emissions into water and air due to heavy use of chemical materials being used in the process. In one of the largest REE mines (Bayan Obo in China), a large number of environmental and health issues have been identified due to the huge amount of gas, liquid and solid waste generated by the mining operation. Even in the few REE mines that do not contain radioactive elements (e.g. thorium), many environmental and health issues were identified. Many illegal mines also exist in China, where environmental, health and safety issues are more or less ignored. China has also either restricted or blocked their export on a number of occasions.

Many actors along the value chain of ICT products, moreover, have traditionally tried to avoid the responsibility of the e-waste problem. According to [50], only around 20% of all End-of-Life (EoL) electronic devices are properly recycled, while the remaining 80% is shipped as second-hand goods to developing parts of the world. According to the Basel Convention, while the exportation of second-hand goods is legal, exporting e-waste is illegal. However, only about two-thirds of the second-hand equipment is still functioning and sold in local second-hand markets. The rest is repaired and sold or ends up at local scrap yards. According to Basel Action Network (BAN), the biggest importers of e-waste are China, Pakistan and India, while the biggest exporters are the US, the EU and Australia [18]. From the US, according to [33], between 50 and 80% of all e-waste is exported rather than being recycled nationally. The lack of sustainable e-waste management results in wide-scale environmental impacts as well as health impacts to the people and communities working in or living near these sites [1, 2, 20, 31, 34].

According to the WEEE handbook, e-waste generally contains many different toxic substances, such as mercury, lead, chromium and cadmium, but also various other chemicals including ozone-depleting substances and flame retardants. The amount of toxic substances in e-waste vary, but generally speaking older equipment contains more toxic substances, but also more valuable materials, making these devices more attractive to informal recyclers. Many CRT (Cathode Ray Tube) monitors, for example, contain valuable materials such as cadmium, which should only be managed by professionals. If humans or animals are exposed to cadmium, bones and kidneys can be affected. This substance is now banned by the European Restriction on Hazardous Substance Directive. While CRT monitors have been more or less phased out, flat-screen monitors can also be dangerous to handle, as they may contain mercury which is highly toxic and can cause damage to different vital organs in humans and animals. Also, this toxic substance can be passed on to children when breast-fed by someone who has been exposed to the substance. Cables and wiring are often informally recycled in order to extract the copper. Cables are often coated in plastics (incl. PVC plastics), and the fastest/easiest way to access the copper is to burn the plastic coating away. However, PVC release dioxins when burned, and these dioxins can affect the immune and reproductive systems of humans and animals. Other standard procedures include heating and manual removal of components from printed circuit boards (PBCs), and acid digestion of components, both of these with potential negative effects on the health of the workers. Needless to say, these workers are not trained to properly manage e-waste, but many (including children) are forced to engage in these activities to survive.

This highlights another problem related to e-waste, namely that the whole problem is highly unequal from a global world-system perspective. Lennerfors et al. [32] review the ICT lifecycle from a sustainability perspective, and present a critique toward research, policy and practical initiatives that present ICT as a solution to different sustainability-related problems. They see that while ICT in the use phase can be used for sustainability purposes (dematerialization, optimization, etc.) locally in the developed world, this also results in environmental degradation and social problems in developing countries where much of the extraction, production, manufacturing and disposal takes place. They argue that using ICT to achieve different sustainability-related problems usually resembles a "zero-sum game", where developing countries suffer local environmental and social problems in order to "keep the [developed] core green and clean" [23]. Thus, there is certainly an important aspect of global inequalities related to the e-waste problem that needs to be taken into consideration.

5 Initiatives to Solve the Problem

There are several global initiatives that aim to regulate and create incentives for increased circularity within the ICT industry. As of 2018, two-thirds of countries are covered by a national e-waste management policy [4]. Almost all national and international policies include a take-back system, often based on an Extended Producer Responsibility (EPR) clause, in which the producer or distributor is obliged to collect used electronic and electrical products for reuse and recycling. Even though "policymakers, producers and recyclers in various countries have created specialized 'take-back and treatment' systems to collect e-waste from final owners and process it in professional treatment facilities (…) the collection and state-of-the-art treatment of e-waste is limited, and most nations are still without such e-waste management systems" [5]. In Sweden, where recycling is the norm [21], a sophisticated take-back system is implemented (El-kretsen), and where one of the few high-technological recycling facilities is located, only a very small amount of small electronic devices such as mobile phones are actually recycled.

Perhaps the most well-known global initiative is the Basel Convention on the Control of Transboundary Movements of Hazardous Wastes and their Disposal, which came into place in 1992 and restricts the movement of hazardous waste from high-income to low-income countries [6]. Of the high-income countries, only the USA has not ratified the Convention. In 1995, the Basel Ban Amendment was proposed, which would ban all shipment of e-waste from OECD countries to low-income countries, including export for recycling, but this Amendment remains unratified, because not enough countries support it. The European Union countries and Norway and Switzerland have fully implemented the Amendment in their national legislation [46]. After the Basel Convention, the Partnership for Action on Computing Equipment (PACE) was initiated. PACE is described as a "multi-stakeholder public-private partnership" where many different actors are represented, including producers, recyclers, researchers, environmental groups, and so on. The final guidance documents that were adopted by the parties in 2017 deals with environmentally sound management of end-of-life computing equipment.

In the EU, a Waste Electrical and Electronics Equipment (WEEE) Directive in 2012 promoted the "re-use, recycling and other forms of recovery of waste electrical and electronic equipment (WEEE) in order to reduce the quantity of such waste to be disposed and to improve the environmental performance of the economic operators involved in the treatment of WEEE" [14]. Another organization that focuses on e-waste is The International Environmental Technology Centre (IETC). Their focus is to promote environmentally sustainable technological solutions focusing on holistic waste management. To realize this vision, IETC provides support to governments that want to enhance their use of more sustainable practices, strategies and technologies. They focus on innovative waste prevention methods and technologies and aim to improve human well-being and reduce the impact of e-waste on climate change. IETC is a part of the United Nations Environment Programme (UNEP) and is located in Osaka, Japan. Another UN initiative is the Environmental Management Group, which was established in 2001. In 2016, they started focusing also on e-waste more specifically, by attempting to strengthen collaboration between different policy initiatives within the UN, and to support already existing initiatives and projects related to design and life cycle approaches for sustainability.

There are other initiatives aiming to solve problems related to e-waste, or to design, use, and disposal of electronic equipment in ways that promote circularity and sustainability. Examples include The UN agency International Telecommunication Union (ITU), The International Solid Waste Association, responsible for the well-known report the Global E-Waste Monitor, first released in 2014, Solving the E-Waste Problem (StEP), and more. Another central initiative that works for sustainability in the ICT industry more broadly, but also specifically targets the e-waste problem is the Karlskrona Manifesto for Sustainable Design. According to the manifesto, not only producers of hardware are responsible for sustainable design of technology. Rather, software practitioners who design software systems that "run our world" also have a big impact on the sustainability of ICT and other technological devices. Finally, the International Federation for Information Processing (IFIP) has recently taken a stance in the e-waste discussion with the IFIP Position Paper on e-waste. The work on this paper began in IFIP's Technical Committee 9 in the Autumn of 2017, led by David Kreps, with the goal of setting out some of the details of the problem, as it currently stands, and what role IFIP affirms it can play in trying to redress it. Here, just like in the Karlskrona Manifesto, IFIP establishes which actor (e.g. users, designers and producers of ICT products) has the responsibility for what aspect of the e-waste problem, and how each actor can take their responsibility [30].

6   E-Waste as a Resource

While the magnitude of the e-waste problem is growing, much current research is showing that there are many benefits in recycling e-waste, and the recovery of precious materials such as plastic, iron, platinum, copper, aluminium, gold, silver and palladium. While finding a solution to the e-waste problem is likely to be costly initially, there are thus important synergies that need to be taken into consideration. Since virgin materials have traditionally been both cheaper and of better quality than recycled materials, initiatives for ICT companies to adopt more circular business models have been driven either by good will/CSR or by regulations. According to [58] Zeng et al. (2019), much research has focused on how to recover different types of materials from e-waste. However, few studies have focused on the economic feasibility of recovering such materials from e-waste rather than from virgin-mined - materials. Recently, however, it has been suggested that many precious metals (such as gold and copper) are becoming cheaper to extract from e-waste than from virgin ore. The biggest potential for recycled materials compared with virgin materials is according to [22] that the content of precious metals in e-waste is usually much higher than in virgin ores. This means that while ore usually exists in larger quantities in each specific location compared with e-waste, it can be very profitable to extract metals from e-waste instead, given that it is possible to gather large enough quantities [11]. According to Cucchiella et al. CRT monitors, smart phones, LCD TVs, cellphones and LCD notebooks are probably the products with most potential to be profitable when recycled, due to the high amount of precious materials in them [11]. The Global E-waste Monitor [5] concludes that the total value of all raw materials present in e-waste is estimated at approximately €55 billion in 2016. However, Cucchiella et al. [11] estimate that the potential profit from recycling materials in e-waste is €2.15 billion. This much lower figure is affected by a number of factors such as transportation, collection rates, etc. However, given the increased interest in circular business models, and increased regulatory pressure, it would be surprising if not more ICT companies started to see the potential of e-waste as a resource in the near future. After all, the ICT industry is heavily dependent on metals such as copper and gold and utilizes about 30 and 12% of the total consumption respectively [58].

According to the WEEE handbook (p. 5), "from a resource perspective, e-waste is an urban mine providing tremendous resources for manufacturing and refurbishing". Zeng et al. [58] argue that as virgin-mined materials are getting more expensive, and e-waste more easily accessible, recycled materials will soon be more profitable than virgin-mined materials. They show that in China, a country with large quantities of e-waste available for recycling, pure gold and copper recovered from e-waste is now cheaper compared with virgin mining of ores. More specifically,

> the cost of urban mined gold from [e-waste] has been far lower than the world commodity price each year, and is falling as per the learning curve associated with the processes of demanufacturing involved. By 2015 the estimated cost of urban mined gold had fallen to US $1,591 per kg in 2015, compared with the world commodity price of just under US$4,000 in the same year [58].

As China will soon be the biggest importer and producer of e-waste, the economic benefit of recycling will most likely increase in the future, given the investment in proper recycling facilities. Zeng et al. [58] argue that this could also be the case for other materials and in other geographical contexts. However, at the moment many OECD countries lack the required infrastructure and collection systems, making alternatives to formal recycling more attractive, as they provide a smaller but immediate short-term benefit [25].

There are obviously many other benefits to recycling materials found in e-waste. For example, metals can be extracted from e-waste with far less environmental impact than by extracting the same amount of metals from ore, given that the waste is formally recycled. The approximate content of different metals in e-waste is often known beforehand, making the refining process more efficient. Furthermore, much less solid waste material is generated from extracting metals from e-waste compared to from virgin ore [25]. There are also obvious social benefits from formal recycling, such as the cleaning up of "e-waste villages", and replacement of harmful informal recycling practices with formal recycling. Three problems that arise with increased formal recycling is that initial costs are high before proper regulations, take-back systems and recycling facilities are in place; that many people today make a living out of informal recycling practices; and that take-back systems and regulations need to be more impactful than they are today. As emphasized by [25], increased recycling rates and improved processing of end-of-life products are necessary in order to achieve sustainability in metal life cycles.

7 Conclusions

In conclusion, it is clear that although e-waste is a pressing problem, it can also be seen as, and become a resource. The shift in perspective required is towards a life-cycle perspective on all materials in the production, marketing, and end-of-life processes of ICT artefacts.

Such a perspective includes attention to:

- Sustainable (social + environmental + economic) extraction of materials (both virgin materials but more importantly from existing (e-)waste).
- Sustainable production of hardware and software (for repair, longevity, dismantling, upgradeability, etc.)
- Reparation and refurbishing of discarded products
- Effective take-back systems
- Effective dismantling and separation of precious materials (e.g. iron, platinum, copper, aluminium, plastic, gold, silver, palladium and more).
- Re-use of precious materials.

Any attempt to address the issue of electronic waste and sustainability needs first, therefore, to consider the interdependence of the different aspects of the issue as discussed in this chapter: design, resource depletion, environmental degradation, and human health impacts are all interwoven. For example:

- Design for repairability can extend the lifespan of ICTs through plug-and-play upgrades and improvements, both hardware and software [27], as well as a modular design that encourages repair [9].
- End-of-life design results in a less complex disassembly process and less scrap [53].

The combination of Design for repairability and End-of-life design can contribute to a set of electronics design guidelines that meet circular economy principles [7]. In addition, a Best of 2 Worlds (Bo2W) approach, in which informal disassembly of electronics is combined with formal high tech recycling, may diminish health and environmental impacts [54].

These changes are challenging, but not insurmountable. They will need to be supported by supra- and national policy and regulations, encouraged by taxation and other levers of behaviour change; and CSR. They will increasingly be driven by virgin resource scarcity.

The responsibility for rising to these challenges lies, therefore, with the ICT industry, first and foremost, but also with policymakers and governments, ICT professionals working in the industry, and ultimately the users/consumers of ICT products, who can help to drive change through consumer choice. Lastly, waste handling companies must be engaged more by the industry, to ensure their own requirements are built-in to the design of artefacts, streamlining the life cycle from design to disassembly.

References

1. Asamoah, A., Essumang, D., Muff, J., Kucheryavskiy, S., Søgaard, E.: Assessment of PCBs and exposure risk to infants in breast milk of primiparae and multiparae mothers in an electronic waste hot spot and non-hot spot areas in Ghana. Sci. Total Environ. **612**, 1473–1479 (2018)
2. Awasthi, A., Zeng, Z., Li, J.: Environmental pollution of electronic waste recycling in India: a critical review. Environ. Pollut. **211**, 259–270 (2016). https://doi.org/10.1016/j.envpol.2015.11.027
3. Bakker, C., Wang, F., Huisman, J., Hollander, M.: Products that go round: exploring product life extension through design. J. Clean. Prod. **69**, 10–16 (2014). https://doi.org/10.1016/j.jclepro.2014.01.028
4. Balde, C.P., Wang, F., Kuehr, R., Huisman, J.: The global e-waste monitor – 2014. United Nations University, IAS-SCUCLE, Bonn, Germany (2015). https://i.unu.edu/media/unu.edu/news/52624/UNU-1stGlobal-E-Waste-Monitor-2014-small.pdf
5. Baldé, C.P., Forti, V., Gray, V., Kuehr, R., Stegmann, P.: The global e-waste monitor – 2017. United Nations University, IAS-SCUCLE, Bonn, Germany (2017). https://www.itu.int/en/ITU-D/Climate-Change/Documents/GEM%202017/Global-E-waste%20Monitor%202017%20.pdf
6. Basel Convention Text (1992). http://www.basel.int/TheConvention/Overview/TextoftheConvention/tabid/1275/Default.aspx
7. Bovea, M.D., Pérez-Belis, V.: Identifying design guidelines to meet the circular economy principles: a case study on electric and electronic equipment. J. Environ. Manag. **228**, 483–494 (2018). https://doi.org/10.1016/j.jenvman
8. Brundtland Commission: Our common future: report of the world commission on environment and development (1987). http://www.un-documents.net/our-common-future.pdf
9. Cordella, M., Sanfelix, J., Alfieri, F.: Development of an approach for assessing the reparability and upgradability of energy-related products. Procedia CIRP **69**, 888–892 (2018). https://doi.org/10.1016/j.procir.2017.11.080
10. Crutzen, P.J.: The Anthropocene. In: Ehlers, P., Krafft, D. (eds.) Earth System Science in the Anthropocene, pp. 13–18. Springer, Heidelberg (2006). https://doi.org/10.1007/3-540-26590-2_3
11. Cucchiela, F., D'Adamo, I., Ko, S., Rosa, P.: Recycling of WEEEs: an economic assessment of present and future e-waste streams. Renew. Sustain. Energy Rev. **51**, 263–272 (2015). https://doi.org/10.1016/j.rser.2015.06.010
12. Daly, H.E. (ed.): Economics, Ecology and Ethics: Essays Toward a Steady-State Economy. Freeman & Co., San Francisco (1973)
13. Daly, H.E.: Beyond Growth. Beacon Press, Boston (1996)
14. EU Directive 2012/19/EU of the European Parliament and of the Council of 4 July 2012 on waste electrical and electronic equipment (WEEE). https://eur-lex.europa.eu/eli/dir/2012/19/oj
15. Ferris (2015). https://www.eenews.net/stories/1060011478
16. Fors, P.: Problematizing sustainable ICT. Doctoral thesis, Uppsala University (2019). https://www.diva-portal.org/smash/record.jsf?pid=diva2%3A1282900&dswid=-6325
17. Foster, J.B., Clark, B., York, R.: The Ecological Rift. Monthly Review Press, New York (2010)
18. Geeraerts, K., Illes, A., Schweizer, J.: E-Waste from the EU: A Case Study on Illegal E-Waste Export from the EU to China. A Study Compiled as Part of the EFFACE Project. IEEP, London (2015)
19. GFN (2020). https://www.footprintnetwork.org/

20. Grant, C., et al.: Health consequences of exposure to e-waste: a systematic review. Lancet Global Health **1**(6), 350–361 (2013). https://doi.org/10.1016/S2214-109X(13)70101
21. Hage, O., Söderholm, P., Berglund, C.: Norms and economic motivation in household recycling: empirical evidence from Sweden. Resour. Conserv. Recycl. **53**(3), 155–165 (2009)
22. Hagelüken, C., Corti, C.: Recycling of gold from electronics: cost-effective use through 'Design for Recycling'. Gold Bull. **43**(3), 209–220 (2010)
23. Hornborg, A.: The Power of the Machine: Global Inequalities of Economy, Technology, and Environment. AltaMira Press, Lanham (2001)
24. Humphries (2013). www.crs.gov
25. Izatt, R., Izatt, S., Bruening, R., Izatt, N., Moyer, B.: Challenges to achievement of metal sustainability in our high-tech society. Chem. Soc. Rev. **43**(8), 2451–2475 (2014)
26. Jolly (2014). https://www.nytimes.com/2014/03/27/business/international/china-export-quo tas-on-rare-earths-violate-law-wto-panel-says.html?_r=0
27. Karlskrona (2015). http://sustainabilitydesign.org/karlskrona-manifesto/
28. Kassem, M., et al.: Metals in our IT equipment: social and economic impacts, geopolitical conflicts. Other social impacts of ICT manufacturing. Int. J. Eng. Innov. Res. **4**(6), 2277–5668 (2015)
29. Kreps, D.: Against Nature: The Metaphysics of Information Systems. Routledge, London (2018)
30. Kreps, D., et al.: IFIP Position Paper on E-Waste. IFIP, Vienna (2019)
31. Krugman, P. (2010). https://www.nytimes.com/2010/10/18/opinion/18krugman.html
32. Lennerfors, T.T., Fors, P., van Rooijen, J.: ICT and environmental sustainability in a changing society. Inf. Technol. People **28**(4), 758–774 (2015)
33. Lepawsky, J., Araujo, E., Davis, J., Kahhat, R.: Best of two worlds? Towards ethical electronics repair, reuse, repurposing and recycling. Geoforum **81**, 87–99 (2017). https://doi.org/10.1016/j.geoforum.2017.02.007
34. Li, H., et al.: Brominated and organophosphate flame retardants along a sediment transect encompassing the Guiyu, China e-waste recycling zone. Sci. Total Environ. **646**, 58–67 (2019)
35. Löser, F.: Strategic information systems management for environmental sustainability: enhancing firm competitiveness with Green IS, vol. 6. Universitätsverlag der TU Berlin (2015)
36. MacDonald, C. (2015). https://www.bbc.co.uk/news/magazine-33133712
37. McNeill, J.R., Engelke, P.: The Great Acceleration: An Environmental History of the Anthropocene Since 1945. Harvard, Belknap (2014)
38. Meadows, D.H., Meadows, D.L., Randers, J., Behrens, W.: The Limits to Growth. Signet, New York (1972)
39. Moore, G.E.: Cramming more components onto integrated circuits. Electronics **38**(8), 114 (1965)
40. PACE: The platform for accelerating the circular economy: a new circular vision for electronics: time for a global reboot. E-Waste Coalition (2019). https://www.itu.int/en/ITU-D/Climate-Change/Documents/2019/A-New-Circular-Vision-for-Electronics.pdf
41. Rattle, R.: Computing our Way to Paradise?: The Role of Internet and Communication Technologies in Sustainable Consumption and Globalization. Rowman & Littlefield, Lanham (2010)
42. Raworth, K.: A Safe and Just Space for Humanity: Can We Live within the Doughnut. Oxfam, Oxford (2012)
43. Raworth, K.: Doughnut Economics. Penguin Random House, Milton Keynes (2017)
44. Richter, F.: Battery life is a key feature for mobile devices (2012). https://www.statista.com/chart/563/improvements-wanted-by-mobile-device-users/
45. Reck, B.K., Graedel, T.E.: Challenges in metal recycling. Science **337**(6095), 690–695 (2012)

46. Rucevska, I., et al.: Waste crime – waste risks: gaps in meeting the global waste challenge. A UNEP Rapid response assessment. United Nations Environment Programme and GRID-Arendal, Nairobi and Arendal (2015). www.grida.no
47. Schüler, D., Buchert, M., Liu, R., Dittrich, S., Merz, C.: Study on rare earths and their recycling. Öko-Institut eV Darmstadt (2011)
48. Steffen, W., Broadgate, W., Deutsch, L., Gaffney, O., Ludwig, C.: The trajectory of the Anthropocene: the great acceleration. Anthr. Rev. **2**, 1–18 (2015)
49. StEP White Paper: One global definition of e-waste (2014). http://www.step-initiative.org/e-waste-challenge.html
50. Umair, S., Anderberg, S., Potting, J.: Ewaste imports and informal recycling in Pakistan. J. Solid Waste Technol. Manag. **42**(3), 222–235 (2016)
51. United Nations Environment Management Group: United Nations system-wide response to tackling e-waste (2017). https://www.unenvironment.org/news-and-stories/story/end-ele ctronic-waste-united-nations-organisations-highlight-their-commitment
52. U.N. (2020). https://www.un.org/sustainabledevelopment/
53. Xing, K., Abhary, K., Luong, L.: IREDA: an integrated methodology for product recyclability and end-of-life design. J. Sustain. Prod. Des. **3**(3), 149–171 (2003). https://doi.org/10.1007/s10970-005-3925-9
54. Wang, F., Huisman, J., Meskers, C.E.M., Schluep, M., Stevels, A., Hagelüken, C.: The best-of-2-worlds philosophy: developing local dismantling and global infrastructure network for sustainable e-waste treatment in emerging economies. Waste Manag. **32**(11), 2134–2146 (2012). https://doi.org/10.1016/j.wasman.2012.03.029
55. Wieser, H.: Beyond planned obsolescence: product lifespans and the challenges to a circular economy. GAIA – Ecol. Perspect. Sci. Soc. **25**(3), 156–160 (2016). https://doi.org/10.14512/gaia.25.3.5
56. Wilson, G.T., Smalley, G., Suckling, J., Lilley, D., Lee, J., Mawle, R.: The hibernating mobile phone: dead storage as a barrier to efficient electronic waste recovery. Waste Manag. **60**, 521–33 (2017). Special Thematic Issue: Urban Mining and Circular Economy
57. WSJ (2016). https://www.wsj.com/articles/chinas-rare-earths-bust-1468860856
58. Zeng, X., Li, J.: Measuring the recyclability of e-waste: an innovative method and its implications. J. Clean. Prod. **131**, 156–162 (2016)

On Diversity, Equity, and Inclusion in Computing: Finding Allies in Overrepresented Populations

Christopher Leslie[1,2]([envelope])

[1] South China University of Technology, Guangzhou, China
chrisleslienyc@hotmail.com
[2] Zhejiang Hexin Group Co. Ltd., Yunhe, China

Abstract. Participation in science and engineering after the nineteenth century has largely been skewed toward men, computing being no different. However, the history of diversity in computing offers an unexpected insight. Some might assume that there has been a smooth progression from originally a few women in computing to a slightly more representative proportion at the present time. This article reviews the significant and growing body of scholarship that has challenged this linear assumption. In addition to the female pioneers who are now well known, there were many women who made the transition from hand calculators to computer operators at the time IFIP was established. An historical analysis of the decrease in the participation of women after their initial dominance shows that the rhetoric of rigorous computing coincides with the decreasing percentage of women. Thus, computing offers important lessons into the way policy and ideology can inadvertently cause a lag in representation for some demographic groups. Based on the author's own experience in fostering an inclusive environment at a U.S. engineering school, this paper then describes the challenges and opportunities for programs to enhance diversity and reverse the historical exclusion of certain groups. IFIP has been a leader in incorporating the history of computing into technical education, which can result in creating curricula that foster diversity and make a more inclusive atmosphere by incorporating the arts, broadly conceived, into STEM to create STEAM.

Keywords: STEM education · History of computing · Diversity · Unearned privilege · Stereotype threat · Microaggressions · Imposter syndrome · STEAM

1 Introduction

A few years ago, I was working on a grant proposal with two faculty members in the dean's office to support diversity at a university dedicated to science and engineering. Based on my continuing research into diversity, equity, and inclusion (DEI) in science, technology, engineering and mathematics (STEM), I wrote in the rationale that introductory courses negatively impacted all students, but particularly historically excluded

L. Strous et al. (Eds.): Unimagined Futures, IFIP AICT 555, pp. 142–161, 2020.
https://doi.org/10.1007/978-3-030-64246-4_12

groups, such as women, indigenous people, and people of color. Research supported this claim: large lecture courses seem to ratify existing patterns of representation. My collaborators surprised me by suggesting my comment was inaccurate.

As a student, professor, and advisor, I had observed the phenomenon many times. First-year engineering students are admonished to demonstrate their rigor, many receiving failing scores on their midterm exams. Every student feels the stress of gateway courses that seem like an effort to "weed-out" unqualified undergraduates, but members of historically excluded groups are disproportionately affected, reversing efforts to diversify. The resistance to my assertion about the deleterious effects of first-year courses struck me as odd because my university had committed to increasing diversity in engineering. I learned that not everyone was familiar with the processes that conspire to maintain STEM as a field dominated by men with Asian and European roots.

Lessons about diversity in the U.S. are applicable to some extent in a worldwide context. The conversation about diversity in the United States centers around local definitions. Thus, one sees articles about the overrepresentation of white and Asian-American men when compared to these groups' percentage of the population. Certainly, U.S. racial categories are not universally applicable to universities and industries around the world; however, the lessons learned about individuals who are not in the majority – whether it be ethnically, economically, or in national origin – can be applied elsewhere. After all, there is no evidence that abilities are uniform within different groups, and there is no evidence that those groups have different aptitudes for STEM overall. Although racial tensions may seem unique to U.S. history, the U.S. also has a long history of working to overcome prejudice of all types. In addition, racial and gendered attitudes in the U.S. are in part based on science from the age of empires, creating an opportunity to link the effort to end discrimination in the U.S. to the effort to ameliorate the legacy of colonialism in STEM internationally.

Comparing the demographics of the U.S. population to the demographics of STEM professions, one sees how opportunity is unevenly distributed. To be sure, demographic categories are gross generalizations that only show symptoms of underlying inequities. People who understand the spectrum of gender will bristle at the binary separation of populations into men or women. Similarly, given biological research, the eighteenth-century notion that humanity can be reliably divided into four or five discrete categories is laughable. My students from southeast Asia are quick to point out that the assertion that Asians are overrepresented in STEM should not lead people to believe that there are too many Khmer or Burmese students in the university. Even though the demographic categories could be improved, they offer a window into the ways that the opportunity to pursue a career in STEM is not equal for everyone.

This conversation has the potential of upsetting struggling students who feel they have succeeded based on their merits alone. However, it is wrong to expect the members from historically excluded groups do all of the work to promote DEI. To be sure, recent work on promoting diversity in STEM like Dunbar-Hester [1] seeks to bring a positive attitude toward the situation, turning a problem into an opportunity. Diversity benefits all members of the community, not just people from groups that have been historically excluded. The community- and merit-based culture of computing provides a potential for change that might be more difficult to realize in other professions.

When trying to secure allies from current individuals in STEM, it is important to remember they are likely from overrepresented groups. Some express the feeling that they or their peers will have to give up their places so that STEM can be more diverse. It is important to state upfront, then, that increasing diversity in STEM is not a zero-sum game. The truth is, continuing technological advancement and bringing the benefits of scientific progress to a wider proportion of the world's population have created a demand for workers that is increasingly difficult to fulfill. In 2012, for instance, the U.S. determined that it would be short 1 million STEM professionals in the coming ten years. In other words, as shown in Fig. 1, it would be unproductive to replace anyone. Proponents of increasing diversity suggest that the easiest way to recruit more people to STEM is to utilize the pool of untapped talent from students who tend to avoid choosing STEM or leave STEM programs. Even though women and people of color represent more than 70% of the workforce, they are only 45% of the workers in STEM. Thus, they represent a "large underutilized source of potential STEM professionals" [2]. Doubling the number of female students, though, is not an ambitious goal when the starting point is so low. The U.S. has relied on policies like retaining international students with restrictive H1b visas, instead of fostering an inclusive environment.

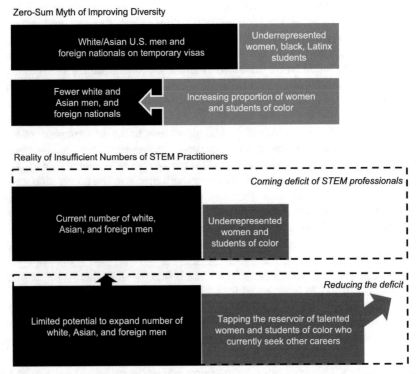

Fig. 1. Increasing diversity in STEM is sometimes thought of a zero-sum game. However, there are not enough students and professionals in STEM fields.

Although this paper focuses on university experiences, the implications of these ideas are clear in other contexts. In fact, fostering an inclusive environment will improve research and working conditions for everyone. A workplace environment where all can be included is one where ideas are shared more openly, bringing about more successful outcomes. This paper begins with an historical overview of diversity with an emphasis on women in computing. Counter to some people's expectations, the underrepresentation of women in computing was not something experienced in its early days, going a long way to dispel the notion that it is somehow natural that women are not interested in computing. Finally, the paper provides an overview of some current ideas about DEI in STEM as a starting point for those who might wish to help create a more inclusive environment.

2   The Decline of Diversity in Computing

When IFIP was established in 1960, computer science and computer engineering were barely recognized as fields. Although this was a different age in terms of diversity in the workplace, computing was actually a field that had a healthy presence of women. As the workplace overall became more diverse, though, STEM generally and fields related to computing specifically have been outliers. Women and people of color are no longer the underrepresented minority overall, but STEM student populations and workforces have persistently failed to diversify.

2.1   Initial Diversity in Computing

Surprisingly, at the time IFIP was founded, the percentage of women in computing had reached a high point and would soon start to decline. As has been noted by Light and others, the electronic devices that took the place of women also "would take their name": the legions of women who had made calculations by hand [3]. In spite of this, the female "human computers" were experts in setting up problems who had an important role in the early days of electronic computing. Six women, for instance, were part of the first team that programmed ENIAC. When the project was transferred to Aberdeen, Abbate says at least seven more women joined the team. Two followed the leaders who went on to create UNIVAC [4]. Of course, while working on UNIVAC, Hopper would go on to pave the way for computing by inventing the software compiler.

As electronic computers became more widespread, some of the women who had been doing calculations by hand continued their work, preparing equations so that they could be fed into machines. They taught classes about computing, and they also had an influence on programming. Abbate notes that the women who worked on ENIAC invented break points (a technique of inserting stops in a program for debugging), they created a system to visualize the timing of digital analysis, and they adapted techniques from applied mathematics to computerize numerical analysis [4]. Even so, women received little recognition for their work. Abbate suggests that the erasure of the women was mirrored by many of their male counterparts; the machine and its inventors took center stage at a time when hardware seemed more important than the programmers who made it function. As pointed out by Ensmenger [5], the reason for this is partly one of methodology: a "bias in the traditional emphasis of the history of *computing* on the history of the *computer*." Because few women had the opportunity to create machines, the mistaken impression that there were no women involved arose.

Shortly before IFIP was founded, computing jobs were increasingly located in private companies, and there is (perhaps unexpectedly) evidence that women were welcome. In 1956, the U.S. Labor Department noted that some industrial laboratories hire women for computing groups exclusively, others at a high percentage. Abbate points to a 1957 brochure to recruit women to IBM. Entitled "My Fair Ladies," the brochure claimed that a job at IBM would give a woman a "highly important position" that would allow her to use her "talents and aptitudes." Abbate also refers to a 1963 advertisement promoting English Electric's software services entitled "Why pick a woman to pep up your accounting department?" The fashionable woman in the advertisement, pensively chewing on a pen, "simultaneously positioned female programmers both as eye candy for male managers and as competent, no-nonsense technical experts" [4]. Despite this implicit bias, Abbate notes that the advertisement claims women are competent and possess a "logical flair" for writing programs.

From this base, one would expect to see only a greater participation in computing from women as the 1960s drew on, given the general attention toward civil rights and, specifically, anti-discrimination legislation in the U.S. Quite the reverse would turn out to be true. One of the key moments in the development of modern computing was the creation of time-sharing systems, where multiple users could work simultaneously on a single mainframe, helping to create the notion of a community. This turn from individualistic problem-solving to communities of practitioners is often lauded as a pivotal shift in computing, but given the social norms of the 1960s, not all parts of the change were positive. Some of the key work in time-sharing was done at Dartmouth University, which was at the time a single-sex university. Joy Lisi Rankin has pointed out that, as one might have predicted, the university's computer center employed women. However, the student programmers and their achievements demonstrated what Rankin describes as a "macho computing culture" [6]. Even when Dartmouth became coeducational, female students tended to avoid the computing center. As Rankin notes, the social world reinforced the growing norm of computing as a privileged domain. Seven of the nine secondary schools working with Dartmouth before 1967 were all-male, private schools. Interestingly, Rankin notes, the teachers who supervised the high school students were also male, even at a time when teaching was assumed to be a profession dominated by women [6]. Despite the initial prominence of women, access to computing was mediated through gender and class biases of this time.

This transformation of computing into a male field is now well documented. Mar Hicks has noted how programmers in the U.K. computer industry were once thought of as skilled professionals when the work seemed less valuable, but when men learned how precious computing would be, it soon became a management position, where women were underrepresented [7]. This attitude was reinforced by policies that required women to have college degrees at a time when there were not so many women in college, as memorably depicted in the book *Hidden Figures* by Margo Shetterly [8] and in the film, particularly as portrayed by Janelle Monáe [9]. Abbate notes that a college degree was not a useful prerequisite; policy makers thought of it as an indicator of general intelligence and not of skill in computing. Abbate writes, "given the economic and class barriers to attending college during this period, it could not be assumed that only those with a degree had the ability to think" [4]. This had the perhaps unintended consequence of decreasing access to the profession of computing.

This policy did not reflect experience. Abbate points out that education was not found to be a good proxy of intelligence; in 1968, she writes, General Electric in Albany, New York created a program to prepare black residents for jobs in computing even if they did not have college degrees. The organizers found that some of the students who did not complete high school were still at the top of program participants. Evidence of how relaxing the requirement that computing professionals must have a college degree could change the field, though, did not result in a new policy. Abbate surmises, "Accepting black high-school dropouts as potentially talented programmers might have threatened the privileged status of technical skill." As a result, larger social forces contributed to a bias against addressing exclusion, even though the people enforcing the policy might have thought they were making merit-based decisions.

A computing expert in the 1970s and beyond might think it was natural, however unfortunate, that there were so few women in computing. It would be hard for most professionals from this period to say that groups were actively excluded from computing – but even so, Abbate, Rankin, Hicks, and other scholars have demonstrated how policy rather than personal interest created a palpable bias that resulted in a community that decreased in diversity and was less inclusive.

2.2 Creating Underrepresentation

Around the time when IFIP was founded, only about a third of college degrees in any field were earned by women. Although women would continue to have important roles in computing in the 1970s and beyond, their presence would peak around 1985 and then go into decline. As a marker of the erasure of the initial diversity in computing, no women were invited to the 1968 Garmisch conference where the term "software engineering" was coined. Their absence "should give us pause," Abbate says, who then proposes several well-known women who conceivably could have been invited [4]. Paradoxically, the women's and civil rights movements seemed to have resulted in a backlash against diversity in engineering in particular, computing specifically.

As shown in Fig. 2, science, law, medicine, and engineering saw fewer than 15% women in 1950. The women's movement, along with a more general attention to civil rights in the U.S., made the lack of diversity unpalatable in many fields. Due to antidiscrimination legislation (such as the 1964 Title IX of the U.S. Civil Rights Act), a resolution by Association of American Medical Colleges (AAMC) to foster diversity, and the general spirit of feminism, some professions began to change. For instance, medical programs actively began to mentor and recruit women, with the result that today men and women are nearly equally represented in medical school [10]. A similar trend can be seen in law. As a result, membership in these professions is closer to national demographics of the professional class overall. This trend is even more troubling because engineers are only one constituent in a modern engineering project; they must work with managers, investors, government officials, residents. STEM students who are not used to diverse environments will find themselves unprepared for a multi-unit enterprise where demographics match national averages.

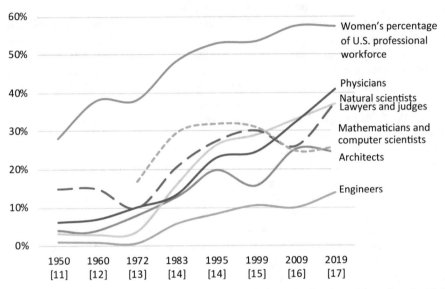

Fig. 2. Since 1950, the percentage of women in the U.S. professional workforce has doubled, growing from 28% to 57% [11–17]. Despite an initial increase, computing has declined in diversity.

Contemporaneous with the civil rights movement, computing saw an environment that was hostile to diversity. As noted by Dunbar-Hester [1], the cultural values of the open-source movement included a "tenacious devotion to free speech" that "provided a fertile ground for confrontation and hostile speech – including sexist speech – to flourish." At the same time that open-source and maker communities seem to be divested from politics, asserting instead an individualistic mindset that has personal benefits, Dunbar-Hester reminds us that progressive politics are unwelcome in these communities. Nonetheless, Dunbar-Hester points out the many ways that feminists and others have taken advantage of the community-based protocols of these groups, which rely on consensus and participation, to create spaces that support DEI. She cites groups like LinuxChix, Debian Woman, Ubuntu Women, the Geek Feminist project, and PyLadies as groups that strive to make a welcoming environment.

When engineering fields in general became dominated by men, it may have seemed proper to "fix" computer science by making it seem more like other engineering fields. As Abbate describes, the "crisis" that software engineering was expected to resolve did not go away when the masculinist rhetoric of rigor and technical merit were infused into the profession. Indeed, by devaluing "the aspects of software production that rely on stereotypically feminine skills of communication and personal interaction," a whole new series of problems developed. By 1990, evaluators of the field noted that practitioners were too closely focused on technical issues, economics, and rationality. Failures resulted because computing professionals were unable to communicate with their clients and understand their needs and constraints – let alone the unintended social consequences of their work. The interpersonal or "soft" skills, which Abbate describes sardonically as "elusive," were the values once imparted as part of a liberal education before the invention of specialized education for computing. The study of culture and the resulting sense of citizenship it should impart were the casualties of software engineering reforms in the name of rigor.

Certainly, the early generations of computer science professionals had not shied away from the arts and sciences, but they were not graduates of computer science programs because they did not yet exist. Even as other professions began to address diversity, computing's effort to become more like engineering unfortunately changed the path one took to become a computing professional. By the 1990s, the liberal arts had been devalued in computing education, and diversity was on a downward trend.

2.3 Bringing Diversity Back

In 1991, Ellen Spertus wrote a report about women's experiences based in part on her online data collection while she was an undergraduate student at MIT [18]. She reports some disappointing experiences but also makes positive assertions: her mentors at MIT were supportive of her effort, and the deficit of trained computer professionals was leading to efforts to improve recruiting of women.

The efforts to reverse the historical exclusion of groups in computing that began in the 1990s, however, should actually be described as *returning* diversity to computing. In spite of efforts by educators and admissions staff, a study by the U.S. National Science Foundation did not find much improvement in the early days of the 21st century. Undergraduate enrollments in STEM seemed to be following existing trends. Although first-year college students nationwide are nearly evenly split between genders and reflect the ethnic diversity of the country well, significant gender and racial differences in the sciences persisted. In math, statistics, and computer science, 1.4% of women were interested, as compared to 5.2% of men. The difference was much greater in engineering overall. In terms of race, Asian students were more than twice as likely than other groups to choose a major in engineering (15.0% of all first-year students) or in math, statistics, or computer science (5.6%) [19]. If one is committed to the idea that gender or race do not somehow give a student a biological advantage, then social biases must be considered.

Some students, faculty, and administrators believe that STEM fields are already quite diverse. Even though the STEM workforce has drawn traditionally from white and Asian men, universities claim they meet diversity goals with international students and by incrementally increasing the number of women [20]. Classrooms might seem diverse due to a diversity of national origins, for instance, masking the absence of other demographic groups. I remember one student who attended a DEI program I organized only because he wanted to make the point that at our university there were not enough white men and increasing the number of white men would improve diversity. He asked us to notice that most people in our classrooms were not white men.

The social encouragement (or discouragement) is even more pronounced when one figures in recent data from the College Board, the company that administers the SAT. When a high-school student signs up to take the SAT, the College Board asks pointed questions that can show prospective students' preparation for and interest in college majors. In the past decade, the College Board found that the proportion of college-bound students from historically excluded groups had never been higher, as was the percentage of black and Hispanic students who surpassed the College Board's benchmark for college readiness [21]. Differences in the math portion of the SAT, although they varied as much as 200 points between races, were not so different between genders of each race. In fact, as shown in Fig. 3, the College Board found that women were slightly more prepared in terms of mathematics than their male classmates – about 50% of each group having four or more years of math that included calculus and AP or honors classes – and yet men were much more likely to say they would study engineering or computer science when they were getting ready to take the SAT. Thus, the persistent lack of diversity must be seen as a contradiction to the increasing preparation and interest of those from groups that have been historically excluded.

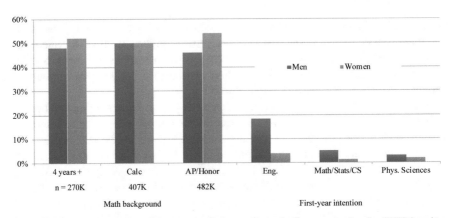

Fig. 3. The college board found that men and women have similar preparation for STEM majors. Nevertheless, men outnumber women in their intention of studying STEM.

Although about 50% of students who start in STEM do not finish, the attrition of students of color is higher than 75%. The overrepresentation of white and Asian students widens at higher degree levels [22]. This phenomenon has been called a "leaky pipeline." Some blame falls on the first-year experience. Abbate notes that the tradition of getting rid of what was seen as an excess of students through "daunting workloads" started in the 1980s; these caused people to drop out who have less experience or confidence (i.e., women). The study of a bottleneck course, Calculus 1, by Colorado State researchers surveyed more than 2,000 students. They found that women were 50% more likely to switch out of the required sequence (and leave STEM). In addition, they discovered that confidence levels in men after the course were much higher than women. Based on their understanding of the students, this lack of confidence was not a matter of ability but self-perception [23]. Given the strong preferences some STEM educators have for this sort of first-year experience, it will be difficult to ameliorate the effects.

As historian of science Londa Schiebinger asserts, broader changes in gender-based social expectations from many domains are required to correct underlying causes of inequality. It is not natural or necessary for some groups to be underrepresented in STEM. Schiebinger likes to point out that in 17th century Germany, a higher percentage of astronomers were women (14%) than there are today (5%) [24]. She points to well-known studies that show men are reviewed more favorably than women in hiring and promotion. Recognizing that there have been many efforts since the 1950s to improve opportunities for women, Schiebinger downplays efforts to "fix the women," supposedly making them better prepared for STEM. Seeing women as the problem, Schiebinger writes, is not the best or only way to change inequality [25]. Cultural assumptions about classrooms, research labs, and academic departments – not to mention everyday life – work against all women, and especially in STEM.

To Schiebinger, though, it is not so difficult to accept unfairness in STEM and work to become conscious of it. A bigger challenge is thinking about how research results can be improved by ameliorating bias. As seen in Fig. 4, Schiebinger is not alone in this regard. In the 21st century, compelling arguments have been made to increase diversity in STEM. Removing bias in STEM makes improvements for all.

Benefits of improving diversity in STEM	
Better knowledge	Improve epistemology, eliminating gendered metaphors to understand scientific concepts [25, 26]
Cultural competency	Prepare students for diverse workplaces [27]
Improved innovation	Challenge preconceptions about users of technology and recipients of medicine [25, 27]
Social justice	Provide access to well-paid, prestigious jobs [26]
Talented workforce	Utilize the best thinkers; intelligence and insight are distributed evenly among all demographics [26]

Fig. 4. The arguments for supporting diversity have been well articulated [25–27]. Notably, diversity benefits professions and society as a whole, not just historically excluded groups.

3   Becoming an Ally Who Fosters DEI in STEM

In his famous 1902 book *Souls of Black Folk,* W.E.B. DuBois asks, what does it feel like to be a problem? As the first African-American to earn a Ph.D. from Harvard, DuBois was often asked about what was then referred to as the "Negro Problem": what to do for the 3.5 million formerly enslaved people after the Civil War. As he describes, this terminology is a small insult to someone who is trying to be a public professional [28]. As DuBois might remind us, it is important to think about how others hear the conversation about DEI in STEM if one wishes to have a positive impact.

These days, it is common to hear members of a male-dominated STEM extracurricular club state that they would welcome any woman who volunteered to participate. People from overrepresented groups seem mystified as to why their environments lack diversity. In the past twenty years, many people interested in equity have developed a rich palate of concepts and best practices. It is beyond the scope of this article to discuss each fully, but this section will provide a brief overview of the concepts and terms that are helpful to people who seek to foster an inclusive environment.

3.1 Unearned Privilege

The concept of "unearned privilege" can be used to understand how disparities in representation in STEM are symptoms of problems that affect many people. Macintosh invokes a metaphor of an "invisible, weightless knapsack of special provisions, maps, passports, codebooks, visas, clothes, tools, and blank checks" to describe the unacknowledged advantage a member of a majority group can draw on [29]. The items in the backpack provide dominance in social settings, but this is not the only impact; Macintosh points out that the idea that one's skin color will not be a factor in judgements about you or the expectations that people around you will treat you equitably "should be the norm in any decent society." STEM policy and programs have not been designed well to improve representation of marginalized groups and, as described below, may in fact reinforce preexisting inequalities.

This concept of unearned privilege does not suggest that obstacles to careers in STEM that white women face, for instance, are the same as Latino men, nor that all Latino men and white women will find less success than white and Asian men. Similarly, one should not suppose that white and Asian men find it easy to gain their achievements in STEM. The concept of unearned privilege suggests, though, that some groups have more confidence that the educational and industrial environment will work for them: someone without a backpack will not see the same success from the same amount of effort as someone with a backpack. Science and engineering, after all, require intense preparation that causes most students uncertainty and doubt. It would not be surprising, then, that those who feel that their effort will not yield meaningful results would leave STEM and seek a career in a field that needs their technical skills and analytical ability but offers less intense identity-based challenges, such as financial analysis or medicine, which have been more successful in promoting DEI in the past 60 years.

Some might say that unearned privilege is simply a euphemism for sexism or racism, and perhaps it is. The goal of using this term, though, is to broaden the understanding of racism and sexism beyond being kind and respectful to people from different demographic groups to provide a better understanding how erasing inequity requires more than politeness. It is helpful to qualify the word "privilege" with "unearned" for another reason. The white and Asian men who predominate STEM in U.S. universities and industries are not always individuals who have economic or political advantages. In my own experience, many students in the overrepresented groups were, in fact, from backgrounds that are often called underprivileged, in the sense of lower-income. Calling a student "privileged" whose parents left his home country and made many sacrifices so that he could study engineering – and who likely worked one or more jobs while he did so – is likely to earn the retort that "I am not privileged." Care must be taken in this conversation, especially when asking current engineers and educators to support it.

3.2   Stereotype Threat

The term stereotype threat was coined by Claude Steele to help understand performance differentials between overrepresented and underrepresented groups [30]. At every stage of testing in schools, lower scores are earned by historically excluded groups, such as women or students of color. This was startling to Steele and his associates because the comparatively poor performance could not be attributed to lack of kills or preparation. "The underperformance phenomenon documents lower performance by these groups at each level of skill – that is, when skill and preparation ... are essentially held constant" [31]. Through more research, Steele learned to describe the cause of this phenomenon.

In one article, Steele likens the additional cognitive load on a member of an historically excluded group to a person who is late to a dinner party. Although the other guests are unconcerned about the lateness, the late person feels ill at ease and is preoccupied with unnecessary tasks in a vain effort to compensate. To Steele, this analogy explains the performance differential: during an assessment, some of a student's effort is wasted on worrying whether the student will confirm the stereotype or, at least, be perceived as confirming it. This phenomenon was also demonstrated among other historically excluded groups.

The performance differential is frequently seen with challenging assessments, so Steele developed a methodology to reveal the involvement of stereotypes. The team recruits students who have mathematical ability and believe mathematics is important to their future plans. These students are asked to complete a challenging assessment, but one group receives different instructions than the other. In the first group, students are told that they are going to take a difficult mathematics assessment that many female students find difficult. In the second group, the instructions are simpler: just do your best. Steele and his associates found that in the first group, where the fear of a stereotype was activated, the performance gap between overrepresented and underrepresented students increased dramatically. In this way, Steele has shown how what should be an objective assessment does in fact exhibit bias. All students have similar background preparation, they are all answering the same questions, and they are all sitting at a similar desk. Nevertheless, perceptions of bias can vary the outcome depending on one's demographic membership. This challenges the assumption that test scores can be the basis of merit-based decision-making.

There is some good news in this research: Steele found that an awareness of stereotype threat is a good way to overcome it. However, there is a potential downside as well. Programs to provide simpler curricula or offer extra help to students who are already committed to success in STEM may backfire if they unintentionally reinforce the stereotype. Challenging problems and meaningful support are the best help for students from historically excluded groups if they are determined to succeed. Overall, Steele says, educators should emphasize the expandability of the human mind: no one is born with a natural ability to solve math and engineering problems. Instead, people can learn.

3.3   Imposter Syndrome

Imposter syndrome is the feeling that one's accomplishments do not come from one's ability. The phenomenon was first noticed in 1978 by psychologists Clance and Imes among women with exemplary credentials, who internally and inexplicably create various scenarios that negate "any external evidence that contradicts their belief that they are, in reality, unintelligent" [32]. Men are likely to believe their success is an intrinsic characteristic, whereas women attribute their success to luck, accident, or hard work in order to compensate for what they think is their lack of natural ability. This is not unique to STEM fields. In the context of STEM education, though, it helps to explain performance differentials and why students do not persist in their degree programs or careers.

The feeling that one's abilities are substandard and that only the kind graces of mentors and professors allow a student to continue can be debilitating. The sensation is worsened by the first-year weed-out pedagogy. Students typically receive very low grades in their initial assessments. Those who have friends or family who have attended engineering school before know that it is not uncommon to receive a score below 50% on the first exam; they know that it is traditional in many schools for the professor to "curve" students at the end of the term on a range from A to C even though their term averages are much lower. It seems as if this is a way for faculty to impress upon students the importance of rigorous thinking and encourage them to try harder.

Students I have spoken to have been gratified to learn the name for imposter syndrome because it matches their experience. Imagine the feelings of members of historically excluded groups in this situation. They are already feeling as if they may have made a poor career choice. They have been told that rigorous thinking is important and they believe that they must succeed on their own merits. Everyone then receives devastatingly low scores on early assessments. Some students will feel that their poor scores are evidence that they are unable to master the material. Even though those around them are having similar experiences, those in underrepresented demographics already feel the deck is stacked against them. They may develop defensive habits, like coming to class late or refusing to hand in homework, while they consider other options, with the result that they do not learn any of the course material. The feeling of their overrepresented peers – that everything will be ok at the end of the term – is not an adequate motivation for students from historically excluded groups to move forward. In this context, a student may feel simply that they are allowed to pass a class where the evidence clearly showed they failed because of the desire to diversify engineering.

Imposter syndrome can be demonstrated empirically. For instance, in a study of data gathered about 1,143 students in astronomy (40% women) [33], women report fear of that their lack of knowledge will be discovered and other symptoms of imposter syndrome. This is unfortunate for many reasons, but among graduate students, it is particularly upsetting because they are the most knowledgeable about their topics. By asking other questions, researchers found that those who reported imposter syndrome were also likely to report an unwelcome environment and lack of mentorship.

As was seen before, social factors and not ability are the cause of this factor that stymies efforts to diversify. Dunbar-Hester [1] notes that this topic was a common theme in the free software conferences for social change. At the workshops devoted to diversity she attended, Dunbar-Hester noted that people can overcome the feeling that they are imposter by "claiming more authority in the face of these feelings." In other words, an alternative social environment can improve diversity in STEM.

3.4 Microaggressions

The impact of imposter syndrome and stereotype threat can be said to be magnified by microaggressions. Discussing the concept of microaggressions has become an effective way of promoting an inclusive environment at a time when overt bias and threats have become socially unacceptable. In a social justice circle, discussing microaggressions is a way to explain how people who do not think of themselves as prejudiced might nevertheless create adverse environments for members of historically excluded groups.

John F. Dovidio provided some of the theoretical foundation of this concept in his work on averse racism. He and his colleagues note that after the 1960s, white people have modified the appearance that they are racist while at the same time cultivating "a private self-concept of being non-prejudiced" [34]. In the different approaches to understanding racism since that time, Dovidio et al. note that averse racism is expressed by people who are "politically and socially liberal." Instead of blatant racism, these individuals harbor "unconscious negative feelings and beliefs" that are expressed "in subtle, indirect, and often rationalizable ways." In spite of their professed support for equality and righting past wrongs, these people have interior, conflicting notions that are expressed in discomfort or anxiety. In short, they feel an "aversion" against black people, whence the name. It is unlikely that a person perpetrating averse racism will take actions that can readily be identified as racist. At times of ambiguity, though, they might express themselves in ways that can harm black people while at the same time help them to "maintain their self-image as non-prejudiced" [34]. This form of racism has been studied in a variety of contexts, helping to explain biases in hiring as well as problems in intergroup dynamics.

The term "microaggression" has come to be used to describe incidents where averse racism is expressed. Researchers have provided a taxonomy that includes microassaults, microinsults, and microinvalidations [35] or assumptions of inferiority, assumptions of criminality, and exoticization [36]. To the person expressing averse racism, the beliefs they espouse may seem bland or inconsequential. However, to the person experiencing the prejudice, the impact can be severe – especially for individuals who receive signals of averse racism many times throughout the day. Repeatedly experiencing microaggressions can magnify stereotype threat and imposter syndrome, but to the perpetrator, the racism does not exist or it is ambiguous. Calling averse racism a "microaggression" is an effort acknowledge to the perpetrator that what they think may be a minor slight (the "micro" part of the name) is in fact an act of violence (the "aggression" part of the name). Investigators have noted that students are more likely to report microaggressions in the classroom than will faculty [37]. The same research points out that students' greatest complaint is when microaggressions go unchallenged. As with stereotype threat, knowledge about the phenomenon is the best way to combat it.

3.5 Adding the Arts to Create STEAM

The founder of IFIP's Working Group 9.7 (History of Computing) was a proponent of restoring women to computing through the study of history. John A.N. Lee tells a personal anecdote, explaining how he has forgotten the family name of the woman in the computing center who did his calculations, but her work led to his degree. Without her, he later recognized, his graduation would have been delayed for years, but at the time he thought of her as "part of the furniture." He writes that his only excuse is that his colleagues thought the same about women in the computing center [38]. By the time he founded IFIP Working Group 9.7 in 1992, he had championed placing prominent women, like Grace Hopper, into their rightful place.

Lee oversaw a special issue of the *Annals of the History of Computing* dedicated to ENIAC in 1996. Thelma Estrin, one of the contributors to this issue, noted that women's studies and computing were established at roughly the same times and can have an influence on each other. She suggests improving computing education with concepts from women's studies, such as the effort to replace abstract thinking with concrete, practical projects. She writes, "Feminist epistemology, with its dedication to concrete learning, introduces new ideas for gaining knowledge that may make CS more relevant for minority and lower-income students as well as women" [39]. In 1998, WG 9.7 along with IFIP TC 3 adopted the "History in the Computing Curriculum" guidelines. The history of computing "allows students and scholars to explore the thinking and decisions of people as well as the socio-technical dynamics" in computing [40]. Concomitant with the growth of feminist science studies at the end of the 20th century, these scholars began to investigate how bringing the liberal arts back into STEM might improve outcomes in education and research.

This work has proven to have even greater importance when thinking about DEI. When students who have left STEM programs explain their reason in interviews, sometimes they state that their personal interests changed. Digging deeper, though, reveals their unexpected way of defining "personal interests." Listening carefully to these students, one realizes that the concerns they have about STEM seem out of step with the civic-minded personae of so many people who work in STEM fields. One way to counter this mistaken impression of STEM is by adding the arts, which can be broadly conceived as the liberal arts.

Georgette Yakman coined the term STEAM in 2008 [41]. Pointing out the long tradition of educational theory that proposes to develop an individual holistically, Yakman applauds the way that STEM educators have moved away from teaching disciplines as discrete "silos." Instead, Yakman favors an interdisciplinary approach that demonstrates how various fields are interrelated. This is important in an advancing world because transferring knowledge is insufficient when technological devices and scientific knowledge are in constant flux. According to Yakman, only an "integrative education" can help students be "continuously adaptable to the changes and developments of society." Building on the work of holistic educators like Maria Montessori and Rudolph Steiner, Yakman proposes STEAM as a framework for integrative pedagogy.

The foregoing discussion should make clear that Yakman, in terms of computing at any rate, is calling for the *return* of the liberal arts to STEM because they were present from the beginning. With the advent of software engineering and the call for increased rigor in computing, the attention to holistic education faltered. For Yakman, a middle school educator, putting the arts into STEM to create STEAM is important because they explain "how society develops, impacts, is communicated and understood with its attitudes and customs in the past, present and future." According to her definition, the fields of the arts include some obvious candidates, such as the fine arts and literary study.

However, she also includes broader studies of humanity on her list, such as psychology, sociology, history, and philosophy. Interestingly, she also includes physical arts – such as sports and dance – as well as the manual arts, or making things, which used to be constrained in the U.S. to vocational training. This echoes Estrin [39] in the effort to improve education with hands-on, practical activities.

STEAM is often championed as a means to create innovative scientists and engineers. One famous example of the unexpected technical innovation that comes from the arts was mentioned by Steve Jobs in his 2005 Stanford University commencement address [42]. As he was dropping out of Reed College, he stopped taking required courses and chose courses that interested him. He took a course in calligraphy, learning about serif and sanserif typefaces and proportional spacing. "It was beautiful, historical, artistically subtle in a way that science can't capture, and I found it fascinating," he says. At the time, he had little hope studying the western tradition of hand lettering would serve any practical purpose in his life. However, ten years later when he was imagining the Macintosh, he designed a computer that could produce beautiful typography. Today, all consumer electronics use different typefaces. This anecdote demonstrates how an appreciation for history and the arts can inspire technical innovation.

It may be underappreciated, though, how STEAM can support DEI. Some students leaving STEM will say that they wanted to have more time for their so-called creative side, by which they seem to mean that their love for aesthetic experiences felt out of place with the rigorous, algorithmic education in their STEM majors. A student with technical capabilities will successfully develop an interest in photography, for instance, and then abandon a career in STEM altogether. Students in a 6-year preparatory program for STEM, similarly, surprised me by choosing college majors that were only tangentially related to STEM. One, for instance, went on for a major in graphic design. These students, who are obviously very capable, take the basic skills they learn in their foundational courses and become successful. The problem for STEM is, a colleague pointed out to me, that these students are very bright and they can thrive in multiple fields. When faced with negative social pressures, they take their talents elsewhere.

In a way that is somewhat similar, other students will say that their culture or history is important to them, and they do not feel as if their training in STEM has any relationship to their personal identity. For instance, a black student who is studying urban infrastructure proclaimed his dismay that his classes did not address the experience of people of color in cities, even when his courses covered the history of infrastructure in cities. For students with a strong sense of ethnic identity, the way in which a typical STEM curriculum strips away the social realm can be distasteful. The movement of students away from STEM and into other fields should be seen as a failure of the STEM programs and not as evidence that the students were never suited to STEM in the first place. For instance, Donna Riley and Alice L. Pawley write about a Latinx student who chose engineering as an undergraduate major because she felt it would be a field that honored her commitment to social change and because it is an interdisciplinary field that would have allowed her to pursue a variety of interests [43]. After her first year, though, those same values led her to consider a change in major to cultural studies, hoping to learn more about her Latin American heritage. Her desire to maintain positive social change remained intact, but unfortunately the way that culture and ideology are typically absent in STEM education made it seem like an unwelcome choice. The rigid and analytical curricula may be satisfying to some students and employers, but they are not necessarily supportive of DEI.

This does not mean, of course, that hard work and deep learning in STEM must be sacrificed. In creating an interdisciplinary science and technology studies (STS) program inside of a school of engineering, a colleague and I were thinking of students who wanted to pursue careers in science or engineering but at the same time had significant interest in the humanities and social sciences. As members of a department that offered general education courses for engineering students, we built on the general premise of what would later be called STEAM, allowing a student to graduate from an engineering school by taking a minimum of one-third humanities or social science courses and one-third engineering courses along with other students in STEM majors, with the remaining third decided by the student. This kind of curriculum is not suitable for every student; it requires extra thought and planning. Our students went on to typical careers in STEM ranging from medicine to manufacturing.

After 10 years, though, the program showed an unexpected outcome: the percentages of women and non-white students were twice that of the overall student population. In retrospect, the efficacy of our interdisciplinary major in promoting DEI was simple. Students were not dissuaded from taking difficult courses in engineering or science; they stayed in the same classrooms with students in traditional engineering majors. They did appreciate the flexibility to choose more of their own classes, and they enjoyed courses in STS where they could study science and engineering in the context of history, ethics, literature, philosophy, and other fields of the arts. I cannot imagine an entire school of engineering changing its curriculum in this manner, but having an STS major as an option for some students would certainly improve outcomes. Taking some of the features of this program – such as the ability to choose electives, incorporating STEAM, and offering courses that address the social issues related to STEM – would be a benefit as well.

4 Conclusion

It is clear that current STEM pedagogy is successful for many students, including some women and people of color. However, it is also clear that there are other students who are not served well by current thinking in STEM education. If one accepts the premise that talent in STEM is spread throughout the human population and is not confined to white and Asian men alone – as we must – then the current disparities in participation can only be explained by social causes. In order to recruit and retain a larger number of diverse students, it seems unavoidable that the structure and social environment of STEM education must be examined.

The story of computing as a profession is relatively recent, and it is easy to see how its initial freedom from engineering education led to different outcomes. To be sure, the separation of science from the liberal arts is a legacy of the industrial revolution, and C.P. Snow [44] famously decried the "two cultures" split even before IFIP was founded. However, the familiar landscape of universities and workplaces when modern computing was established helps to show how the lack of diversity in computing – and thus in STEM overall – was not inevitable. Likewise, it should be possible to promote policies and cultures that can reverse the trend, as was done in medicine and law.

IFIP was a pioneer in advocating the inclusion of the liberal arts into STEM education. The way that STEAM can promote not just innovative designs but also a more effective workplace should be explored further. In addition, attention to the so-called "soft" skills in engineering will make engineering students more effective in their careers but also less abrasive to their peers. Factoring in time to discuss privilege, stereotype threat, imposter syndrome, and microaggressions to the classroom will make students and professors more efficacious in the promotion of an inclusive environment, improving diversity as a result.

References

1. Dunbar-Hester, C.: Hacking Diversity: The Politics of Inclusion in Open Technology Cultures. Princeton University Press, Princeton (2020)
2. President's Council of Advisors on Science and Technology: Engage to excel: producing one million additional college graduates with degrees in science, technology, engineering and mathematics. Executive Office of the President, Washington, D.C. (2012)
3. Light, J.S.: When computers were women. Technol. Cult. **40**(3), 455–483 (1999)
4. Abbate, J.: Recoding Gender: Women's Changing Participation in Computing. The MIT Press, Cambridge (2012). Kindle Edition
5. Ensmenger, N.: The Computer Boys Take Over: Computers, Programmers, and the Politics of Technical Expertise. MIT Press, Cambridge (2010)
6. Rankin, J.L.: A People's History of Computing in the United States. Harvard University Press, Cambridge (2018)
7. Hicks, M.: Programmed Inequality: How Britain Discarded Women Technologists and Lost its Edge in Computing. MIT Press, Cambridge (2017)
8. Shetterly, M.L.: Hidden Figures: The American Dream and the Untold Story of the Black Women Mathematicians Who Helped Win the Space Race. HarperCollins, New York (2016)
9. Gigliotti, D., Chernin, P., Topping, J., Williams, P., Melfi, T.: Hidden figures. Fox 2000 Pictures, United States (2016). (producers)
10. Braslow, J.B., Heins, M.: Women in medical education—a decade of change. New England J. Med. **304**, 1129–1135 (1981)
11. U.S. Department of Commerce: Statistical abstract of the United States. Washington, D.C. (1953). https://www.census.gov/library/publications/1953/compendia/statab/74ed.html. Accessed 31 Aug 2020
12. U.S. Department of Commerce: Statistical abstract of the United States. Washington, D.C. (1963). https://www.census.gov/library/publications/1963/compendia/statab/84ed.html. Accessed 31 Aug 2020
13. U.S. Department of Commerce: Statistical abstract of the United States. Washington, D.C. (1976). https://www.census.gov/library/publications/1976/compendia/statab/97ed.html. Accessed 31 Aug 2020
14. U.S. Department of Commerce: Labor force; its distribution by occupation. Washington, D.C. (1995) https://www.census.gov/prod/2/gen/96statab/labor.pdf. Accessed 31 Aug 2020
15. U.S. Department of Labor: Employed persons by detailed occupation, sex, race, and hispanic origin (1999). https://www.bls.gov/cps/aa1999/AAT11.TXT. Accessed 31 Aug 2020
16. U.S. Department of Labor: Employed persons by detailed occupation, sex, race, and Hispanic or Latino ethnicity (2009). https://www.bls.gov/cps/aa2009/aat11.txt. Accessed 31 Aug 2020

17. U.S. Department of Labor: Employed persons by detailed occupation, sex, race, and Hispanic or Latino ethnicity (2019). https://www.bls.gov/cps/cpsaat11.htm. Accessed 31 Aug 2020

18. Spertus, E.: Why are there so few female computer scientists?. http://hdl.handle.net/1721.1/7040. Accessed 1 July 2020

19. National Science Foundation: Women, minorities and persons with disabilities in science and engineering. http://www.nsf.gov/statistics/wmpd/2013/tables.cfm. Accessed 1 July 2020

20. Academies, N.: Expanding Underrepresented Minority Participation: America's Science and Technology Talent at the Crossroads. National Academies Press, Washington, D.C. (2012)

21. The College Board: 2013 SAT report on college and career readiness. http://media.collegeboard.com/homeOrg/content/pdf/sat-report-college-career-readiness-2013.pdf

22. Chang, M.J., Eagan, M.K., Lin, M.H., Hurtado, S.: Considering the impact of racial stigmas and science identity: persistence among biomedical and behavioral science aspirants. J. High. Educ. **82**(5), 564–596 (2011)

23. Ellis, J., Fosdick, B., Rasmussen, C.: Women 1.5 times more likely to leave STEM pipeline after calculus compared to men: lack of mathematical confidence a potential culprit. PLoS ONE **11**(7), 0157447 (2016). https://doi.org/10.1371/journal.pone.0157447. Accessed 1 July 2020

24. Schiebinger, L.: Women in science: historical perspectives. In: Women at Work: A Meeting on the Status of Women in Astronomy, pp. 11–19. Space Telescope Science Institute (1993)

25. Schiebinger, L.: Getting more women into science and engineering – knowledge issues. In: Gendered Innovations in Science and Engineering, pp. 1–21. Stanford UP (2008)

26. Intemann, K.: Why diversity matters: understanding and applying the diversity component of the national science foundation's broader impacts criterion. Soc. Epistemol. **23**(3), 249–266 (2011)

27. Chubin, D.E., Malcom, S.: Making a case for diversity in STEM fields. Inside Higher Education (6 October 2008). http://www.insidehighered.com/views/2008/10/06/chubin. Accessed 1 July 2020

28. Dubois, W.E.B.: The Souls of Black Folk. 1903. Penguin Books, New York (1982)

29. McIntosh, P.: White privilege: unpacking the invisible knapsack. In: Plous, S. (ed.) Understanding Prejudice and Discrimination, pp. 191–196. McGraw-Hill (2003)

30. Steele, C.M.: A threat in the air: how stereotypes shape intellectual identity and performance. Am. Psychol. **52**, 613–629 (1997)

31. Steele, C.M., Spencer, S.J., Aronson, J.: Contending with group image: the psychology of stereotype and social identity threat. In: Advances in Experimental Social Psychology, vol. 34, pp. 379–440 (2002)

32. Clance, P.R., Imes, S.: The imposter phenomenon in high achieving women: dynamics and therapeutic intervention. Psychother. Theory Res. Pract. **15**(3), 241–247 (1978)

33. Ivie, R., Ephraim, A.: Mentoring and the imposter syndrome in astronomy graduate students. In: Proceedings of the Women in Astronomy and Space Science Conference (2009)

34. Dovidio, J.F., Gaertner, S.L., Pearson, A.R.: Aversive racism and contemporary bias. In: Sibley, C., Barlow, F. (eds.) The Cambridge Handbook of the Psychology of Prejudice (Cambridge Handbooks in Psychology), pp. 267–294. Cambridge University Press, Cambridge (2017)

35. Sue, D.W., et al.: Racial Microaggressions in everyday life: implications for clinical practice. Am. Psychol. **62**(4), 271–286 (2007)

36. Nadal, K.L.: The racial and ethnic microaggressions scale (REMS): construction, reliability, and validity. J. Couns. Psychol. **58**(4), 470–480 (2011)

37. Marcus, A., Mullins, L.C., Brackett, K.P., Tang, Z., Allen, A.M., Pruett, D.W.: Perceptions of racism on campus. Coll. Stud. J. **37**, 611–626 (2003)

38. Lee, J.A.N.: Well behaved women rarely make history! SIGCSE Bull. **34**(2), 14–15 (2002)

39. Estrin, T.: Women's studies and computer science: their intersection. IEEE Ann. Hist. Comput. **18**(3), 43–46 (1996)

40. Impagliazzo, J., Lee, J.A.N., Cassidy, D.C.: Integrating historical and societal contexts in the computing curricula. In: Berleur, J., Avgerou, C. (eds.) Perspectives and Policies on ICT in Society. IIFIP, vol. 179, pp. 239–255. Springer, Boston, MA (2005). https://doi.org/10.1007/0-387-25588-5_17

41. Yakman, G.: ST$\sum$@M education: an overview of creating a model of integrative education. In: The Proceedings of the Pupils' Attitudes Towards Technology (PATT-19) Conference: Research on Technology, Innovation, Design & Engineering Teaching, Salt Lake City, pp. 335–358 (2008)

42. Stanford Report: You've got to find what you love. Jobs Says (14 June 2005). https://news.stanford.edu/news/2005/june15/jobs-061505.html. Accessed 1 July 2020

43. Riley, D.M., Pawley, A.L.: Complicating difference: exploring and exploding three myths of gender and race in engineering education. In: Proceedings of the American Society for Engineering Education 2011 Conference, AC 2011-1381 (2011)

44. Snow, C.P.: The Two Cultures and the Scientific Revolution: The Rede Lecture. Cambridge University Press, New York (1959)

Preserving the Legacy of IT Innovation

Doron Swade(✉)

Kingston upon Thames, Surrey, UK
doron.swade@blueyonder.co.uk

Abstract. IT challenges museological conventions. There are issues of physical scale at both extremes – large mainframes on one hand and microscopic devices on the other. The social utility of collections is widely measured by public exhibition. But 'Black-box' syndrome is a nightmare for exhibition designers and content developers: in the case of computer cabinets and integrated circuits there is no transparency of function to speak of and this stresses established techniques of display and interpretation. Software poses a near-intractable challenge for traditional object-centred museums and it is unclear upon whom, and on what institution, custodial responsibility falls. The impermanence of storage media is incompatible with archaeological timescales. Whether software has meaning without the capability of running it is an open question. Yet running legacy software has formidable resource implications: the need for working historic machines or their physical surrogates, and/or expertise to migrate applications to contemporary platforms. We look to museums to preserve for posterity the material culture of these transformative technologies. There are formidable challenges. How are we to meet them?

Keywords: Collecting IT · Museums and IT · Software preservation · IT innovation legacy · Computer preservation · History of computing

1 Introduction

Information technology represents a substantial human endeavour. The intellectual, economic and material resources involved in production, distribution and use represent major social, cultural and technological movements. There is a prevailing sense that, given the scale and transformative influence of these technologies, their social and technical histories should be preserved.

The mandate of museums is to preserve a material record of change. So it is to museums and museum-like institutions that we turn as repositories and custodians of the technological narratives of our times. What privileges physical objects in preservational practice is the 18th-century concept of 'permanence of substance' – that objects are durable and unchanging and are therefore appropriate evidentiary sources for the preservation, in perpetuity, of meanings [1]. In the case of IT, it is to museums of science and industry, and to specialised computing museums, that we look to preserve a permanent record of technological change.

© IFIP International Federation for Information Processing 2020
Published by Springer Nature Switzerland AG 2020
L. Strous et al. (Eds.): Unimagined Futures, IFIP AICT 555, pp. 162–176, 2020.
https://doi.org/10.1007/978-3-030-64246-4_13

2   Material Culture

IT hardware artefacts fall within traditional collecting criteria, and there are well-established protocols and practices for their acquisition and preservation. In the case of computers, historical significance is framed in different ways. We collect 'world firsts', technological breakthroughs and major innovations – Fleming's diode, the first transistor, the first sub-micron integrated circuit. We collect physical examples that are typical of their kind or representative of widespread practice – PCs, smartphones, electronic calculators – mass produced artefacts where what is distinctive about them is, paradoxically, their uniformity. We collect objects with special provenance – an original lens from Colossus's optical tape reader, a console clock from a Ferranti *Pegasus* (a signature feature of several though not all Ferranti machines), the distinctive red logo from an Elliot 803, Alan Turing's pen – artefacts that have actual or mythical associations with legendary inventors, designers, makers or systems. We collect failures, real and virtual, that stumbled for whatever reason before viable realisation or, if realised, that failed commercially or simply were not favoured by the roulette of success (Apple Newton). We collect objects at the extremes of physical scale, performance and history – substantial chunks of mainframes; supercomputers (Cray-1, the Russian BESM-6), electromechanical race-track Totalisators [2, 3]; and the Harwell Dekatron aka WITCH that dates from 1951 [4], respectively. We collect objects as cultural artefacts without any necessary technical distinction – the National Savings ERNIEs which generate Premium Bond winning numbers [3, 5], acoustic hoods for daisy wheel printers, product packaging, and ephemera - trade literature, an Apple lapel badge [Fig. 1].

Fig. 1.   Apple lapel, badge (1982). Picture credit: Doron Swade

3   Part for the Whole

Curators, archivists and museum store managers are said to have two recurring nightmares. The first is that nothing will survive. The second is that everything will survive.

While the mandate to collect items of IT hardware is relatively unproblematic, in practice IT hardware presents dilemmas for curators and collections managers. Mainframes from the 'Big Iron' era are impractically large to collect in their entirety and there are few complete systems to be found in protective custody that include duplicated peripherals, console furniture and a full set of processor cabinets. It remains unclear whether there is a complete IBM System/360 to be found in a museum collection. Computing is not alone in this. The last remaining hot-metal printing press used in Fleet Street, the Woods press dating from the 1930s, measures nine metres tall, nine-and-a-half metres long and weighs 140-tonnes. The Press was acquired as part of the Science Museum's printing collection and is stored in an aircraft hangar outside London [6]. Locomotives and aircraft pose similar problems of physical scale.

Faced with the improbable size of first-generation computing installations, and later, mainframes, curators resorted to what might be called 'artefactual synecdoche' – acquiring parts to stand for the whole. The struggle for increased speed and power was a perennial priority especially in the pre-chip era. Given the mismatch between physical scale and available storage space, curators and collectors chose the central processor or processor cabinets as placeholders for what was seen to be the essential significance of the whole, resonating perhaps with the idea of preserving only a brain as the pre-eminent organ of the human body. The same was largely true of memory and the wish to reflect the challenges of storage capacity. Magnificent examples of magnetic core memory, with the visually arresting layered arrays of minute ferrite beads, survive, torn, as it were, from their operational environments in a process we might call 'chainsaw acquisition' where only the severed part survives. [Fig. 2]

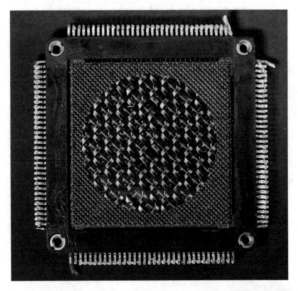

Fig. 2. Magnetic Core Memory (Digico 1972)) (Inset: detail). Picture credit: Doron Swade

The downside of reduction by selection was to lose an artefactual record of the operational environment and physical context – office furniture, for example, and enough kit, not always visually distinguished and often many times duplicated, to convey the physical scale of the original installation. In the case of Olivetti's computers, reduction by selection loses one of the signature features of Olivetti machines – cabinet design, floor layout, colour and overall appearance. To collect anything less than the machine in its entirety loses an historic convergence of design, technology, ergonomics and human machine interaction – an expression of Adriano Olivetti's personal philosophy about industry and society and the company culture of elegance and ergonomics in product design [7]. A legacy of the prohibitive size of early systems is that none of the great first-generation machines survives complete, and some are barely commemorated through even partial relics – ENIAC, EDVAC, EDSAC, UNIVAC, SAGE, Whirlwind, and the Manchester 'Baby' (SSEM), LEO.

Another selective reduction was to acquire control consoles which straddled techno-logical and cultural meanings. SAGE, a radar command and control air defence system, built in the US, in response to the threat of Soviet nuclear attack during the Cold War is an example. In cultural terms the sober grimness of its consoles, a small fraction of this vast system, conveys vigilance, the seriousness of the threat it was intended to neutralize, and the high stakes of Cold War tensions [Fig. 3].

Fig. 3. SAGE Console (1960) Picture credit: Computer History Museum

Increased miniaturisation came to the rescue of despairing museum store managers. Starting with the mini-computer era of the 1960s, when complete machines were mod-estly sized and could be manageably stored, the problem of prohibitive space require-ments for 'Big iron' acquisitions was for the most part self-resolving. For the first three generations of computers, machines and systems were defined localised entities that hap-pily conformed to traditional categories of artefact. With the challenges of distributed processing, embedded devices and especially networks, the earlier era of collecting seems, in comparison, to be blithely innocent.

4 Exhibition and Interpretation

Maintaining a material of technological change through collections can legitimately be regarded as the core mandate of museums. Yet the social utility of collections is widely measured by public exhibition, interpretation and display. 'Inform/inspire, educate and entertain' is a tired but typical aspirational mission. In presentational terms the importance and transformative influence of early rail transport is conveniently symbolized by the massiveness of steam locomotives. In much the same way, up to the early 1960s, the fact that computer systems were big, conveyed significance and complexity, and there was a happy congruity between meanings and external form. As a free-standing object, function was largely opaque but this was masked by wonder at their size which supported the message of technological and historical significance. If it's big, it matters, is the perceptual equation.

But from the early 1960s, developments in solid-state physics began to stress traditional exhibit presentation in a new and distinctive way. More and more was happening at component and device level, and there was less and less to see. What was of significance in an integrated circuit was invisible, whether live or not. 'Black-box syndrome' was the exhibitor's dread where external form and internal function, however innovative, agreed to amicable divorce. With diminished visual appeal, long-accepted display conventions were challenged in an unprecedented way. New techniques were called for to unpack meanings from small items with no functional transparency to speak of. While difficult, the problem of the chip, as museum artefact, is not intractable. Creative use of existing techniques – panel graphics, illustration, imaginative comparisons, screen-based layered interactive exposition – provide solutions. No such obvious relief is available for software.

5 Software in an Object-Centred Culture

The acquisition, preservation and interpretation of software poses near-intractable practical and philosophical difficulties for museums. Traditional museums are part of an object-centred culture, and privileged in this culture are physical artefacts, their meaning, significance and their care. Items of hardware, the physical stuff of IT systems are, by the conventions of traditional curatorship, unproblematic candidates for acquisition– monitors, keyboards, disk drives, system boxes, printers and the like. Software, a term in general use by the early 1960s, was defined negatively. *The Oxford Dictionary of Computing* defined software as 'a generic term for those components of a computer system that are intangible rather than physical' [8]. Prentice Hall's *Illustrated Dictionary of Computing* severs any link with the physical by noting that that 'software is independent of the carrier used for transport' [9]. We habitually refer to CD distribution disks, and previously to floppy disks, as 'software'. However, this fudges the distinction between the carrier, or medium of record, and the program. Strictly the software is a non-material logical abstraction, and the disk, PROM, mem-stick, punched cards, punched paper tape, are carriers [10].

We do not collect polynomials or prime numbers, but we do collect mathematical instruments, physical models, mathematicians' workbooks, drafts of seminal publications, first editions and, in the case of prime numbers, hardcopy printouts. The mathematics gallery at the Science Museum, London completed in 2016 [3] does not display number or mathematical operations, but computational machines and devices used in various arenas of human affairs, trade, war, finance, vital statistics, and structures i.e. ways in which number, an abstraction, has been physicalised for computational purposes. In this way abstract meanings are abducted by material artefacts. Similarly, when we 'collect software' we are not strictly collecting algorithmic logic but the physical media of creation representation, distribution, and storage – coding sheets, flow charts, written deliberation of designers and programmers, manuals, publicity literature, punched cards, and carriers in various forms – optical, magnetic, solid-state, paper. The distinction is not an entirely pedantic one. If software falls outside the mandate of object-centred museums then upon whom, and on what institution, does custodial responsibility for preservation fall?

Even when we collect, say, shrink-wrapped software products, we do so, at least partly, in their capacity as cultural artefacts – historical placeholders – rather than as archival records of a working product. The model for Museum preservation practice is essentially an archaeological one in which we retard physical degradation by passivating the physical environment – protection against physical trauma, low light, temperature and humidity control. The effectiveness of this model is limited when it comes to ensuring the data integrity of software carriers. Optical media and, *a fortiori*, magnetic media are notoriously impermanent, and manufacturers are loath to commit to figures for service lifetime. At best we are talking about decades, which is negligible in the archaeological timescales we envisage. Software is not alone in this. A curator of medicine might acquire a pack of Aspirin. There is significance in the branding, advertising graphics, tablet form, blister-pack press-through dispenser, logo and packaging – cultural content. But a pack of Aspirin would not be acquired and preserved as a permanent record of its chemical structure which it is accepted will degrade, and with it, its therapeutic potency. The inventoried Aspirin pack in a medical collection is not preserved as a pharmaceutical record of the product as it would be by retaining its chemical formula and/or the recipe for manufacture [10]. Similarly, it is accepted that passivating the environment will not ensure the operational viability of software when stored on its native medium. In short, there is a basic incompatibility between life-expectancy of the medium-of-record and the long-term custodial aspirations of museums.

6 Software Preservation

A working party was set up by the Computer Conservation Society [11] in the early 1990s to address the issue of software preservation and take account of the impermanence of storage media and the resources required to ensure content renewal in perpetuity. The group disbanded after three months with the conclusion that the only credible way to preserve software systematically was to record the content as a bit stream on paper and entrust this printed record to archivists who have well-proven techniques for the indefinite preservation of paper media.

There is a variety of initiatives that have risen to meet the formidable challenges of software preservation. Perhaps the most broadly-scoped programme is that of the Computer History Museum (CHM), California, where the collecting emphasis is on source code – a form more revealing than most, of programmers' intent and approach [12]. Enviably, the Museum supports a dedicated Software Curator, Al Kossow, who has developed protocols and practices to ensure the integrity of stored content including measures to prevent and detect corruption. In the UK David Holdsworth heads up the software conservation activity of the Computer Conservation Society, London. Here the mission is to preserve software in machine-readable form with a view to current or future capability to execute [13]. There are countless software preservation initiatives by societies, by national libraries and archives, and through the efforts of enthusiasts some dedicated to a specific class of products, computer games, for example. All face a variety of common issues, principal amongst which are the limited life of storage media, the impermanence of contemporary hardware platforms, and the portability of virtual platforms for emulators and simulators.

7   Software Recovery

As with hardware, the historical significance of software was rarely evident at the time of its creation or implementation and, if it survived at all in whatever form, it did so for the most part by accident or, occasionally, through the agency of a conscientious practitioner. There are cases where the original medium survives intact but nothing is known of its contents. There are other cases where the original medium did not survive but there is a non-electronic record which may or not be complete. And yet other cases where software is known to have existed but nothing at all exists in material form. Only in the last of these cases can the software strictly be considered 'lost'. In each of the other cases software, taken as the logical algorithmic content, survives, whether or not in executable form. However, in all these cases, before the software can be preserved for future use, it needs first to be recovered, whether retrieved from the original medium, translated from a non-electronic medium, or reconstructed from scratch.

An example of retrieval from an original medium is the restoration to working order of the Elliott-NRDC 401, an experimental vacuum-tube machine dating from 1952-3. Only one 401 was made and the restoration, begun in the early 1990s by the Computer Conservation Society, was obstructed by the absence of any documentation for the drum store – no data, metadata, or information on the file structure. The restoration team headed up by Tony Sale and Chris Burton built read heads, ran the drum and captured the bit stream on a PC where it could be inspected, analysed and decoded. That the data was readable from a 40-year old drum puts in a slightly more favourable light the notorious impermanence of magnetic media. Len Shustek at the Computer History Museum has recovered source code from degraded magnetic tapes from Whirlwind – this by digitising the streamed analog waveforms and using software to reconstruct the original data [14, 15].

There are more extreme examples involving retrieval from other than native media. David Holdsworth recounts the recovery of software for the KDF9 computer from lineprinter listings [16]. The texts were copy-typed after OCR proved inadequate as a recovery tool for the 40-year old hardcopy. Two assembler language programs were recovered in this way and the code runs on an emulator.

8 Love Letters

David Link's reconstruction of Christopher Strachey's program to generate love letters is an example of software recovery that combines computer archaeology and art [17]. Strachey wrote his love letter generator for the Ferranti Mark 1 (1952) at Manchester. Nothing of the original storage medium appears to have survived. Link located the source code in the Bodleian Library in Oxford but found it impossible to decode the algorithmic structure or internal dynamics of the program. He concluded that the only way to analyse the program was to reconstruct it and run it live – this by first constructing a software emulator, and later a functional physical replica using contemporary parts including simulations of Williams-tube memory using WWII radar tubes. He rewrote a critical missing subroutine (the original was subsequently found) and the system formed the basis of an art installation which displayed continuously generated love letters on a screen, and also provided some interactivity with the visitor [18].

It is clear from these examples that there are substantial, ingenious, and significant initiatives to recover and preserve software. It is also clear that such initiatives, which require high levels of specialised expertise, are not centralised or co-ordinated and do not have a shared mission. Perhaps most importantly, they do not have the long-term security conferred by statutory responsibility as is the case for state-funded national museums with its mandate defined in law, the UK government's 1983 Heritage Act, for example. This is not a criticism. Quite the reverse – let a thousand flowers bloom. The observation is intended simply to flag that if our concern is preservation in perpetuity then the long-term future of these remarkable efforts is not secure.

The creation of new institutions to preserve new informational media is not without precedent. The National Sound Archive (NSA) was founded in 1955 as the British Institute of Recorded Sound and was absorbed into the British Library in 1983. As part of the British Library the sound archive is state funded. The National Film Archive was founded in 1935. As part of the British Film Institute (BFI) the film archive is sponsored by the government's Department of Digital, Culture, Media and Sport (DCMS). Both archives are secure for as long as society continues to value these media as part of its cultural heritage. If it is time for institutionalised software preservation with the security of state funding, how do we articulate answers to the questions, what, and who is it for?

9 Functionality

Whether the preservation of software, without means to run it, is meaningful is a fraught question. Gerard Alberts argues that software is a dynamic artefact and not to preserve user experience and interaction with it is to lose essential elements of its meaning [19]. Web archiving, which preserves 'snap shots' of static screen pages, has a very different outcome to preserving the experience of web-surfing in real time. David Holdsworth is of like mind in writing that 'a basic tenet of the CCS's software conservation activity is that software is only truly conserved when it can be run on current hardware and has the prospect of being run on hardware in the foreseeable future' [16]. This is a judicious formulation in that it sanctions and encourages responsible preservation without making a contemporary hardware platform, or an operational equivalent, a prerequisite. We are enjoined to preserve, as a holding operation, before the material is lost and while specialised expertise survives.

Two areas come to mind where running software might be thought to be indispensable to meaning. The first is computer games. Gaming has significantly driven innovation and it is questionable whether the preservation of only the physical paraphernalia of gaming can meaningfully replace the ability to run these programs live on contemporary platforms [20]. A second example is that of art installations. Computer-enabled or computer-dependent art installations are largely meaningless unless run live. David Link's *Poetry Machine* and his self-regenerating book, *Meditationes*, are examples [21–24] [Fig. 4].

Fig. 4. Poetry Machine by David Link. Picture credit: David Link

The demands of exhibition are usually time-bound and any given platform will last the duration before terminal obsolescence. *Poetry Machine*, which involves sophisticated software and interactivity was revived after twenty years by migrating the software to a Windows platform and refreshing the hardware – a non-trivial process even for Link, its original creator. Archiving an installation scarcely qualifies as meaningful preservation without the resources to renew it and without the security of continuity. A related context in which functionality impacts preservation is the art market where the installation is seen as product. If an installation is sold what is it one owns without the resources to maintain in perpetuity the original system, or migrate the software to a later platform? Paintings and sculpture are not plagued in this way. They do not require the mediation of complex technology to render them intelligible.

10 Platforms

There are countless initiatives to provide contemporary hardware platforms or functional facsimiles, primarily through the restoration to working order of surviving machines, or through the reconstruction of historic machines of which there are no surviving examples [25, 26]. The hallmark of such initiatives is the expertise, ingenuity and commitment of largely volunteer effort. Teams at the Computer History Museum have successfully restored a DEC PDP-1 (1959) and an IBM 1401 (1959) [27]. At The National Museum of Computing (TNMoC) at Bletchley we find working restorations of the Harwell Dekatron ('WITCH') a hybrid relay-valve machine dating from 1951 [4], a Marconi TAC (1959), the discrete component germanium transistor Elliott 803 (early 1960s), an Elliott 903 (late 1960s), an IBM 1130 (1965), an ICL 2966 (1980s), ICL System 25 (1980s) and ICL DRS 6000 (1990), a Cray EL98 (1993), and a variety of classic personal computers [28].

In instances where no original exists to restore or replicate, reconstructions have been resorted to. Prominent amongst these is the Manchester SSEM ('Baby') at the Science and Industry Museum in Manchester. At TNMoC there are several substantial working reconstructions of WWII machines [28] – Colossus, Heath Robinson, and the Turing-Welchman Bombe, as well as the post-war Cambridge EDSAC [29].

Restorations and reconstructions provide contemporary hardware platforms, or functional equivalents, for running legacy software as well as new programs. Through these restorations and reconstructions, the fidelity of programming practices, performance, interactivity, and the user experience are preserved. These initiatives have other historiographical as well as social benefits: the practicalities of restoration or reconstruction draw one into a level of intimate detail with the machine that rarely occurs by other means; physical realisation almost invariably results in contingent or unexpected findings not foreseen by analysis or theory; operating the machines gives insights into contemporary ideas and practice and captures generational experience that would otherwise be lost; tacit knowledge is regenerated; documentary completeness is a contingent outcome; and the working system provides an authentic benchmark for simulation [25].

In addition to the historical and historiographical value of restorations and reconstructions there is the social capital they create i.e. their value to those who make up the project teams, to visitors who view and experience them on public display, and to museums and organisations that host these exhibits. The projects provide meaningful engagement within an organisational context for veteran experts to share expertise, exercise their craft, and extend their professional activities in historically and educationally meaningful ways. Demonstrating the machines has pedagogic value to users and visitors. Large machines on public display act as foci for visitor attention and provide a platform for storytelling through live demonstration and conventional exhibition graphics. Finally, large systems publicly displayed memorialise important episodes and practices for which they act as both placeholders and monuments that serve as generational bridges to an otherwise lost past.

11   The End of the Road

However successful are such efforts to extend the operational life of historic machines or to provide historically authentic reconstructed platforms, we have to accept the eventual demise of such systems if our aspirations are to extend to archaeological time spans. While degraded wiring can be replaced, and any part, vacuum tubes for example, can, in principle at least, be refactored as replacements, a point will arrive where the effort and cost will become prohibitive even if the relevant expertise can be migrated inter-generationally. It is anyway the case that any replacement programme compromises the physical integrity of the original artefact and, if the machine is unique, violates the central primacy of the original in the central tenets of museum practice. There are also political insecurities. The priorities of host institutions change. At the Science Museum, London, a Ferranti *Pegasus* (1959), a vacuum-tube computer with magnetic drum storage, was restored to working order by the Computer Conservation Society and successfully run and demonstrated from the early 1990s for over 25 years. There was no technical reason preventing further extending its operational life. Its maintenance and public demonstration were ended following a policy shift away from working exhibits, and the machine was moved off public display into storage.

The construction of an historic machine is essentially an act of physical replication. There is of course logical replication in the form of emulators and simulators. Emulators allow us to run contemporary software on a non-native platform and this offers liberation from the need for working original or non-original hardware. Simulation captures the operational persona of the machine in providing a virtual functional equivalent that allows a user to program, run, and interact with an operational facsimile. While the logic of virtual machines may be faithful to the original there are performance issues that are not automatically portable, real-time execution being one.

Emulation and simulation offer the promise of indefinite migration to new platforms and, as the languages used for the simulations become increasingly machine independent, indefinite migration from one generational platform to the next appears to offer a form of logical immortality. In practice, however, the independence of software from hardware is rarely absolute and there are interdependences that compromise the prospect of indefinite preservation by these means. There is also the question of the longevity of the languages that host the emulators. When these are superseded, we have a new migration problem.

12   Justification for Working Software

In a bid for state or institutional funding for software preservation a question that will inevitably be asked is, to what purpose i.e. what benefits would accrue from having an archive of software whether running or not? The tendency is to begin to stutter. The point is that we have little idea how these artefacts will be interrogated by those who follow. We cannot foresee what features may be of interest or significance. A researcher may be interested in the historic use of subroutines, the practice of altering instruction codes under program control, trawling early programs for forgotten techniques that could inventively be repurposed, algorithmic structures and precedents, the first use of nested looping, the first use of number as symbol rather than quantity, response and execution times, the speed of a compiler, latency… a gallimaufry of practical, philosophical, logical and technical inquiry. We do not ask this question of traditional museum objects nor of the specific utility of sound or film. It is accepted that these have cultural and historical value and are saved to be available for unforeseen and unforeseeable interrogation, and cultural appreciation. I have argued elsewhere [1] that what underpins the primacy of the original in museum culture is that only the original embodies predicates, properties and features the significance of which we cannot fully know nor anticipate. It is precisely this epistemic incompleteness that is responsible for the elevation of the original above object surrogates, replicas, or imitations. What underpins the value of the original, and is responsible at least in part for its mystique, is the sense that understanding is never complete, that knowledge is never total, that the original artefact embodies evidence the meanings which may not be accessible by other means, and whose significance cannot be foreseen. Software, as a digital object, is no different.

Exhibiting software poses daunting difficulties, and very few museum-like organisations have embraced the challenge. The deterrents are already familiar: abstractness, arcane complexity and the absence of anything physically meaningful upon which traditional object-based exhibition routinely relies. A bold exception is the exhibition *Make Software: Change the World* that opened in 2017 at the Computer History Museum [30]. The exhibition features seven exemplars of software products or classes of software identified as transformative: Photoshop, MP3, MRI, Car Crash Simulation, Wikipedia, Texting, and World of Warcraft i.e. applications regarded as 'game-changing' in computer-mediated virtual reality, compression, simulation, gaming, and crowd-sourced knowledge. This treatment leapfrogs attempts to treat software as a traditional museum object, dumps otiose agonising about the relationship between software and hardware, and confidently abandons much else that has so far daunted and paralysed wishful exhibitors. The subtext of the exhibition is that these are wondrous objects and they are created or enabled by software which is demonstrably powerful, important and ingenious. This treatment uses widely known outcomes to raise interest in the generative process. This turns on its head the traditional approach that favours focusing on the generative process (programming, compiling, software engineering…) in an attempt to provide some kind of explanatory account for the outcome.

13   Summary and Conclusions

Non-working hardware devices and systems fall within the traditional collecting mandates of object-centred museums which have well-established preservation practices and protocols. Exhibiting these as static objects is amenable to existing interpretative display techniques. In the case of smaller devices, especially solid-state devices, opacity of function, uniformity, and physical size stretch conventional techniques of interpretation, but not unmanageably so.

Working historic machines and systems are heavily concentrated in the independent sector. Private collections and independent smaller museums are the primary hosts of restoration and reconstruction activity that heavily relies on the expertise, interest and commitment of volunteers. There tends to be little co-ordination between these groups for acquisition, exhibition or restoration activity, and security of support, not to mention their artefactual holdings, are perpetually at risk.

Prominent in the independent sector are subject-specialist museums dedicated to computing. These include the Computer History Museum, California, the Heinz Nixdorf MuseumsForum (HNF) in Paderborn, Germany, The National Museum of Computing (TNMoC) at Bletchley. With company funding, philanthropic and sponsorship support these collections are relatively secure for the time being. There are many regional museums with local focus, small departmental collections in universities, and small museums funded by universities, where financial security is partly assured by their organisational hosts. Overall, the future of smaller private collections is precarious especially when viewed in the context of archaeological time scales.

Running historic software requires functional intactness in the form of bit-perfect records as well as contemporary hardware or a physical or virtual functional equivalent.

Software preservation is a growing activity though still tends to be localised and fragmented. The levels of specific expertise for effective preservation through capture and emulation are high, and dedicated volunteers, many retirees, tend to be the drivers here. When it comes to storage methods, formats, and media there is little standardisation.

The resource implications of running software on contemporary platforms, or on functional equivalents, act as formidable deterrents for traditional museums. High levels of expertise are required in skills areas that have high market value outside the museum sector. Organisational commitment is required to ensure continuity, and social, technical and historical utility is difficult to justify through cost-benefit arguments. The resources required to sustain an indefinite programme of copying, renewal, and integrity-checking are non-trivial and few organisations have yet been willing to commit to preservation programmes of this kind.

The dream is for an independently resourced organisation with a mandate to pro-actively acquire software, preserve executable versions in perpetuity, to maintain working contemporary hardware platforms, develop emulators and simulators, and migrate this material to new generational platforms on an indefinite basis, this to provide a gene pool of software evolution. Systematic pro-active collecting of this kind is rare even as an agenda for object-based state-funded museums. What tends to survive are artefacts seen to be important enough for people to care about. Advocacy for much of this collecting comes from outside the museum sector, from enthusiasts, practitioners, specialists and professionals. What survives for the most part is through the happenstance of history. Software, so far, is no exception.

References

1. Swade, D.: Virtual objects: threat or salvation? In: Lindqvist, S. (ed.) Museums of Modern Science. Watson Publishing International, Canton (2000)
2. Swade, D.: Forgotten machines: the need for a new master narrative. In: Haigh, T. (ed.) Exploring the Early Digital. HC, pp. 41–68. Springer, Cham (2019). https://doi.org/10.1007/978-3-030-02152-8_3
3. Rooney, D.: Mathematics: how it shaped our world, pp. 89–90. Scala Arts and Heritage Publishers Ltd., London (2016)
4. Harwell Dekatron Computer aka W.I.T.C.H: The National Museum of Computing. https://www.tnmoc.org/witch. Accessed 26 Feb 2020
5. Swade, D.: The three ages of windfall fantasy. Guardian, 6 October 1988

6. Good news for historic press: BBC News, 20 November 2001. http://news.bbc.co.uk/1/hi/sci/tech/1665086.stm. Accessed 25 Feb 2020
7. Mori, E.: The Italian Computer: Olivetti's ELEA 9003 Was a Study in Elegant Ergonomic Design. IEEE Spectrum (2019). https://spectrum.ieee.org/tech-history/silicon-revolution/the-italian-computer-olivettis-elea-9003-was-a-study-in-elegant-ergonomic-design. Accessed 26 Feb 2020
8. Software: In: Illingsworth, V., Glaser, E.L., Pyle, I.C. (eds.) Dictionary of Computing. 2nd edn. pp. 352. Oxford University Press, Oxford (1986)
9. Nader, J.C.: Software. Prentice Hall's Illustrated Dictionary of Computing, pp. 412. London: Prentice Hall (1992)
10. Swade, D.: Collecting Software: preserving information in an object-centred culture. In: Hashagen, U., Keil-Slawik, R., Norberg, A.L. (eds.) History of Computing: Software Issues, pp. 227–235. in particular page 230. Springer, Heidelberg (2002). http://doi.org/10.1007/978-3-662-04954-9_19
11. CCS: Computer Conservation Society. https://www.computerconservationsociety.org/about.htm. Accessed 29 May 2020
12. Software Preservation. Computer History Museum, Software History Centre. https://computerhistory.org/software-history-center/. Accessed 26 Feb 2020
13. Holdsworth, D.: History, nostalgia and software. In: Tatnall, A., Blyth, T., Johnson, R. (eds.) HC 2013. IAICT, vol. 416, pp. 266–273. Springer, Heidelberg (2013). https://doi.org/10.1007/978-3-642-41650-7_24
14. Shustek, L.: Decode the analog waveform extracted from old computer mag tapes (2019). https://github.com/LenShustek/readtape. Accessed 26 Feb 2020
15. Stachniak, Z.: Software recovery and beyond. IEEE Ann. Hist. Comput. **41**(4), 110–118. IEEE Computer Society, Washington D.C. (2019)
16. Holdsworth, D.: Rescuing software from lineprinter listings. Resurrection: The Bulletin of the Computer Conservation Society 57, CCS (2012). https://www.computerconservationsociety.org/resurrection/res57.htm#e. Accessed 26 Feb 2020
17. Link, D.: Machine Heart (das Herz der Maschine). Hatje Cantz Verlag, Ostfildern (2011)
18. Roberts, S.: Christopher Strachey's Nineteen-fifties Love Machine. The New Yorker, 14 February 2017. https://www.newyorker.com/tech/annals-of-technology/christopher-stracheys-nineteen-fifties-love-machine
19. Alberts, G., Went, M., Jansma, R.: Archaeology of the Amsterdam digital city; why digital data are dynamic and should be treated accordingly. Internet Histories: Digital Technology, Culture and Society 1(1–2), pp. 146–159. Taylor&Francis Online, London (2017). https://doi.org/10.1080/24701475.2017.1309852
20. Guins, R.: Game After: A Cultural Study of Video Game Afterlife. MIT Press, Cambridge (2014)
21. Link, D.: Poetry Machine. In: Brouwer, J., Fauconnier, S., Nigten, A. (eds.) ART&D: Research and Development in Art, pp. 196–205. V2 and Nai Publishers, Rotterdam (2005)
22. Link, D.: Poetry Machine (2005). http://alpha60.de/art/poetry_machine/. Accessed 27 Feb 2020
23. Link, D., Einheit, F.M.: "Radar Angels: Art and Artificial Text Generation." The Turing Conversation. ETH Zurich. https://www.turing.ethz.ch/the-turing-conversation/contribution-8.html. Accessed 12 Aug 2020
24. Vega, A.: Meditationes: A metaphysical laboratory by David Link (2016). http://alpha60.de/art/meditationes/. Accessed 25 Feb 2020
25. Swade, D.: The historical utility of reconstruction and restoration. In: Campbell-Kelly, M. (ed.) Making IT Work, pp. 7–21. British Computer Society and The National Museum of Computing, London (2017). http://www.computerconservationsociety.org/miw/Proc%20MIW%202017.pdf

26. Swade, D.: Historical reconstructions. IEEE Ann. Hist. Comput. **27**(3), p. 3. IEEE Computer Society, Washington D.C. (2005)
27. Garner, R.: Restoring and demonstrating 1960s vintage computers at the computer history museum. In: Campbell-Kelly, M. (ed.) Making IT Work, pp. 54–67. British Computer Society and The National Museum of Computing, London (2017), http://www.computerconservati onsociety.org/miw/Proc%20MIW%202017.pdf
28. Explore the Galleries, The National Museum of Computing, https://www.tnmoc.org/galleries. Accessed 27 Feb 2020
29. EDSAC - Electronic Delay Storage Automatic Calculator, The National Museum of Computing, https://www.tnmoc.org/edsac. Accessed 27 Feb 2020
30. Make Software: Change the World, Computer History Museum, https://www.computerhist ory.org/makesoftware/exhibit/. Accessed 26 Feb 2020

Founding IFIP as an International Computing Organization

David Alan Grier[(⊠)] [iD]

Djaghe LLC, New York, Washington, DC, USA
grier@gwu.edu

Abstract. IFIP was founded with the help of UNESCO and it captured some of the scientific idealism that marked the early days of UNESCO. Identifying the presence of this idealism helps explosion why the organization could be successful at some kinds of activities and challenged by others.

Keywords: International organizations · Professional societies · Computing milieu · Computing history

1 Introduction

The 1950s were marked two phenomena that foreshadowed the founding of IFIP in 1960. It was a decade in which internationalism flourished. After the cataclysm of the second world war, national governments were interested in rebuilding their countries, establishing their place in the global economy and developing institutions that would limit the widespread conflict. The decade saw the rise of the computer industry. The first commercial machines appeared in 1951 and 1952. By the end of the decade, more than 3,000 machines were operating in government offices, corporate organizations, and university computer centers.

To some, it might seem obvious that these two phenomena might combine in an international organization that would promote computing. However, it was far from obvious to the members of the computing community how this organization might be formed and what it might do. At the time, computing was still an engineering discipline and hence tightly connected to national security and the fate of the nation state. Hence the most likely form of an international computing organization might have been a multi-national organization that shared information and promoted the peaceful uses of computing.

IFIP, however, did not follow this model. It became an organization that represented professional societies and looked for ways to support computing developments across nations. This approach was the result of nearly 8 years of careful work, study and negotiations. IFIP achieved its current form because its early leaders, leaders that included people such as Isaac Auerbach and Alwin Walther, had a clear vision sense of computing's universality. They also felt that the universal nature of computing should be

© IFIP International Federation for Information Processing 2020
Published by Springer Nature Switzerland AG 2020
L. Strous et al. (Eds.): Unimagined Futures, IFIP AICT 555, pp. 177–187, 2020.
https://doi.org/10.1007/978-3-030-64246-4_14

captured by an international organization that transcended national borders and provided benefits to all. In the early years of IFIP, they spend much of their efforts trying to build such an organization, and to learn what that kind of organization could and couldn't do to promote computing and computer science.

2   The Founding Generation

Isaac Auerbach (1921–1991) helped to organize IFIP in the late 1950s. Yet in many ways, he was more a creature of the 1940s, an era that rejoiced at the end of the second world war and hoped that nations could cooperate to maintain the peace. In scientists, these hopes were seen in a form of scientific idealism, an idealism that believed that scientific knowledge was the property of all human-kind, that it could be a force for good and that scientists could collaborate across national boundaries in a way that would establish a model for all collaboration. This idealism was not unique to scientists, but the scientist community embraced it fervently. "Part of this optimism stems from central tenets of classical liberalism," explain two scholars of international organizations, which viewed International Organizations "as a peaceful way to manage rapid technological change and globalization, far preferable to the obvious alternative - war" [7].

Auerbach was member of that post-war generation of scientists. He came of age during the last years of the war and might be described as being "almost a member" of the founding cohort of computer designers. He first came in contact with computers at Harvard, where he was an undergraduate. Harvard professor Howard Aiken (1900–1973) built a mechanical computer in 1943, a machine that presaged developments in electronic computation less five years later [4]. Auerbach did not work on this machine but he did take one undergraduate course from Aiken, a course in numerical analysis [10]. His relations to the undergraduate Auerbach, seems to be friendly but not close. He helped to spark Auerbach's interest in computation but was a little upset when Auerbach decided to join the Eckert and Mauchly Computer Corporation rather than pursue graduate study at Harvard.

The Eckert and Mauchly Computer Corporation was first company that came out of the ENIAC Project at the University of Pennsylvania. The ENIAC has been described as the most important result of second world war research that was never used in the second world war. It was not quite an electronic computer when it first began operating in the fall of 1946 but it led directly to the ideas of the modern stored program computer architecture and the construction of many electronic computers in the late 1940s and 1950s.

Auerbach described himself as perhaps "the number three man in the company". He worked as an electrical engineering in the company and claimed that he was ultimately responsible for "all of the manufacturing of the product" as well as doing research and developing all the electronics for the memory. He eventually grew disenchanted with the way the founders were managing the organization and moved to the laboratory of the Burroughs Adding Machine Company. Burroughs had created this laboratory in downtown Philadelphia in order to build its expertise in electronics and move into the market for electronic calculators and computers. To lead the laboratory, they had been able to recruit Irven Travis (1904–1986), who had worked with Eckert and Mauchly on the ENIAC project during the war [4]. For his first job at Burroughs, Auerbach had the opportunity to return to the ENIAC and study its design as Burroughs had been given a contract to build new memory units for the machine that would extend its capacity and lengthen its life [2].

While working for Burroughs, Auerbach began to look beyond his employer and think about the bigger computing community. In 1949, he was one of the founding members of the Computer Interest Group of the Institute of Radio Electronic Engineers, the organization that would eventually become the IEEE Computer Society. He also served as a member of the organizing committee of the Joint Computer Conferences [4].

In the 1950s and 1960s, to be on the organizing committee of the Joint Computer Conferences was to be at the center of the American computing community. These conferences assembled most of the serious researchers in computing. Their proceedings contained most of the important computing papers of the era, certainly far more than the journals of the three professional societies that sponsored the conference, the Institute of Radio Engineers, the American Institute for Electrical Engineers and the Association for Computing Machinery. At the time, most of the interesting computing development was being done by private corporations such as Eckert and Mauchly Corporation, ERA (both later to merge as UNIVAC), IBM, Burroughs, Honeywell, RCA and General Electric [1].

Auerbach had a restless mind that kept pushing him into bigger and bigger communities. At the Fall Joint Computer Conference of 1955, he posed an innocent question about the work that was being done outside of the United States that led him to the founding of IFIP. As he later recalled it, he was "sitting in the bar with three or four other guys" when he observed that they came "back to these meetings every year" and in the process met "the same people and kind of talk about the same kinds of things. Does anybody have any idea what's going on overseas?". The Joint Computing Conferences had few attendees from outside the United States and most of that group came from the United Kingdom [4].

At this point, most industrialized countries were supporting some kind of computing development but the connections between these projects were haphazard. Sometimes a laboratory would publish a book or article that was well circulated. In 1951, for example, the first major book on programming, which was written by Maurice Wilkes (1913–2010) of Cambridge University. More often than not, the connections were made by the movement of computing personnel. Harry Huskey (1916–2017), the assistant to the late Alan Turing (1912–1954), had brought his experience to the University of California and to Bendix Corporation. The Computing laboratory at the University of Sydney also relied on connections to Turing's laboratory as well as connections to the University of Illinois. Some of the pioneering computing work was done isolation. In Kyiv, Serge Lebedev (1902–1974) worked behind the barriers of the Soviet Union and in Germany, Konrad Zuse (1910–1995) labored with little contact to British or American projects.

Auerbach wanted to build a more systematic way of connecting computer projects and immediately rallied the support of the Joint Computer Conference board. As a member of the board, he argued that the group should develop an international meeting or congress for computer developers and users. He seems to have gotten their approval relatively easily but instead of arranging for the Joint Computer Conferences board to manage the conference, Auerbach turned to the United Nations Educational Scientific and Cultural Organization (UNESCO) [4]. He knew no one in the organization and had only an outsider's understanding of how it worked. Yet, Auerbach did not seem particularly concerned by his lack of knowledge or connections. He drafted a proposal that the UN group sponsor an international conference in computing. With the help of two friends, "mailed out 40 or 50 copies of this proposal to UNESCO representatives from various countries" and asked those representatives to support this idea. "Much to everybody's pleasant surprise they agreed," he recalled [4].

3   The Two Sides to UNESCO

It is possible to argue that Auerbach did not need UNESCO to create his conference. He could have planned a conference in one of the European capitals, raised money through his connections at the Joint Computer Conferences, and managed the conference himself. That argument probably underestimates the difficulty of running an international conference in 1955. International borders hindered the movement of both assets and people. Furthermore, it was often difficult to hold a meeting in Europe without a local organization to take responsibility for the event. Seven years later, the new IFIP board was a little surprised to discover that it needed a legal presence in Germany if it was to hold a conference in that country [14].

However, it seems that Auerbach was interested in building connections with UNESCO from the time that he first conceived of an international meeting on computation. In his notes, he never discusses any alternatives to a connection with UNESCO and never considers running the conference as an independent entity. From his subsequent actions and writings, he clearly wanted to have a connection between his envisioned computer conference and UNESCO [5].

At this point in its history, UNESCO was at the zenith of its reputation. It was viewed as pristine organization that was promoting scientific cooperation throughout the world and through that cooperation, peace. "UNESCO's early science programs were designed to serve science and scientists rather than states," explained one student of the institution. "They aimed to increase the world sum of scientific knowledge and access to that knowledge without regard to national boundaries" [4]. If Auerbach was working to raise the profile of computing and connect it to the major international institutions of his time, he would do well to connect it to the UNESCO of the early 1950s.

Yet, UNESCO was already starting to show the first signs of moving away from the international scientific idealism that it had espoused in the early part of the decade. Scholars have called this a shift from "Kantian Transnationalism" and a slow movement towards a "Cold War Hobbesian Nationalism" [7]. Expressed more bluntly, the leadership of UNESCO realized that national governments were supporting it and hence these governments needed to have a bigger voice in the leadership of the organization. This shift was most clearly seen in a re-organization of UNESCOs governing board. Initially, that board had consisted of individual scientists, educators and cultural voices. After 1954, the board was dominated by 22 national representatives [12].

If UNESCO was starting to serve governments more than scientists, it is perhaps a bit of an anomaly that IFIP became an organization that was supported by professional societies rather than those governments. Initially, neither UNESCO nor the IFIP founders may have pondered that distinction but they quickly began to discuss the ramifications of that issue. In 1957, Auerbach started holding meetings to plan the International Conference on Information Processing, which was eventually held on June 15–20, 1959 in Paris. In all, 1,800 people attended [6].

During these initial meetings, Auerbach raised the question of how the conference might establish a permanent existence. "I broached the issue about how to continue the cooperation and relationships that we had established with each other on an ongoing basis," he recalled. At this point, "UNESCO made it very clear that they wanted no part of that. If we wanted to do it, we could either do it as an inter-governmental activity or a professional activity." After a certain amount of discussion, Auerbach agreed to delay any further discussion until the end of that first conference [4].

From the descriptions of the 1959 conference, it seems to have been based on a combination of ideas drawn from the Joint Computer Conferences and the organizational goals of UNESCO. As he had at the joint conferences, Auerbach viewed computing as being strongly based by the businesses and the business community. "We felt that IFIP was an opportunity for us to enlarge the market by reaching out and teaching people something about computers and how they can be used," he recalled. It "was not difficult" to convince American firms, such "IBM, or UNIVAC, or Burroughs, or NCR" to participate. He was also able to reach German companies such as Siemens [4]. The conference was far from being a trade show, as the group was able to secure Auerbach's one-time teacher, Howard Aiken, as a keynote speaker [6].

Most observers agree that the first conference was a success, though all could identify shortcomings that they wished to rectify in any future conference. Many felt that the U. S. dominated the conference. Auerbach felt that this judgement was not surprising as the meeting had been initiated by a group of Americans who had wanted to "find out what's going on over there" [4]. Too "many of the papers were out of date and lacked the originality that should have prevailed," noted Auerbach. He argued that the "program was controlled by UNESCO's obsession with protocol and International politics, and thus was flawed by excessive concern for national distribution of the participants rather than the absolute quality of the papers" [6].

During the conference, Auerbach and the other organizers reconvened to discuss how they might hold a second meeting and how they might build an organization to support it. "All of us agreed that dealing with the bureaucracies of government was not something with which any of us were enamored," he said, "and so if we're going to do it why don't we do it as professional societies". With this discussion, IFIP embarked on the path that would lead it to its present organizational structure. At the same time, they did not abandon UNESCO nor did UNESCO entirely abandon them. It is clear from their early actions, that they appreciated their connections with UNESCO and were grateful for some of the things that the agency had done for them [4]. They regularly praised their early contact at UNESCO, Jean Mussard, and followed his advice [13]. Most notably, Mussard helped IFIP build connections with the International Council of Scientific Unions and to get consultative status within UNESCO [15]. In later years, UNESCO would provide funds, help organizations technical meetings, and support the work of the IFIP Technical Committee on Education, TC-3 [30].

In the work of strengthening its organization, the IFIP board was closely assisted by Mussard and other UNESCO personnel. In particular, UNESCO encouraged many a country to organize a professional society for computing [12]. He also helped IFIP win a financial support from UNESCO and build cooperative relations with other international groups, notably, the International Council Of Scientific Unions or the Union Of International Engineering Organizations, (a precursor to the UN Federation of Engineering Organizations). Mussard urged the IFIP Board "to one of these two large nongovernmental organizations, as this would facilitate formal relations with UNESCO and ensure a link with other international scientific organizations" [13].

In its early days, IFIP underscored its commitment to that scientific idealism. At its first meeting, the group selected Alwin Walther (1989–1967) as its vice president. During the second world war, Walther had stood in mirror image to Auerbach and the ENIAC team. He had led computing at the Technische Hochschule in Darmstadt, Germany. This was the major computer organization at the time. He had led both teams of human computers and the development of new automatic computing machinery. Among other things, this group had done the ballistics and targeting calculations for the V-2 rocket. He was declared to be a person of interest in the waning days of the war and was captured (in what appears to have been a fairly friendly manner) by the British mathematician John Todd. Todd had run the computing operation for the British Navy during the war and, in May 1945, had been given the assignment of seizing the Third Reich's computing assets [11, 29].

4   First Steps as an International Organization

Beginning in 1960, IFIP took the first steps that any organization has to make. They had to establish their legal existence and legitimacy, secure themselves, and determine what they were going to do. All of these activities were shaped by the form of governance that they chose. As a professional organization, they decided that they would be a membership organization. The members would be professional societies and that they would accept no more than one member from each country. (As the organization evolved, they would make an exception for the United States, which had multiple professional organizations for computing.)

The initial organizational structure of IFIP challenged the plans of the board. They had decided to incorporate their organization in Belgium, which had become a center for international and trans-European scientific work that was symbolized by the Atomium, the iconic structure that represented the 1958 Brussels World's Fair. The Belgian government seemed to be pleased to provide a home to IFIP but felt the organization did not meet the requirements set forth in the Belgian incorporation law. In particular, Belgian law required all members of a federation, such as IFIP, would be "duly incorporated" entities. It was far from clear that all the founding organizations would meet this requirement, much less those that they might wish to admit in the future. This issue would be eventually resolved, but it would suggest some of the challenges that IFIP would have in the future [13].

To plan for the future, the IFIP board would have to secure the future of the organization. Securing the future of IFIP meant expanding the number of organizations. The first meeting of its board, in 1960, was attended by the representatives of ten societies. Not all of these groups were professional computing organizations. The Spanish representative, for example, came from the government Higher Council of Scientific Research. (Consejo Superior di Investigaciones Cientificas.) To build its membership, IFIP would have to identify real and potential professional societies, help them meet the organizational requirements and encourage them to apply. Through 1970, this remained an important task for the board. The board received regular reports about organizations that might be ready to apply, those that actually applied and those that were accepted to membership.

Auerbach, who served as the first president of IFIP, was concerned with both the position of IFIP in the computing community and its relationships to other organizations. He told the board that "many external bodies come into existence in our vast field and that they impinge into our domain of interest". He added that IFIP "must develop suitable policies to take care of this situation, otherwise the status and the influence of IFIP will gradually diminish" [18].

5   Strategy and Structure

Beyond the task of securing the future IFIP, the board had to plan what the organization would actually do. In the classic theories of administrative behavior, structure follows strategy, an organization decides what it needs to do and then creates a structure that will accomplish that goal [9]. IFIP seems to have followed that pattern to a certain extent. As it identified new tasks, it created technical committees to undertake those tasks and constantly modified the structure of those committees in order to make them effective.

At the same time, the IFIP leadership was trying to identify the things that the group could do and could do well. It did not have a lot of models to follow [28]. Perhaps the best antecedent of the group could be found in the International Statistical Congresses of the 19th and early 20th centuries. These congresses met to standardize statistical practice and to develop common definitions of data and statistics. However, it seems unlikely that the IFIP founders were aware of these congresses. Furthermore, these meetings had a strong governmental component. The true successor to these congresses, the Organization for Economic Cooperation and Development, was founded at roughly the same time as IFIP and was a true intergovernmental organization.

From the start, the IFIP leadership had one clear goal, to sponsor a regular conference on the subject of computing [3]. It had begun planning of these conferences (following the 1959 Paris conference) as part of the work to build the IFIP organization. Beyond that goal, the board felt that IFIP should be involved in other activities but was unsure about what those activities should be. At its second meeting, the board decided that the organization would publish a bulletin containing articles "of information on meetings, professional societies, etc., but no scientific articles". It also created a technical committee "on the Standardization of Terminology and Symbols". This committee would soon produce a glossary of computing terms, a glossary that dealt with the not insignificant problem of the differences between British and American terms. However, it would take 18 months for the committee to find its place in the organization [14].

IFIP first had to deal with how this committee would fit into the international standards regime. For the most part, the International Organization for Standardization (ISO) takes standards that have been developed by a national standards organization and helps them get international support. However, IFIP was not a national organization and needed a plan to get its work before the ISO. Furthermore, it needed a broader base from which to develop its ideas. To make progress towards both goals, the committee developed a partnership with the International Computing Center (ICC).

The ICC was a UN sanctioned agency that offered computing time to organizations from countries that lacked adequate computing facilities. Conceived in 1952, it had created a facility in Rome and begun operations in 1960. At a time when universities did not have computer science departments, computer centers were often a site of technical research and development. The MIT Computation Center, for example, had developed a pioneering timesharing operating system in the late 1950s and early 1960s. It was expected that the ICC would play a similar role [21–23].

The collaboration between IFIP and the ICC was genuine and, perhaps, effectual but it was not long lasting [19]. After changing the name of its technical committee to be "Joint IFIP-ICC Terminology Committee" in 1961, it reverted the name of the committee to "Committee on Terminology and Symbols" with the added designation of TC-1 in 1962 [16]. The group finished its work in 1964 but as it did so, it revealed some of the structural challenges faced by IFIP. Auerbach noted that the committee had undergone substantial changes and that "little work is getting done at the present time". He said that the "chairman and other members have moved to other countries, and regrettably some have not replied to correspondence or even to telephone communication" [20].

IFIP would face this problem regularly in its history. It would set goals and then struggle to keep a committee working to achieve those goals. In part, this problem also came from the fact IFIP was not really a representative body. Though it was clearly influenced by its members, it set its agenda independently, as most international organizations do. International Organizations "can become autonomous sites of authority, independent from the state 'principals' who may have created them," note scholars of these organizations [7]. Rather than doing the things that their members have decided that the organization should do, these groups tend to identify activities that their members are not doing or cannot do. They then attempt to complete their activities utilizing individuals that come from their member organizations. This challenge was most clearly seen when IFIP decided to support the development of the ALGOL.

ALGOL was an important project in the early years of computer science and established a pattern of work that would be repeated throughout the history of computing. It was one of the first computing languages, along with languages such as Fortran and Cobol. Unlike those two languages, which were developed by a private corporation and the US Department of Defense respectively, ALGOL was created by a volunteer international committee. It grew out of a 1958 conference that had been jointly sponsored by the Association for Computing Machinery and the German Gesellschaft für Angewandte Mathematik und Mechanik, two groups that would be represented on the IFIP board.

From its founding, the ALGOL project was coordinated by the ALGOL Bulletin, a newsletter that was supported by the Danish Government and edited by Peter Naur, a Danish computer scientist. The aim of the Algol Bulletin, Naur wrote, "will be to act partly as a correspondence column for the active members of the [ALGOL Development Group], and partly as an instrument for making agreements" [24]. In 1962, IFIP agreed to take responsibility for ALGOL and created a new technical committee to support it. "The Working Group has been mainly set up to establish an authoritative body which can serve as a home for ALGOL," reported Naur. "The incentive for this was derived from a request of ACM to IFIP" [25].

From our current perspective, ALGOL was an early example of a collaborative or open source project. Like IFIP, it had no real example or model to follow. IFIP treated it like a standardization project and was generally successful in completing the first task it undertook, creating a portable subset of the language [17]. This subset represented an admission by those involved with the project that the language had overly ambitious goals. The "generality of some of the features of ALGOL 60 and the disagreement concerning the exact meaning of others have proved a considerable discouragement to some of the groups who have contemplated implementing the language," reported Naur, "and have caused most of the existing implementations to be based on subsets defined locally" [26].

The ALGOL subset proved to be reasonably successful but subsequent efforts reve-lated the challenges that IFIP faced as a language development organization in the early 1960s. Again, from our current standpoint, we know that such development is best done with rapid feedback, when a group is able to posit questions, suggest answers to those questions, and assess those potential answers within a short period of time. Naur identi-fied it as "the principle of feedback in well-adjusted systems." At this period, IFIP was simply not able to maintain that kind of process [27].

Auerbach, as President, seemed to grasp that IFIP faced some special challenges as a organization. It was, after all, a tertiary organization. The volunteer workers, the people who served on technical committees, were not employees of IFIP they were not employees of the organizations represented in the IFIP leadership but were volunteers to those organizations. At one meeting, Auerbach recognized this challenge and "pleaded that IFIP can only perform its several duties if all committee members who have accepted assignments will carry these out promptly and carefully" [14].

In 1964, after the group had completed three full years of operation and had five years of experience, the leadership realized that it needed to think clearly and carefully about the kind of organization it could be and the kinds of things that it could do. It created a "Futures Plans Committee" to consider how IFIP should work with other organizations and "with the important question of how IFIP should be organized in the future". It even raised the question of whether the organization should run a single large conference. "It may be possible," Auerbach explained to the group, "that the Congress 65 is the last congress of its kind, and that we will have to hold meetings on a smaller scale" [18].

6   The Organization You Have and the Organization You Desire

Auerbach and the other founders created IFIP over roughly a ten-year period that started at a 1955 Joint Computer Conference in the United States and ended with Auerbach stepped down from the presidency in 1965. If we take his reminiscences at face value, we would conclude that IFIP proved to be the kind of organization that Auerbach hoped to create. It is an international body. It cooperates closely with UNESCO. It actively disseminates information about international computing activities. Finally, it bases its legitimacy on professional societies and not nation-states, an activity that was hard to accomplish given the direction that UNESCO was moving in the mid 1950s.

Yet, these descriptions only illustrate the structure of the organization and do not describe what it does or how it operates. While such issues need a fuller and more detailed analysis, we can get at least a first hint about those operations from its annual reports and its celebratory books. It is certainly an independent organization that sets its own agenda. It certainly takes advice from its members but it largely deals with questions that are international in scope, questions that may or may not directly affect national organizations. It has learned that there are some things that it can do well and some things that are more challenging [8, 31, 32].

At almost every point in its history, IFIP has had to confront the same questions that Auerbach and the founders faced in late 1960s. "Is its current organization structure the correct structure for our time?" and "What are the activities that it can do best?" These questions are all the more urgent because IFIP itself is being affected by the forces of globalization that it helped unleash. At least three of its members and one of its former members operate globally. They hold conferences outside their national borders, they publish globally, and they build international standards. Only IFIP can determine if its organizational structure is still relevant, if these other organizations are going to become the dominant international organizations or if there is yet a new organization that we do not yet understand that will be an improvement on what we have seen to date.

Three years into his term as president, Auerbach recognized some of the basic questions that IFIP was facing at the time and would face in the future. Addressing the leadership he needed that there might be "external bodies that come into existence in our vast field" and "impinge into our domain of interest," he told the IFIP leadership. "We must develop suitable policies to take care of this situation, otherwise the status and the influence of IFIP will gradually diminish (Report on Second Council Meeting 1961). Auerbach and the others built a successful professional organization at a time when UNESCO was discouraging that model. As with all organizational leaders, the next generation of leadership will face questions equally vexing as they move IFIP into the future.

References

1. Aspray, W., Williams, B.: "Arming American scientists: NSF and the provision of scientific computing, facilities for universities, 1950–1973". Ann. Hist. Comput. **16**(4), 60–74 (1994)
2. Auerbach, I.: A static magnetic memory system for the ENIAC. In: Proceedings of the 1952 ACM National Meeting (Pittsburgh), pp. 213–222, May 1952
3. Auerbach, I.: Just as bridges are made of wood. CACM **8**(11), p. 656, November 1965
4. Auerbach, I.: Oral History, Charles Babbage Institute, April 10 1978. https://conservancy.umn.edu/handle/11299/59495
5. Auerbach, I.: Personal recollections on the origin of IFIP. In: Zemanek, H. (ed.) A Quarter Century of IFIP. North Holland, Amsterdam (1986)
6. Auerbach, I.: Oral History, Charles Babbage Institute, 2–3 October 1992. https://conservancy.umn.edu/handle/11299/104351
7. Barnett, M.N., Finnemore, M.: "The politics, power, and pathologies of international organizations". In: International Organization, Vol. 53, No. 4, pp. 699–732, Autumn (1999)

8. Brunnstein, K., Zemanek, H. (eds): 50 Years of IFIP - Developments and Visions, IFIP, Laxenburg (2010)
9. Chandler, A.: Strategy and Structure, MIT Press, Cambridge (1962)
10. Cohen, I. B.: Howard Aiken: Portrait of a Computer Pioneer. MIT Press, Cambridge (1999)
11. de Beauclair, W.: Alwin Walther, IPM, and the development of calculator/computer technology in Germany 1930–1945. Ann. Hist. Comput. **8**(4), 334–350, October (1986)
12. Finnemore, M.: International organizations as teachers of norms: the united nations educational, scientific, and cultural organization and science policy. In: International Organization, vol. 47, no. 4, pp. 565–597. Autumn (1993)
13. IFIP 1960, Report on First Council Meeting (1960). https://www.ifip.org//images/stories/ifip/public/Archive/MinHist/1960%20council%20jun%20rome%20(it).pdf
14. IFIP 1961a, Report on Second Council Meeting (1961). https://www.ifip.org//images/stories/ifip/public/Archive/MinHist/1961%20council-1%20feb%20darmstadt%20(ge).pdf
15. IFIP 1961b, Report on Third Council Meeting (1961). https://www.ifip.org//images/stories/ifip/public/Archive/MinHist/1961%20council-2%20oct%20copenhagen%20(dk).pdf
16. IFIP 1962a, Report on Fourth Council Meeting (1962). https://www.ifip.org//images/stories/ifip/public/Archive/MinHist/1962%20council-1%20mar%20munich%20(ge).pdf
17. IFIP 1962b, Report on Fifth Council Meeting (1962). https://www.ifip.org//images/stories/ifip/public/Archive/MinHist/1962%20council-2%20aug%20munich%20(ge)%20.pdf
18. IFIP 1963, Report on Sixth Council Meeting (1963). https://www.ifip.org//images/stories/ifip/public/Archive/MinHist/1963%20council%20sep%20gola%20(no).pdf
19. IFIP 1964a, Report on Seventh Council Meeting (1964). https://www.ifip.org//images/stories/ifip/public/Archive/MinHist/1964%20council-1%20may%20prague%20(cz).pdf
20. IFIP 1964b, Report on Eighth Council Meeting (1964). https://www.ifip.org//images/stories/ifip/public/Archive/MinHist/1964%20council-2%20nov%20rome%20(it).pdf
21. Informations Statistiques 1958, Revue de l'Institut International de Statistique, vol. 26, no. 1/3, pp. 163–166 (1958)
22. International Computation Centre 1952, *Current Science*, vol. 21, no. 2, p. 36, February 1952
23. International Laboratories for Research 1952, Current Science, vol. 21, no. 7, p. 36, July 1952
24. Naur, P.: ALGOL Bulletin, vol. 1, 16 March 1959
25. Naur, P.: ALGOL Bulletin, 15 June 1962
26. Naur, P.: ALGOL Bulletin, 16 May 1964
27. Naur, P.: ALGOL Bulletin, 28 July 1968
28. OECD 2011: A majestic start: how the OECD was won. In: OECD Yearbook 2011, OECD Observer, Paris (2011)
29. Todd, J.: Applied Mathematics Research in Germany with Particular Reference to Naval Applications, British Intelligence Objectives Subcommittee, His Majesty Stationers Office, London (1946)
30. Watson, D.: Computers and education – a landscape. In: Brunnstein, K., Zemanek, H. (eds.) 50 Years of IFIP - Developments and Visions. IFIP, Laxenburg (2010)
31. Zemanek, H. (ed.) A Quarter Century of IFIP, North Holland, Amsterdam (1986)
32. Zemanek, H. (ed.) IFIP Leads into the Future (1996)

The Role of National, Regional and International Professional ICT Bodies

Roger Johnson[1] and Leon Strous[2(✉)]

[1] School of Computer Science and Information Systems, Birkbeck University of London,
Malet Street, London WC1E 7HX, UK
rgj@dcs.bbk.ac.uk
[2] Gistel 20, Helmond, The Netherlands
strous@iae.nl

Abstract. National, regional and international professional ICT societies, associations and federations have played important roles in the past in advancing the computing field. The ways these roles can be fulfilled and the ways these bodies are organized depend on the state of technology and of society in general. Technological and societal developments make it necessary for these bodies to evolve, both in their roles and in their structure. This chapter is addressing challenges facing ICT societies and opportunities for change.

Keywords: ICT societies · Professional ICT bodies · IFIP · Regional associations · Global associations · Federations

1 Introduction

In his chapter in this book, David Alan Grier describes how Isaac Auerbach fulfilled his vision for an international body built on national representative computer bodies with a mission to promote the use of what today we would refer to as Information and Communication Technology (ICT) through the advancement of the technology and the dissemination of knowledge about it.

The purpose of this chapter is to look at some aspects of what has happened since those early years. It will focus primarily on the role of the national, regional and global bodies with which IFIP interacts either as its members or as external agencies. It does not look in detail at the contribution to IFIP of the individual computer scientists and other ICT professionals. Our approach will be essentially thematic rather than chronological since the development of professional ICT bodies has been influenced by changes to many different factors in a rapidly changing world.

For example, many of the professional ICT bodies which are the focus of this chapter were only being founded around 1960 and exist today in a world where communication has been transformed by, for example, high bandwidth digital links, cheap air travel and the elimination of many earlier political barriers enabling researchers and practitioners to travel and communicate freely across the globe. Again, since the 1960s, there have been

© IFIP International Federation for Information Processing 2020
Published by Springer Nature Switzerland AG 2020
L. Strous et al. (Eds.): Unimagined Futures, IFIP AICT 555, pp. 188–199, 2020.
https://doi.org/10.1007/978-3-030-64246-4_15

dramatic changes in the power of computer processor technology, latterly combined with high bandwidth digital communications, to create application systems with capabilities that were at best science fiction in the 1960s if envisaged at all.

Looking back over 60 years it is clear that the decision to finally adopt the name International Federation for Information Processing (IFIP) rather than the earlier International Federation of Information Processing Societies (IFIPS), was well judged in that it focused on the motivation for IFIP's endeavor, promoting the effective processing of information worldwide, rather than either the nature of IFIP's membership or the technologies employed to undertake information processing.

2   Ambitions and Goals

When a professional society is founded, it has to decide on what role it wants to play. It has to define ambitions and translate these into goals, strategies and activities. During its lifetime each society has to regularly evaluate this and decide how it wants and needs to evolve. In this section we describe such an evolution with IFIP as an example but similar evolutions have taken place in other societies, including IFIP's members.

2.1   Initial Ambitions

The founding President, Isaac Auerbach, records that the initial idea for IFIP occurred to him during a break at a conference late in 1955 [2]. From then it took nearly four years of determined negotiating to reach the point on January 1st 1960 when thirteen national technical bodies came together to form IFIP. The founding statutes of the International Federation of Information Processing Societies, dated 6 July 1959 state:
Name and Aims, article 1.

An International Federation of Information Processing Societies shall be constituted in order to achieve the following basic aims:

a) *Sponsor international conferences and symposia on information processing, including mathematical and engineering aspects.*
b) *Establish international committees to undertake special tasks falling within the spheres of action of the member societies.*
c) *Advance the interests of member societies in international cooperation in the field of information processing.*

Given the focus in this chapter on the role of IFIP and IFIP's membership, it is worth spending a moment examining each of these aims in turn from a member body's perspective.

The first aim, the sponsoring of international events about information processing, is an obvious aim for a global organization such as IFIP although the concerns of some early groups about the scope of "information processing" can be detected by the inclusion of the words "including mathematical and engineering aspects". IFIP conferences were not to be focused only on practitioner events such as the large trade fairs which were popular at the time but also to include events addressing the needs of researchers and academics as well. Since the 1960s trade shows in ICT have diminished in importance and IFIP's remaining conferences and congresses are mostly conventional academic events aimed primarily at individual researchers rather than the broader membership of national ICT bodies.

The second aim is less clear-cut because it depends on the "spheres of actions" of the member societies. It is on the one hand easy on the other hand more difficult to crystalize. If we take the ACM as an example of such a member society we can read on the history pages of the ACM website that: *"The original notice for the September 15, 1947 organization meeting stated in part: The purpose of this organization would be to advance the science, development, construction, and application of the new machinery for computing, reasoning, and other handling of information."* [1]. Conferences and symposia are one way to achieve such advances, so the easy part of achieving IFIP's second aim of was the creation of Technical Committees and Working Groups, doing (scientific) research and organizing events (and is thus linked to the first aim). The clause enabled IFIP's member societies to set up committees to carry out joint endeavours although the historic record shows that these have been few in number.

Looking at the early history of IFIP it is clear that the volunteer leadership in the 1960s were very close to their member societies, as Presidents or holders of other senior leadership roles in their home countries and that as a result there was a close alignment of the objectives of the member societies and the activities undertaken under the IFIP umbrella. For example, the United States were represented by Isaac Auerbach, the nominee of the American Federation of Information Processing Societies (AFIPS) while the UK was represented by the founding President of the British Computer Society, Maurice Wilkes. The Soviet Union was represented by a leading Russian academician Anatoli Dorodnicyn from the Soviet Academy of Sciences. NB: it should be noted that throughout the history of IFIP many officers and GA representatives were presidents or officers in their societies.

2.2   IFIP's Evolving Mission

Since the first version of the statutes and set of goals and ambitions, IFIP has regularly updated them following developments in technology and society but also as a consequence of the growth of the federation. The mission statement, although sometimes rephrased, has in essence remained the same: "The International Federation for Information Processing (IFIP) is a global non-profit federation of societies of ICT professionals. It aims to achieve the worldwide professional and socially responsible development and application of information and communication technologies" [7]. In 2013 IFIP, after lengthy discussion, adopted a set of Strategic Aims which state that IFIP provides a global platform to:

1. **Advance information and communication technologies (ICT)** by supporting the advancement of knowledge, fostering excellence in research and development, organizing international events, disseminating high quality ICT related information through a variety of appropriate means, promoting the adoption of global standards, supporting policies that stimulate research.

2. **Advance the responsible application of ICT**, by promoting responsible use of ICT, awareness of ethical issues, robust international legal frameworks, public understanding of ICT, providing policy statements on socially relevant topics and developments.
3. **Advance the role, position and effectiveness of professional ICT societies**, by sharing knowledge, experiences and good practices, advocating the role of its member societies, providing opinions on important developments, cooperating in activities, acting as the representative global body for societies of individual ICT professionals.
4. **Advance professionalism in ICT**, by appropriate bodies of knowledge for ICT practitioners, common skills and competencies frameworks, accreditation and certification, high quality ICT education, life long learning.
5. **Advance digital equity**, by promoting accessibility of ICT, promoting good practices, promoting and enhancing appropriate access to knowledge and experiences, organizing and contributing to activities aimed at achieving the UN Millennium Development Goals (MDGs) and the goals of the World Summit on the Information Society (WSIS).

The 2013 list appears challenging given IFIP's three members of staff and a large body of volunteers just a small proportion of whom ever meet other than to discuss issues related directly to their area of technical expertise.

This paper will argue that a close alignment of IFIP's activities with the objectives of the member societies has a track record of success at delivering successful outcomes. But there are also challenges and while these have been there from the start and will probably always be there, in the following sections we will reflect on some challenges that need to be addressed faster and perhaps in a more fundamental way due to the speed of changes and the impact of some changes.

There is little doubt that, with maybe a few exceptions, other societies face similar challenges. We will also make some suggestions to address the challenges and increase the capacity and impact of professional societies.

3   Challenges

3.1   Resources

One of the ironies of the position in which IFIP finds itself today is a direct consequence of the revolutionary changes brought about by the information processing technology which IFIP has been promoting. Even in 1965 when 5,000 delegates from 35 countries attended the best ever attended IFIP World Computer Congress in New York or in 1974 in Stockholm when 4,300 delegates from 55 countries attended, the global reach implicit in the agenda set out in 2013 would have seemed an impossible dream.

However, the development of ICT in the intervening years and especially the coming of the internet, which facilitated the creation of social media, has resulted in even individual bloggers aspiring to influence agendas worldwide. Nonetheless undertaking significant work programs depends on the generation of resources to match the ambition.

If IFIP and ICT societies in general are to continue to "make a difference" then they need skills at capacity building. Over the years the authors have witnessed good ideas not taken up because of their feasibility being unfavorable given the available resources in terms of time and money. Perhaps not surprisingly, these resources, especially busy volunteers, can only provide very limited capacity for innovation. To achieve common goals, partnering with other organizations of all types has become more and more essential.

Financial resources for an ICT society typically come from membership fees, publications, events and sponsorships. Many societies and federations struggle to increase or even retain membership. It is harder nowadays to convince individuals and societies that membership of a professional body pays off. Employers are less willing to pay membership fees for their employees or allow them to spend time on activities. Publications are also moving in the direction of open access. Pressure from national and international funding agencies for scientific research is showing results. If publications are free to read, the business model for publishers must change which has an effect on their income. Events have grown in number, making it difficult to financially break-even or make a profit. Concerning sponsorship we face the fact that organizations that have sponsored activities financially and in kind in the past have changed over time. These changes include financial means and priorities. For instance UN agencies in the past could fund activities but that has become more and more problematic because these agencies depend in turn on financing by member countries and in some cases UN agencies now depend on sponsorship for their own activities.

This also applies to governmental support. The series of World IT Forum (WITFOR) conferences have been major successes which has done much to advance the understanding of the practical contribution of ICT in developing regions with an array of national leaders and government ministers from around the globe. An essential component in the success of each WITFOR conference has been that each host was the national government. They have provided substantial human and material resources – not least world class conference facilities. However, in the latest editions this support had decreased compared with the earlier events, due to changes in the economic situation and hence the priorities of the governments involved. The organizational burden imposed on a tiny number of IFIP shoulders has proved to be difficult to sustain. Perhaps as a result, the objective of leaving legacy projects in the host countries and their neighbors has proven to be very difficult.

The IFIP Digital Library (DL) project has been a technical success insofar as having a working digital library providing leading edge technical material on a free to read basis [6]. Today all IFIP books published by Springer between 2010 and 2017 are available free to download from the IFIP DL. This is a major achievement and provides a valuable resource to researchers as well as adding significantly to IFIP's visibility and reputation. This is the result of a collaboration between IFIP, its publisher Springer and the French national scientific research institute, INRIA. While IFIP has funded on a project basis the setting up of the DL and the creation of the initial content, maintaining the DL on a free to read (and upload) basis requires a new business model.

The IFIP International Professional Practice Partnership (IP3) was founded in 2007 as a partnership of a number of IFIP Full Members: ACS (Australian Computer Society),

BCS (British Computer Society), CIPS (Canadian Information Processing Society) and the IEEE Computer Society joined in 2009 by three further societies, Information Processing Society of Japan (IPSJ), and what are today called the Institute of Information Technology Professionals South Africa (IITPSA) and Institute of Information Processing New Zealand (IITPNZ). Together they set as their goal the creation of a global ICT profession held in the same respect as the older professions, such as accountants or the medical profession. As a global profession this included the ultimate goal of providing mobility of professionals guaranteed by WTO agreement. Johnson gives an account of the early years of IP3 [8]. This project continues to grow slowly by attracting new member societies. Of particular interest for this section of the chapter is to note, in looking at IP3's progress, the substantial initial investment made by the founding member societies and IFIP and also the substantial support in kind from the member societies and from corporates in pursuit of a shared ambition. Preserving the achievements of IP3 and taking them to the next level requires an improved business model.

The lesson which we take away from these examples is the vital importance of effective and timely capacity building to support projects. This is a challenge not only for IFIP but for many of its member societies. Membership based ICT societies need to build consortia to resource and, moreover, sustain major activities. Corporate bodies can provide very substantial support when a project aligns with their corporate objectives. For other projects, national governments and inter-governmental and non-governmental organizations can all make substantial resources available. Last but not least, teaming-up with each other can help societies reach their goals. Experience has demonstrated that IFIP's member societies will deploy significant resources including finance and skilled staff members if a project is seen to be of sufficient importance to them. To be a major player on the ICT policy world stage resources need to be leveraged, while guarding independence. Partners are needed as well as models for sharing management responsibilities for the activities with partners.

3.2 The Challenges to Membership Based Societies

In the past sixty years both the world of information processing and the world in which that processing is undertaken have been radically changed in ways that would have been unimaginable for the founders.

Information processing is the construction and operation of application software which run on the computers which result from the work of the material scientists and electronic engineers. Many of today's ICT industrial giants began, actually or metaphorically, in garages and attics. Certainly most have grown from tiny start-ups to global giants in much less than a human lifetime and that of IFIP.

Looking at the organizations which form the membership of IFIP, they can almost all be characterized as having one of two primary focuses. Some see their major role as fulfilling the global need of researchers and academics to present papers at conferences and to publish papers in journals. Others have focused on supporting largescale users of traditional ICT such as finance, commerce and government where the development of innovative products delivered by new software applications remains paramount. Member societies have often developed packages to support career development and the certifications of specific skills achieved by individual practitioners. User skills certification and supporting and sustaining the ICT skills of school teachers have also proved commercially valuable for some IFIP members. Programs of this type have generated substantial income for their societies as well as providing useful help to the industry.

Member societies need to sustain their membership numbers to survive. This provides a rather blunt but easily understood measure of success. In order to do so they have turned to professional managers to run the society on behalf of the membership. Those societies who derive their membership by providing services to the research and academic communities have generally had an easier time in managing their membership as the longstanding pattern of conferences and scientific publications survives. However, as already pointed out under the challenges of resources, events and publications are also facing changes that might have a big impact on the resources, activities and attractiveness of professional societies. The numbers of events and publications keep increasing partly because of the way academic performance is measured, namely by counting publications in conference proceedings and journals. It is widely acknowledged that this endangers the quality and hence attractiveness of events and publications. Another consequence of the growing number of events is the difficulty of attracting sufficient participants who are neither authors nor presenters and the efforts to have a financially viable event. This has been exacerbated for many young academics by decreasing support from their institutions due to pressure on many higher education budgets globally.

Societies devoted primarily to the promotion of the concept of professionalism and a long-term objective of giving information processing professionals the same status as older professions are having a much harder time. In a world in which in most countries there is no control on the use of any computer related job title and no limitation on who can undertake various specified ICT jobs, unlike in engineering, medicine or accountancy, professional membership is a "hard sell". Organizations when recruiting staff largely rely on an individual ICT practitioner's proven track record rather than an individual's membership of a professional body in the absence of any statutory requirements.

IFIP was founded by a group of ICT societies and today many membership bodies of all types are facing big challenges, in some cases existential ones, and it is clearly in the interests of everyone interested in promoting ICT in society that we all work together to overcome the challenges and take advantage of the new opportunities opening up for us.

3.3   Regional Associations

A reaction to the growth in the numbers working in ICT as well as to the simultaneous emergence of regional political bodies has been the creation of three regional ICT bodies linking a variety of societies and other stakeholders in the field of information processing [3–5].

The earliest of these was the South East Asian Regional Computer Confederation (SEARCC), held its first regional conference in Singapore in 1976 with sponsorship from IFIP. They have continued to hold major regional conferences ever since. For the participants these conferences offer the benefit of being comparatively close and can be focused on regional issues with top regional keynote speakers. IFIP assisted SEARCC in obtaining UNESCO support for its early conferences and the good relations engendered led to SEARCC membership within IFIP.

The next regional body that became member of IFIP was the Centro Latinoamericano de Estudios en Informatica (CLEI) which had been founded in 1974. CLEI joined in 1984. It has held a major annual regional conference since 1986.

The final regional body that joined until now is the Council of European Professional Informatics Societies (CEPIS) founded in 1989 by 9 European informatics societies. The original motivation for the foundation of CEPIS was to create a pan-European organization who could address the European Commission on matters of interest to the CEPIS membership. CEPIS has always emphasized the raising of the competence and integrity of ICT professionals and users of ICT.

Regional associations have faced and are facing the challenges with respect to membership, resources and activities. A specific challenge for regional associations is to formulate and advocate in a timely way policy statements on topical developments and plans, both legislative and funding programs, of political bodies such as the European Commission or APAC. If the ICT professionals want to be heard by politicians, this is an important challenge to address.

While online webinars have attracted global audiences they have also highlighted the problem arising from the clock of trying to run global organizations. As many businesses have recognized the eight hour working day suggests at least three natural groupings based on time zones. While individuals may be willing to get up early or go to bed late, practical experience suggests even online events should probably be provided on a regional basis offering opportunities for IFIP's regional partners and others to offer activities widely within their time zones.

IFIP has from time to time held regional events, usually in conjunction with local IFIP members. We believe now is the time to develop a coherent strategy to work regionally. The authors have experience of very small societies whose total annual income may not cover a return flight and hotel room to attend a General Assembly. Regional partnerships may have the potential to bridge the gulf that sometimes exists.

While global events may be successful in attracting leading academics for specialist events, it can be observed that attracting practitioners on a global scale has become more difficult. Events aiming to address issues of relevance to information processing practitioners need to be held close to their potential audience.

3.4 Communications, Control and Accountability

Societies and federations that have a realistic ambition to contribute to the development of information processing and to make IT good for society need an organizational structure which is agile and inclusive of the views of their members. The technology that societies and federations like IFIP exist to promote can do much to facilitate the communication needed to gain engagement from the membership.

While a meeting every Spring of the Executive Committee and Board and each autumn of the Executive Committee and General Assembly, may be adequate to manage the affairs of an organization running 30–40 events each year delivered by semi-autonomous technical committees and working groups, it is not effective in the 21st century at managing a program involving multiple stakeholders.

During the recent COVID-19 pandemic, ICT has been put at the center not just of the working lives of healthcare workers but of millions of ordinary people restricted to their own homes who have become regular users of the various video communication packages to maintain contact with family and friends as well as work. This abrupt introduction is likely to continue once the pandemic passes. Organizations of every conceivable sort have arranged online "meetings". In addition, the technology abolishes distance as an inhibitor to communication. Hence many groups have found their virtual talks, tours and religious services "attended" by participants from around the globe. The next big challenge will be whether there is some sort of business model to provide the modest income streams needed to provide what until now have been free offerings.

Organizational structures determine the speed of decision making within the organization. When meetings that make key decisions happen infrequently it is very hard to build up momentum to move projects forward at speed.

The challenge to IFIP is to communicate its program to the leadership within IFIP's member societies much faster and more frequently. When groups of society Presidents or CEOs attend IFIP World Computer Congresses they often immediately recognize how much they have in common with each other. The challenge for IFIP is to maintain and develop the relationships. Presidents often change annually while CEOs can be extremely busy and not necessarily involved in setting the strategy for their own societies. Consequently the relationship with member societies falls back on the General Assembly representatives whose access to the leadership of their societies in many cases may be less frequent than would be desirable.

4   The Way Forward

With all the challenges mentioned one might wonder whether there is a future role for volunteer societies. And by volunteer societies we also mean societies with substantial staff but still to a large extent depending on the activities of volunteers. We believe there is definitely a future and a role and we give some suggestions for the first three strategic aims mentioned in Sect. 2.2. Although these aims are derived from the IFIP documentation, most professional bodies, including the IFIP member societies, will have a similar set. For the last two strategic aims, advance professionalism in ICT and advance digital equity, we refer to the separate chapters in this book.

4.1   Advance Information and Communication Technologies (ICT)

Scientific conferences and publications are a solid base for many professional societies and we believe these activities contribute significantly to the advancement of ICT. Researchers and professionals participate in working groups, technical committees and other types of communities for sharing their work and thoughts. As pointed out in Sect. 3, the numbers of events and publications keep increasing and that is causing concerns with respect to attractiveness, reputation and financial viability.

We see two ways to address this. Firstly, increase cooperation with other societies and for regional and global associations or federations to engage more with member societies. It will be beneficial to work more closely together in starting and organizing activities. Secondly, ICT societies could engage in discussions about potentially other or additional ways to measure academic performance.

Given the huge number of conferences and journals, it is important to decide what is going to be achieved with each event or activity. Clarity and consistency are crucial for the reputation and attractiveness of events. Organizers need to clearly describe and advertise what it is that they want to achieve (goal / objective; type of activity; type of audience / participants; ambition level; potential partners). It should be clear whether an event or group is aiming at top level scientific contributions, or a meeting to engage students and younger professionals in for instance summer (or winter) school type of gatherings, whether a group is a more closed community or fully open, etc.

Another pitfall for ICT societies with respect to events can be bureaucratic processes to get ideas accepted for new activities. It is all too easy to surrender the initial advantage by discussions about the boundaries between existing groups. As mentioned earlier in this chapter, structure and organization should follow the goals and facilitate fast and easy decision making. While 60 years ago it was possible to take one or even two years to decide on new activities, this is no longer an option. A body that doesn't respond speedily to new developments risks becoming obsolete. A society is no different from a commercial company in this respect. With the new communication facilities faster decision making should be no problem. COVID-19 has demonstrated that this can work. And it is not only about starting new activities, the same applies to ending unsuccessful activities and groups much faster and re-engaging volunteers on other activities.

4.2   Advance the Responsible Application of ICT

This strategic aim has great potential for major wins in terms of added value, visibility and reputation. However it depends on societies being able to build a reputation for producing timely and well informed commentary on global hot topics.

As IFIP's strategic aims recognize, in an era of ubiquitous ICT, there is potential for both great benefits and great harm from technologies and their application. As a result there is great public interest in many aspects of ICT. In order to be successful in advancing the responsible application of ICT, societies' organizational structures, governance and mandates need to be in place to entrust small groups of experts on various current and emerging topics to decide on a response and rapidly distribute public statements.

It is important to identify key concerns on which to develop policy statements which can be approved and placed prominently on the IFIP website and published elsewhere. This has to be accompanied by a thorough marketing and media plan. Many of IFIP's member societies spend significant resources on public relations but raising the profile of an organization such as IFIP requires a substantial sustained effort. At the outset IFIP will need to decide why it wishes to raise its profile and who it wishes to influence.

4.3   Advance the Role, Position and Effectiveness of ICT Societies

A major added value of associations and federations of professional societies is learning from each other and sharing experiences. While not everything can be copied one-on-one because of national specificities, both failures and successes are often applicable to more than one society. It is also potentially informative for IFIP to broker international studies of topics which are of interest around the world such as the proportion of women working in ICT. Some member societies publish studies within their own country and many of these are not seen beyond their borders. IFIP could facilitate the sharing of important national studies around the world.

Firsthand experience of the authors assures them that when brought together the leadership of member societies find they share many of the same dilemmas and can learn much from each other. Efforts in the past to get members and member societies engaged in sharing experiences were sometimes successful but not on a continuing basis. Making more use of communication technologies that have proven their value in the recent COVID-19 circumstances is the way forward. Video conferencing could enable meetings with Member Society Presidents and CEOs online and to use the meetings to exchange ideas and to find projects which would attract support from member societies and which are perhaps too big to be done by any one society on its own. In this way IFIP could add value to its members own activities. IP3 showed that member societies are willing to commit substantial resources to projects which match their own work and ambitions.

But that will not be enough. Organizational structures and conditions for cooperation and representation should be evaluated and adapted to this new means. A more direct involvement of the boards of member societies has to overcome the sometimes isolated position of representatives.

Sixty years ago the global approach was obvious and beneficial in advancing ICT. Nowadays a regional approach to sharing experiences can provide additional benefits because of the greater homogeneity within that region in comparison to the wider world. IFIP could increase the cooperation with its regional members, liaise with associations that are not yet linked to IFIP and could add value by taking initiatives to create regional societies where these do not exist yet.

5   Closing Remarks

IFIP was founded 60 years ago as an international federation of information processing societies. Without doubt the role of IFIP in providing an apolitical meeting place for the world's academics and researchers has made and continues to make a major contribution to the development of ICT. IFIP's heavy dependence on volunteers to take the lead in organizing major events, even when supported by professional congress organizers and publishers is a weakness. IFIP's apolitical status in a world of changing alliances remains a core, if understated, strength.

It is imperative that IFIP maintains a close link to the information processing societies around the world. Many of these have influence with their national governments. They share many of the same challenges in their own countries and benefit by meeting together regionally and globally to share their experiences.

A key role for IFIP has been and must continue to be to promote awareness of the transformative power of ICT to facilitate a better quality of life for all of humanity.

References

1. ACM-history, https://www.acm.org/about-acm/acm-history. Accessed 26 Aug 2020
2. Auerbach, I.: Personal recollections on the origin of IFIP. In: Zemanek, H. (ed) A Quarter Century of IFIP, pp 41–67. North Holland (1986)
3. Bobillier, P-A.: IFIP recent history. In: Zemanek, H. (ed) A Quarter Century of IFIP, pp 95–137. North Holland (1986)
4. CEPIS. www.cepis.org. Accessed 14 July 2020
5. ICDL, ICDL Europe website. https://icdleurope.org/about-us/. Accessed 10 July 2020
6. IFIP DL, IFIP Digital Library. https://hal.inria.fr/IFIP. Accessed 13 Sept 2020
7. IFIP Mission. https://www.ifip.org//index.php?option=com_content&task=view&id=255&Ite mid=663. Accessed 28 Aug 2020
8. Johnson, R.G.: IP3 – progress towards a global ICT profession. In: Reynolds, N., Turcsányi-Szabó, M. (eds.) KCKS 2010. IAICT, vol. 324, pp. 177–186. Springer, Heidelberg (2010). https://doi.org/10.1007/978-3-642-15378-5_17

Professionalism in IT

Moira de Roche[1]([✉]), Liesbeth Ruoff-van Welzen[2], Adrian Schofield[3],
and Anthony Wong[4]

[1] IFIP IP3, Cape Town, South Africa
meroche@ipthree.org
[2] LRWA, Voorburg, The Netherlands
l.ruoff@lrwa.nl
[3] IITPSA, Unit 4, Probuild Park, James Crescent, Halfway House, Midrand, South Africa
adrian.schofield@iitpsa.org.za
[4] AGW Lawyers and Consultants, Sydney, Australia
anthonywong@agwconsult.com

Abstract. This chapter considers the history of IFIP and Professionalism in ICT, and why Professionalism in ICT is becoming as critical as for other professions. Examples of the criticality of Professional and Ethical behavior are provided. The founding and work of the International Professional Practice Partnership (IP3) is explained. Requirements for a Profession are provided. The progress in developing Professionalism in different countries is explored.

Keywords: Profession · Professionalism · Technology · ICT · Core body of knowledge · Ethics · Accreditation · Certification · Skills framework · Skills · Competencies · Duty of care · Risk · Liability

1 Introduction

Professionalism is, at its heart, a willingness of one professional to subject their work to the critical assessment of their peers. It is now 70 years since the first commercial ICT systems were built. Today, ICT professionals build, maintain and operate systems of unparalleled complexity in comparison with other engineered artefacts. ICT professionals have an excellent record of success despite, with few exceptions, having none of the professional structures of doctors, lawyers, accountants, engineers and other professional disciplines. These professions have themselves acquired their professional status due to the implications of their roles and decisions, legal responsibility for the wellbeing and the interests of society in general including accountability for injuries, death, damage and loss over the course of their development.

The rapid adoption and pervasive use of digital technology in many diverse areas of our personal and business activities—from transport, education, healthcare, telecommunication through to critical infrastructure, logistics, defence, entertainment and agriculture—have accentuated the importance and prominence of ICT skills and knowledge in recent times. It has also led to the use and deployment of digital technology by these

L. Strous et al. (Eds.): Unimagined Futures, IFIP AICT 555, pp. 200–219, 2020.
https://doi.org/10.1007/978-3-030-64246-4_16

other professions, as tools of their trade and professional work. But as autonomy and self-learning capabilities increase, autonomous and intelligent AI systems feel less and less like machines or tools and will have the ability to interact and work alongside these other professionals to augment their work. They will increasingly be able to take over functions and roles and, perhaps more significantly, the ability to make autonomous decisions.

The need to address digital technology risks and challenges has increased in urgency as the adverse potential impact could be significant in specific critical domains. If not appropriately addressed, human trust will suffer, impacting on adoption and oversight and in some cases posing significant risks to humanity and societal values.

Membership of a professional body is generally not a prerequisite for ICT practitioners to practice, unlike practitioners in disciplines such as law and medicine.

Should government and regulators now hold ICT professionals, developers and providers of these systems to similar professional standards demanded from their professional counterparts in medicine, law, accounting, engineering, finance and architecture?

IFIP founded IP3 – International Professional Practice Partnership - in the belief that this issue deserved careful consideration. Why are the traditional professional structures largely missing in ICT worldwide? Does it matter? Are there risks with the status quo and the opportunities for pro-active interventions?

2 The Maturing of the Profession

Despite passing away in 1929, Herman Hollerith's name was still attached to electric tabulating machines in 1960 – a hundred years after his birth. By 1960, computers were replacing tabulators and companies like International Business Machines and International Computers & Tabulators were filling up space in "computer centres", surrounded by "programmers". For a couple of decades, computing was confined to such centres in medium to large enterprises, serviced by a cohort of skilled people who acquired much of their learning in academia. Their talents were clearly differentiated from those of the user community and they usually worked in separate spaces.

It all started to change in the 1980s, when personal computers began to appear on the desks of managers, administrators and sales staff, replacing the "dumb" terminals that had previously linked them to the mainframe in the computer centre. Although still dependent on the programming skills of specialists for the operating system and main application framework, users were now enabled to decide how to process and see their data and even to write some programs for themselves.

Fast forward to the 21st century and the computing power has moved from the desktop to the hand, with more computing power in a small mobile device than was dreamed of sixty years previously.

But some things have not changed. The way in which the computer is designed, the way in which the operating system functions, the way in which applications interface with the operating system, with each other and with the user, are all dependent on the skills of the people who put it all together. Designers, architects, analysts, programmers, testers – these roles are all vital in ensuring that the technology delivers output according the specifications and expectations.

This is where professionalism becomes a vital component in the creation, construction, and operation of ICTs. When humans began to construct homes, they were single storey and made of local available materials. Trial and error would lead to homes that were weather-proof and durable, with much copying of the more successful techniques. As buildings became larger, the trial and error had to be abandoned in favour of design that took account of all the factors required to create a durable and fit-for-purpose edifice. Registered, professional architects and artisans could be relied upon to deliver the quality of durable buildings that would satisfy the needs of their occupiers.

It is no different when it comes to acquiring fit-for-purpose technology systems that are durable and meet the needs of their users. The same roles of architects, designers, engineers, and the systems equivalent of artisans (programmers, testers, operators and technicians) are relied on to deliver the quality of system expected of them. But, unlike the construction industry, the ICT sector has not demanded such rigorous evaluation of its key role-players, to the extent that a significant proportion of its products and services are purchased with no knowledge of the skills of the people who created them.

This can lead to disaster on a scale that varies from wasting personal money on an "app" that does not work to endangering the lives of hundreds of airline passengers.

3   Why We Need Professionalism

Professionals often overlook and neglect their ethical and fiduciary responsibilities resulting in reputational damage, legal consequences, and ongoing repercussions. Professionalism has long held strong linkages with ethics. The "professional is someone who, amongst other things, behaves ethically with respect to his or her occupation." [20]. The following case studies illustrate why we need ICT professionalism.

3.1   Volkswagen ('Dieselgate') Case Study

In 2017, a Volkswagen software engineer was convicted and sentenced in the USA, for his role in a 10-year conspiracy to defraud regulators and customers by implementing software specifically designed to cheat environmental emission tests in diesel vehicles [25]. The Volkswagen engineer and his co-conspirators designed and implemented software to recognize whether a vehicle was undergoing emissions testing, versus being driven on the road under normal driving conditions, to cheat the emission tests. The 'Dieselgate' software installed in Volkswagen and Audi diesel vehicles "ran the engine cleanly during tests and switched off emissions control during normal driving conditions, allowing the car to spew up to 40 times the U.S. Environmental Protection Agency's maximum allowed level of nitrogen oxides, air pollutants that cause respiratory problems and smog" [22]. The co-conspirators fraudulently certified to regulators that Volkswagen diesel vehicles met environmental emissions standards and complied with legislation.

Did the software engineer and co-conspirators collaborate with management of the organization to advance the 'green status' of the diesel vehicles, meet aggressive sale targets or as a strategy to compete with less polluting gas or electric powered vehicles?

Or did management instruct the software engineer and co-conspirators to design and implement software specifically to cheat environmental emission tests?

Darden Professor Lynch submits that "the presence of three factors contributed to the catastrophic decision made by the engineers—pressure, opportunity and rationalization. When those three factors (known by some as a 'dangerous triad' or a 'fraud triangle') are present simultaneously, we often see employees act unethically" [21].

By August 2020, the scandal has not only tarnished Volkswagen's reputation but has also wiped billions of euros from its market valuation. Fraud charges have also been filed against former board members, including the former CEOs of Audi and Volkswagen [4]. Dieselgate has been reported to cost the Volkswagen group more than €30bn in compensation, fines and costs after numerous legal actions in relation to the 11 million vehicles worldwide including in the USA, Australia, Germany and UK [5].

3.2 Boeing 737 Max Case Study

While not every technology shortcoming or failure, is life threatening or leads to economic loss, many critical infrastructures, including water, energy, transportation, and hospitals, are increasingly dependent on software, AI and autonomous systems. Failure of these systems can potentially lead to injury or damage—or worse death. In addition, automation introduces new vulnerabilities—as a point of error or failure could potentially create catastrophic results and, widespread damage and loss.

This is epitomized by the recent saga with the Boeing 737 Max aircraft. In October 2018, Lion Air crashed shortly after takeoff killing all 189 followed by the Ethiopian Airlines in March 2019, with the loss of 157 lives. These have led to the worldwide grounding of the Boeing 737 Max aircrafts.

To counteract competitive threat, and instead of a major redesign of the previous 737 airframe, the 737 MAX includes an augmentation flight software called the Maneuvering Characteristics Augmentation System (MCAS), which was designed to compensate for the aerodynamic pitch effects associated with the changes in placement and size of the 737 MAX's larger, more efficient engines. The MCAS was designed to activate automatically without any pilot command. The existence on the MCAS was not disclosed to most pilots, and Boeing sought to diminish focus on MCAS as a 'new function' in order to avoid increased costs, and 'greater certification and training impact' [28] The investigations have implicated the automated software MCAS in both crashes and disclosed documents have highlighted company employees' safety concerns about the 737 Max.

"Boeing's economic incentives led the company to a significant lack of transparency with the FAA, its customers, and 737 MAX pilots regarding pilot training requirements and negatively compromised safety" [29].

Should Boeing deploy software to automatically compensate for changes to the hardware design in this instance? Should the existence of the new piece of software be withheld from pilots?

The US Committee on Transportation and Infrastructure report also point to a company culture "where safety was sacrificed to production pressures" [30] and that "the FAA's current oversight structure with respect to Boeing creates inherent conflicts of interest that have jeopardized the safety of the flying public" [31].

The various investigations and reports on the incidents illustrate the complex interplay, and the importance of ensuring that any changes to the automated software is holistically integrated for the proper functioning of the entire aviation system, and not in an incremental and fragmented manner. Should the programmer foresee the potential loss or damage even when it may be difficult to anticipate—particularly with the complex interactions and actions at play?

The U.S. Department of Transportation Special Committee has also recommended "that the FAA should update existing guidance to highlight the vulnerabilities that can develop around multiple adaptations of existing systems, where transfer of historical assumptions may not be appropriate or may require specific validation" [27].

Due to the complexity of these digital technologies and their integration with physical systems, it may be very difficult to discern the boundaries and responsibilities of different stakeholders and actors, and to identify who is responsible for the problems arising and in connection with the design, use and shortcomings of digital technology.

The grounding of Boeing's top-selling aircraft has cost the company billions of dollars. Additionally, Boeing also faces several ongoing criminal and civil investigations [12].

3.3   Equifax Case Study

Equifax, one of the three largest credit reporting agencies in the USA, collects and aggregates credit and demographic information on over 800 million individual consumers and more than 88 million businesses worldwide. In September 2017, they announced a data breach, which impacted the personal information of approximately 147 million people. Also affected were some 693,665 UK consumers and 8,000 Canadian consumers. The sensitivity of the personal information held by Equifax and the scale of the problem was unique at the time.

The data breached included names, home addresses, phone numbers, date of birth, social security numbers, and driver's license numbers. The credit card numbers of approximately 209,000 consumers were also breached. Identity theft can completely derail a person's financial future. Criminals who have gained access to others' personally identifiable information can open bank accounts and credit cards, take out loans, and conduct other financial activities using someone else's identity. Equifax took several weeks to officially announce the data breach, putting millions of people at risk of identity theft.

"We at Equifax clearly understood that the collection of American consumer information and data carries with it enormous responsibility to protect that data. We did not live up to that responsibility." Richard F. Smith, Equifax's former CEO 3 October 2017 [26].

In December 2016, a security researcher examined Equifax's servers and alerted the company that its system was vulnerable to hacks. In May of 2017, the company was first hacked via a consumer complaint web portal, with the attackers using a widely known vulnerability in Apache Struts Software, for which a patch was available in early March. The patch was redistributed by US Department of Homeland Security's Computer Emergency Response Team (CERT) emphasizing the importance of its immediate installation [13]. Due to failures in the company's internal processes, the patches were not successfully applied until late May.

Ten days after the warning, Equifax installed the patch and ran a scan to see if the patch was installed correctly, but they did not scan all of their servers that were using the Apache Toolkit and in some cases did not apply the patch correctly, leaving several servers vulnerable to an attack that had been widely publicized.

On 29 July 2017, the Equifax security department discovered "suspicious network traffic" associated with its online dispute portal. From 13 May to 30 July 2017, hackers were able to utilize simple commands to determine the credentials of network accounts at Equifax to access and infiltrate sensitive personal information. The attackers were able to move from the web portal to other servers because the systems weren't adequately segmented from one another, and they were able to find usernames and passwords stored in plain text that then allowed them to access further systems. The attackers also pulled data out of the network in encrypted form undetected for months because the company had crucially failed to renew an encryption certificate on one of their internal security tools. Equifax eventually patched this vulnerability.

After the discovery on 29 July, the company did not inform the public of the breach. Weeks were spent hiring cybersecurity experts informing select groups of the breach, purchasing an identity protection company so they could sell its services to consumers who had their data stolen.

It is with the intention of mitigating the risk of such outcomes that IFIP's International Professional Practice Partnership (IP3) came into being, to raise the profile of practitioners at all levels, to encourage them to build their careers and skill levels and to register their validated abilities through professional recognition schemes of national professional bodies.

4 Developments Around the World

But not only IFIP/IP3 started initiatives, also other organizations showed work with respect to professionalism, skills and competencies. In the following subsections examples from around the world are listed.

4.1 Africa

The Institute of IT Professionals South Africa (IITPSA) is accredited by the South African Qualifications Authority (SAQA). IITPSAs Professional Membership Grade (SFIA Level 5) was accredited by IP3 in 2015. In 2019, IITSA introduced a new Professional certification Pr.CIO aimed at Chief Information Officers (CIOs) and other officials at a similar level. Pr.CIO is targeted for IP3 accreditation in 2020.

Other African countries that are committed to professionalism in ICT include Zimbabwe, Tanzania, and Botswana.

4.2 Australia

In 2000, the Australian Computer Society (ACS) was admitted to the Australian Council of Professions—now Professions Australia, making the ACS, one of the first computer societies in the world to achieve this status. Professions Australia is the peak body for all professions in Australia including doctors, lawyers, accountants, engineers, and other professions.

ACS' contribution to promoting global standards for professionalism in ICT is long and distinguished. ACS is one of the founding partners of IP3 and was the first computer society to have their certification program accredited by IP3. The accreditation applies to the Certified Professional (CP) at SFIA Level 5 and Certified Technologist (CT) at SFIA Level 3 [1].

In addition, ACS has been able to advocate for the establishment of professional ICT benchmarks through legislation in Australia including the:

1. Professional Standards Legislation: The IP3 accredited certification is recognised under the Professional Standards legislation [3]. This recognition is administered by the Professional Standards Councils in Australia. Certified Professionals are protected by a special ACS member insurance policy and capped liabilities under Professional Standards legislation.
2. Professional Employees Award 2010: which defines minimum wages and employment conditions for ICT professionals [23].

4.3 Asia

IPSJ, Information Processing Society of Japan, founded a certification system named Certified IT Professional (CITP) from 2014. The CITP system was accredited by IP3 in February 2018. The system is operating in two methods: the direct method and the indirect method.

In the direct method, IPSJ certifies individuals by examining application documents that describe the applicant's knowledge level and the demonstration of skill and competency in business experiences.

In the indirect method, IPSJ accredits internal certification systems of companies if they are comparable to the direct method explained above. Once accredited, IPSJ issues the certificates of CITP to the professionals certified within the companies based on the requests from the companies.

As of March 2020, 9853 CITPs have been certified including the ones certified through the indirect method. By the indirect method, nine internal certification systems of companies have been accredited. CITPs had established a professional community called "CITP Community" and held meetings every two months.

From April 2019, IPSJ also recognizes a Professional Engineer, Japan (P. E. Jp) where the technical discipline is Information Engineering (Computer Engineering, Software Engineering, Information Systems & Data Engineering, Information Network Engineering). The qualification will be registered as a CITP, while the registered P. E. Jp is required to fulfill CPD requirement and periodical recertification.

The CITP certification system is designed to conform to ISO/IEC 24773, Certification of software and systems engineering professionals, which is under development at ISO/IEC JTC1/SC7/WG20.

4.4 Europe

In Europe attention for and activities around the IT profession were locally organized in the first years. One of the earliest local initiatives was in the UK. The British Computer Society (BCS) took the lead in 1957. Currently the emphasis is on joint European efforts, resulting in 1989 in the Council of European Professional Informatics Societies (CEPIS) but also in CEN TC 428 ICT Professionalism and Digital Competences, officially launched in 2014 [6].

Most of the activities in the digital skills and professionalism areas are now initiated, financed, and accomplished in the EU context. Within the European Commission 2009-2014 Neelie Kroes as a Vice-President was the first Commissioner to have responsibilities in the digital domain. From that period on a boost of activities was created resulting among other things in The EU Digital Single Market Strategy adopted in May 2015 [11]. Three pillars were mentioned:

- Better access for consumers and businesses to digital goods and services;
- Creating the right conditions and a level playing field for digital networks and innovative services to flourish;
- Maximizing the growth potential of the digital economy.

For IFIP and specially IP3 the report Development and Implementation of a European Framework for IT Professionalism in January 2017 is important [14]. In this report the following was written "Standardizing is a means to further mature a profession. This is also the direction that the European Commission and key stakeholders are following: the European e-Competence Framework (e-CF) evolved in April 2016 into a European Standard (EN 16234-1). The ambition is to do more. A European framework for IT professionalism – as described in this report – would provide a standard that includes not only IT competences, but also other essentials for any IT professional: foundational body of knowledge, education and training qualification and certification, and finally ethics and code of conduct". Indeed in 2018 the European Commission promoted a standardization request to develop standards for the ICT profession in the form of a comprehensive European framework by 2025 [8].

This push was taken serious by CEN TC 428. The first results are visible in 2020:

- A new release of the basic Framework e-CF has been made public. 41 competences are distinguished, divided over the dimensions Plan, Build, Run, Enable and Manage. Important change in this release is the addition of transversal aspects. Those aspects, 7 in total, recognize the relevance of several cross-cutting aspects that are important in the ICT workplace, like accessibility, ICT legal issues and sustainability [7].
- Expert teams are selected and are currently working on different topics within the ecosystem around the e-CF, like Ethics, the Body of Knowledge, Educational and certification aspects and how standards like e-CF can be used in practice. Final products and thus standards are expected to be released in the coming 2 years [19].

In the meantime, a new commission is in place in Europe reacting on the rapidly changing world. That is also seen in the new policies of the European Union. Next to the fact that technology has to work for people and that Europe strives to create a fair and competitive digital economy, Europe's Digital Future is also linked to the climate-neutral by 2050 task. These priorities have as a result that the digital transformation monitor is transformed into the Advanced Technologies for Industry monitor [10]. This monitor is looking at sixteen advanced technologies, that are a priority for European industrial policy and that enable process, product and service innovation throughout the economy, and hence foster industrial modernization. Interesting is the fact that what we formerly called new digital technologies are combined with engineering technologies. Advanced technologies are defined as recent or future technologies that are expected to substantially alter the business and social environment and include Advanced materials, Advanced manufacturing, Artificial Intelligence, Augmented and Virtual Reality, Big data, Blockchain, Cloud technologies, Connectivity, Industrial biotechnology, the Internet of Things, Micro- and nanoelectronics, IT for Mobility, Nanotechnology, Photonics, Robotics and Security. A first report on technology trends, technology uptake, investment and skills in advanced technologies has been published in July 2020 [9]. Also so called "softer skills" are considered in the research about the advanced technologies (see Fig. 1).

Still one element needs to be mentioned. Industry must have access to the relevant technical and digital skills, in order to respond to the disruptive force of today's technological advances. However, in Europe, the number of tech-savvy professionals does not meet the exponentially increasing current demand. The World Economic Forum (WEF) estimated that more than half of all employees will require significant reskilling by 2022 while around 37% of workers in Europe do not even have basic digital skills.

In conclusion we observe that in Europe the importance of having professionalism in the digital environment is on the agenda. It took a long time, perhaps even too long, to realize the importance of a digitally skilled workforce. A combination of the IT sector with other sectors is now seen as the opportunity to accelerate the growth of trained professionals in advanced technologies. Those other sectors have a longer history and a broader experience with standardization, regulation and setting up professional institutes and societies and a positive track record of implementing those skills in business environment.

4.5 North America

The ACM, an international member of IFIP, engages in global support for IT professionalism. In terms of supporting policy decisions, the ACM's Global Policy Council coordinates the work of the European and US Technical Policy committees. The ACM European Technology Policy Committee promotes dialogue and the exchange of ideas on technology and computing policy issues with the European Commission and other governmental bodies in Europe, and the informatics and computing communities.

Recognizing the ubiquity of algorithms in our daily lives, as well as their far-reaching impact, the ACM Europe Technology Policy Committee and the ACM US Technology Policy Committee, have issued a statement and a list of seven principles designed to address potential harmful bias. The US ACM committee approved a statement on automated decision making with Informatics Europe. ACM Europe Policy Committee and

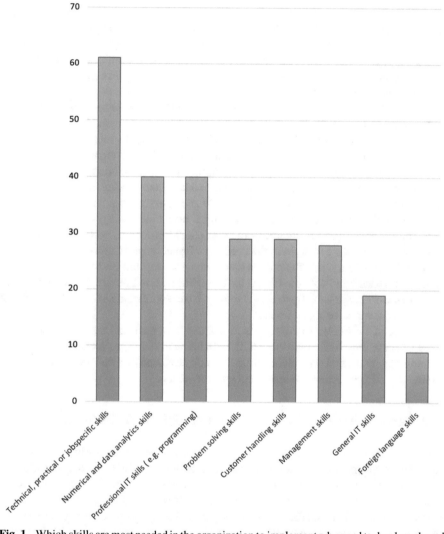

Fig. 1. Which skills are most needed in the organization to implement advanced technology-based products and projects? Figure 44 from the ATI General Findings Report [9]

ACM Europe Council joined with Informatics Europe to produce a white paper for pol-icymakers and industry that outlined the technical, ethical, legal, economic, societal, and educational ramifications of automated decision making (ADM). When Computers Decide: European Recommendations on Machine Learned Automated Decision Making presents 10 specific recommendations addressing the challenges posed by the increased presence of machine learning and ADM.

ACM's US Technology Policy Committee (USTPC) serves as the focal point for ACM's interaction with all branches of the US government, the computing community, and the public on policy matters related to information technology. The USTPC established a subcommittee to provide guidance on issues of Algorithmic accountability and worked to guiding how professionals can address Data Privacy Risks and harms revealed by Facebook/Cambridge Analytica Inquiries.

The ACM revitalized Code of Ethics reflecting the conscience of the computing professional is one of the foundations for most policy documents. ACM is working on support materials for its updated Code of Ethics fortifying its role in contributing to articulating what it means to be a computing professional (https://www.acm.org/code-of-ethics). The ACM Committee on Professional Ethics has presented multiple workshops on using the Code of Ethics in decision making and has produced webinars. They are also developing support materials to support people and organizations who want to use the Code. These documents address: a general ethical reasoning strategy- Proactive CARE, Case studies, techniques to identify potential ethical problems, and examples of the consequences of failure to address the needs of a broad range of stakeholders.

The ACM also models for professional behavior working on several projects for social good: partnering with the UN AI for Good Summit, is a partner of the Partnership on AI, that works with industry to use AI to benefit society. Various ACM Special Interest groups have awards for social impact.

The ACM Continues to contribute to shaping technical ethics policy worldwide. ACM's Computing Curriculum 2020 (CC2020) is a worldwide project to chart the future of computing education on a global scale that was produced by a task force of thirty-six professionals from sixteen countries and six continents.

5   Characteristics of the IT Profession and IT Professionals

The aims of the IP3 Professionalism in IT program are to improve the ability to exploit the potential of information and communication technologies effectively and consistently in all fields of human endeavor and to develop a profession which is respected, trusted and valued. The recognition of the importance of professionalism in IT necessitates a clear and concise understanding of the attributes and obligations that are required of IT professionals. In turn this demands a description of the profession of which its members are the professionals. The IP3 Application and Assessment Guideline (IP3 2020) describes the criteria for the profession, the bodies which govern it and the professionals who belong to it [15]. It serves to define the essence of professionalism upon which all the building blocks of the profession are constructed.

5.1   Profession

The Australian Council of Professions defines a 'Profession' as: "a disciplined group of individuals who adhere to ethical standards and who hold themselves out as, and are accepted by the public as possessing special knowledge and skills in a widely recognised body of learning derived from research, education and training at a high level, and who are prepared to apply this knowledge and exercise these skills in the interest of others" [2].

A profession must:

- be a community controlled by regulation or by a governing body/bodies (most usually professional institutions or associations) which directs the behavior of members of the community in professional matters;
- determine the knowledge, skills, attributes and experience required by professionals;
- give leadership to the public it serves in its specific field of activity;
- adhere to the general standards of professional communities and define those specific attributes and characteristics that distinguish a specific profession from others;
- be valued for its contribution to society.

5.2 Regulated Professional Community

A regulated professional community, e.g. a professional institution or society, must have a means to:

- ensure that members of the community obtain and maintain an acceptable standard of professional competence;
- define the profession's core body of knowledge and competences;
- set appropriate minimum codes of conduct and professional standards set and enforce rules and standards which recognize and protect the public interest;
- take disciplinary action should the rules and standards not be observed or should a member be guilty of unprofessional work;
- support members in their commitment to adhere to the rules and professional standards
- provide enough capacity to implement and manage the above conditions.

Professional communities also undertake other activities (e.g. providing services to members, advising government) but the criteria listed above are the core requirements for a regulated professional community. Figure 2 shows this in a graphical way.

5.3 Professional

An ICT professional, "is someone who has full accountability for their own technical work and responsibilities; whose decisions can impact on the success of projects; who develops business relationships with customers; who must apply fundamental principles in a wide and often unpredictable range of contexts; and, who can analyze, diagnose, design, plan, execute and evaluate work to time, cost and quality targets. In addition, they can communicate effectively, demonstrate leadership, and keep their skills up to date. They are creative, innovative, and aware of their impact on social, business, and ecological environments. Their knowledge and actions are able to influence direction within the organization, their peers and industry" [20].

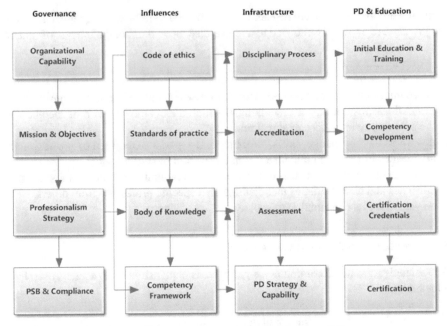

Fig. 2. Key elements of a professional society [17]

"A fully established professional is a practitioner who has specific skills rooted in a broad base and appropriate qualifications, belongs to a regulated body, undergoes continuous development, operates to a code of conduct and recognizes personal accountability" [24].

"Given the reach of ICT in our lives, it is important for an ICT professional to be technically strong (in order to use the right technology for the relevant problem), ethically grounded (to ensure that technology is put to the right use), socially conscious (so that the technical solution takes into consideration elements of sustainability) and business savvy (to ensure commercial viability which is required for social prosperity and funding of new developments)" [16].

And, as with professionals working in other professions, the IT professional must:

- conform to a published code of conduct;
- know, and work within, the limits of their capabilities;
- be accountable for and submit to peer review of their actions;
- undertake continuous professional development;
- have their competence to practice re-assessed on a regular basis;
- explain the implications of their work to stakeholders;
- recognize obligations to the profession as well as to their employer;
- have regard to the public good;
- contribute to the development of the profession;
- support other professionals in maintaining professional standards and developing professional competence.

5.4   National Variations

Implementations of professionalism vary from country to country and discipline to discipline. In some there are autonomous professional institutions while in others there are combinations of nationally approved qualifications and statutory regulation. This guideline does not seek to advance any model but is concerned only that, whatever the model, the professional community meets the minimum standards identified.

6   IFIP/IP3

6.1   Start and Goal of IP3

One of IFIP's strategic aims is to "Advance professionalism in ICT" by:

1. Promoting appropriate bodies of knowledge for ICT practitioners;
2. Promoting common skills and competencies frameworks;
3. Promoting accreditation and certification;
4. Promoting high quality ICT education;
5. Promoting life long learning.

At the IFIP World Computer Congress 2006 in Santiago de Chile a decision was made to "initiate a vigorous program of activity to promote professionalism worldwide". This was the result of a workshop with representatives of IFIP member societies, some of them already having a professional scheme.

IFIP General Assembly (GA) in 2007 confirmed the intention for IFIP to create and launch a global IT Professional Practice Program. IP3 as International Professional Practice Partnership was approved in 2009 and in 2015 formally recognized by incorporating it into the IFIP Statutes.

IP3's primary focus is on the professional behavior of practitioners through the accreditation of association schemes. We also endeavor to influence global policy on Professionalism in ICT through partnerships with companies and other bodies.

Mission
The IP3 mission is to establish a global partnership that will strengthen the ICT profession and contribute to the development of strong international economies by creating an infrastructure that will:

- encourage and support the development of both ICT practitioners and employer organizations;
- give recognition to those who meet and maintain the required standards for knowledge, experience, competence and integrity;
- define international standards of professionalism in ICT.

To carry out this mission, IP3 works closely with its partners who share a commitment to creating a sound global ICT profession.

Vision

A vigorous program to promote professionalism in the IT profession equal to the older and longer established professions; define international standards and create a global infrastructure that will encourage and support the development of both practitioners and employer organizations in the developed and developing world through the creation of a worldwide set of professional certification schemes recognized as the hallmark of true IT professionalism, delivered through independent national member societies and supported by development frameworks for both individuals and organizations.

6.2   Activities – Accreditation

Much of IFIP's focus is on knowledge development and knowledge sharing, through technical committees and working groups. IP3's focus is on the standards applied by the practitioners when using that knowledge to deliver products and services. Many of the bodies representing practitioners around the world had already developed processes for recognizing certain classes of members and IP3 seeks to bring together best practice to enable registered practitioners to be recognized wherever they may be.

To this end, IP3 developed its Accreditation of Professional Member Schemes. The following extracts from the IP3 Application and Assessment Guidelines (2020 edition) set the scene for the Accreditation process [17].

The Accreditation Process followed by the IP3 Standards & Accreditation Council is essentially an audit of the professional body's own process for certifying the professional status of its members, applying the IP3 criteria in measuring performance. For example, the association shall produce a certification scheme (the Scheme) that contains a description of the IT practitioners to be certified. The Scheme should include the following:

- a list of the tasks, jobs, and positions that the certified IT practitioner would be expected to undertake (the Scope);
- a description of the level of accountability, responsibility, autonomy, authority and complexity of the work expected that is easily understood (Professional Competences) and that is compared with the relevant IP3 standard;
- a description of the appropriate Technical Competences expressed in relation to a framework, the body of knowledge, cognitive levels, skills, and performance levels;
- minimum qualifications;
- a description of how competences are evaluated;
- Codes of Ethics and professional Practices, along with disciplinary processes.

The assessment used by the Scheme should be based on a body of knowledge (BoK). For each component of this body of knowledge, the Scheme should state the cognitive level expected of a successful candidate for certification. The Scheme should describe processes for maintaining currency and relevance of the body of knowledge.

The Scheme shall identify those generic practitioner skills expected of a practitioner in the environment in which the candidate will operate.

Mutual Recognition

An important element for a global profession is mutual recognition. It is a requirement of IP3 that all accredited organizations must be prepared to 'recognize' the IP3 accredited certifications of other member organizations when considering transfer applications.

The requirement for such 'recognition' does not mean that transferees have an automatic right of entry to all other IP3 member organisations. But it does imply that each accredited body must attach a value to an IP3 accredited certification - irrespective of which membership body awarded that certification – and that such value must be clear and consistent. It also means that any 'top-up' requirements - i.e. any requirements over and above the IP3 accredited certification - are equally clear and consistent.

Top-up requirements are intended to bridge the gap between the standards evidenced by the IP3 accredited certification and the standards required generally by the receiving organisation and/or to meet specific local requirements. However, it is essential that these gaps or local requirements must be both real and reasonable.

It is an essential principle that any agreed top up requirements must be applied consistently to transfer applicants from all other IP3 member bodies unless such transfers are governed by an overriding mutual recognition agreement. It is open to any accredited body to enter a formal written mutual recognition agreement with another body and this will then set the terms of transfer between the parties to the agreement. In the absence of such agreement all top requirements must be imposed on all transfer applicants without variation or exemption, irrespective of their home association.

In the territories where the IP3 Accreditation has been achieved, there is general agreement that the Scheme is beneficial to both the professional body and to its member practitioners. At its core is the achievement of IP3's goal of "Partnering for Trust in Digital".

6.3   Activities – Other

Conferences

The 20th IFIP World Computer Congress (WCC 2008) took place in Milan, Italy. A specific conference was dedicated to ICT Professionalism and Competences. At the conclusion of this conference, representatives of IP3 and several Computer Societies formally recognized the importance of the ICT Profession: "We recognize that information and communication technologies (ICT) now impact almost every facet of personal and business life. Such technologies are key drivers of innovation and of both economic and social progress, making enormous contributions to prosperity and to the creation of a more open world, enabling pluralism, freedom of expression, and allowing people and organizations to share their culture, interests and undertakings worldwide. We believe that such powerful technologies, and their application, must be driven by competent and reliable professionals who can demonstrate the necessary Competences (including knowledge), Integrity, Responsibility and Accountability, and Public Obligation" [18].

ICT is recognized as a global profession. Several undertakings and recommendations were agreed to by the signatories. This Milan declaration [18] was a serious undertaking that all parties would work towards the same goal, albeit through different structures.

IP3 has held conferences or workshops at all IFIP World Computer Congresses since 2008. We have also held Thematic Workshops at the World Summit for Information Society (WSIS), held in Geneva, every year since 2012. In the first few years, we promoted the Professionalism in ICT, and its importance to the Knowledge and Information Society. Since the launch of the iDOCED campaign (see below), our workshops have explored the Duty of Care the digital landscape requires from all – producers of digital products and systems, consumers, end-users and institutions that procure these services.

iDOCED

IP3 launched iDOCED, the IFIP Duty of Care for Everything Digital Initiative in Sydney on 2 December 2016. iDOCED aims to promote Trust in Digital and the duty of care that everyone including governments; organizations, and other actors and stakeholder have in a digital world. It is designed to remind and support both providers and consumers of digital products and services that they have a duty of care in ensuring that they act responsibly.

Past IP3 Chair, the late Brenda Aynsley, said iDOCED was developed in response to numerous instances of poor ethical behaviour by companies, low quality or underperforming products, or a lack of care by digital consumers in how they use social media or access the Internet – all of which create negative impacts for the community.

Users can be compromised by the way they access the Internet or use software or various online tools. iDOCED seeks to raise awareness of what users can and should do to protect themselves in today's digitally connected world. We often liken it to keeping oneself and our families as safe as possible, only calling on the police and security forces when things go wrong. We need to adopt the same attitude with digital products and services and not leave it to someone else to keep us safe – hence everyone has a duty of care.

IP3 also advocates the need for companies to act responsibly and ethically in the development and implementation of commercial products and services.

Individuals and companies buying digital products and services must apply due diligence and demand that suppliers demonstrate Honour, Integrity and Trust in all their dealings with them. This supports the need for those who produce digital products and services to be professional. The best way for them to demonstrate this is to partner with their local ICT bodies and Computer Societies to become IP3 accredited.

As a global body with members all over the world, IP3 works proactively with professional bodies and other stakeholders in industry and government to raise awareness of iDOCED and encourage its wide adoption. As this happens more widely, consumers will be able to rely on the AI of Everything and the Internet of Everything as being trustworthy and safe for them and their families to engage with and rely upon for communication, transactions and more.

In December 2017, IP3 presented a workshop on Trust and the Duty of Care at the Internet Governance Forum (IGF) in Geneva.

Global Industry Council (GIC)

The support of the international employer community is critical to IP3's goal of building ICT professionalism globally. Recognizing this criticality, IP3 established its Global

Industry Council as the principal forum within which ICT employers can engage with IP3 and influence the development of the global profession.

It is the intention that IP3-GIC is a prestigious organization comprised of recognized thought leaders from major organizations (both private and public sector) with acknowledged experience and expertise in information and communication technologies and that a seat at the Council reflects the global third-party validation that is only possible through a 50+ year old body with UN roots.

Global Industry Council Directors are specially nominated and invited to serve as internationally recognized luminary executives, thought leaders, and visionaries and for their strong history of providing substantive contributions to global business, industry, society, education, and governments. The IP3-GIC is a first of its kind focusing on computing as a profession, which will further align computing with organizational strategy and business agility driving sustainability, education, risk management and security, skills development, professional standards, innovation, entrepreneurship, business growth, regional GDP growth, high yield investment opportunities, and regional economic development.

One of the significant achievements of the Global Industry Council was the development and online publication of the Skills2020 guide in 2015 [16]. This work considered what the ICT skills requirements were likely to be in 2020, with the objective of providing employers with a blueprint for planning the development and acquisition of human capital. It can also be used by an individual to plan their careers.

Developing Relationships
IP3 continually seeks to develop partnerships and engage broadly with industry, government, education and other influencers of ICT professional practice and particularly with other associations such as ISACA, ICCP, FEAPO, ITU, UNESCO, ICC, to name but a few.

IP3 supports the work done by other organisations who are developing ICT as a Profession, most especially the EU. We believe our work is synergistic, and best practice must be shared.

7   Towards the Future

Although a lot has been achieved in the last decade, there is still a lot to be achieved in establishing a true global multi-stakeholder partnership in order to achieve a global profession that benefits everybody. Professionals and professional societies have to increase the efforts because developments in the ICT world continue to go at a speed that gives reason for concern if not done and managed in a professional way. IP3 will continue to work towards ICT as a Global Profession, and partner with organizations who embrace the same goals.

We are developing a project "Digital Skills for Everyone, Everywhere" (working title). both within and across countries. To reap the full benefits of new technologies, investments are needed in education and skills.

The goals and deliverables for this project are:

- Make a repository of best practices, frameworks and use cases worldwide round the development and the usage of frontline digital technology.
- Create a body of knowledge and education program around how to behave in the global professional ICT world.
- Formulate practical recommendations based on findings.
- Start a platform of experts based on the inventory of best practices and use cases around the development of the ICT profession.
- Provide recommendations and platforms for Digital Skills aimed at end-users and consumers, as well as ICT Professionals.

We hold the conviction that any program must address real-world needs and should promote the "FAIR" Principles: Findable, Accessible, Interoperable, and Re-usable.

It is envisaged that the project will partner with UN organisations, Academic Institutes (for research), and global non-profit organisations whose goal is community upliftment. We are confident that the work will align, to a lesser or greater extent, with the UNs Sustainable Development Goals. For example, SDG 9 – Decent work and Economic Growth – for economic growth and sustainability, digital transformation is essential. 21st Century Digital Skills are essential for decent work, and to counteract the negative effects of Automation and Robotics.

References

1. Australian Computer Society (ACS) Certification. https://www.acs.org.au/professionalrecogn ition/certification-landing-page.html. Accessed 8 July 2020
2. Australian Council of Professions. https://www.professions.org.au/what-is-a-professional. Accessed 7 Aug 2020
3. Australian Professional Standards Councils. https://www.psc.gov.au/professional-standards-schemes/what-are-schemes. Accessed 7 Aug 2020
4. BBC News - a, Volkswagen loses landmark German 'dieselgate' case, 25 May 2020. https://www.bbc.com/news/business-52795376?intlink_from_url=https://www.bbc.com/news/top ics/ck3nz6nm8lqt/diesel-emissions-scandal&link_location=live-reporting-story. Accessed 7 Aug 2020
5. BBC News – b. https://www.bbc.com/news/business-53676205. Accessed 7 Aug 2020
6. CEN TC 428. https://standards.cen.eu/dyn/www/f?p=204:7:0::::FSP_ORG_ID:1218399& cs=1600F0DD849DA04F3E3B900863CB58F72. Accessed 5 Sept 2020
7. e-CF, European e-Competence Framework. https://www.ecompetences.eu/
8. European Commission, 2018 Rolling plan ICT standardization, https://ec.europa.eu/growth/content/2018-rolling-plan-ict-standardisation-released_en. Accessed 5 Sept 2020
9. European Commission, ATI General Findings Report 2020, https://ati.ec.europa.eu/reports/eu-reports/report-technology-trends-technology-uptake-investment-and-skills-advanced. Accessed 5 Sept 2020
10. European Commission, Digital Transformation Monitor. https://ec.europa.eu/growth/tools-databases/dem/monitor/content/welcome. Accessed 5 Sept 2020
11. European Commission, Shaping the Digital Single Market. https://ec.europa.eu/digital-sin gle-market/en/policies/shaping-digital-single-market. Accessed 5 Sept 2020

12. Forbes. https://www.forbes.com/sites/siladityaray/2020/08/04/faa-proposes-changes-that-would-allow-boeings-737-max-to-resume-flying/#7fbe306420f2 Accessed 8 Aug 2020
13. Franceschi-Bicchierai, Lorenzo: Equifax Was Warned, VICE, 26 October 2017. https://www.vice.com/en_us/article/ne3bv7/equifax-breach-social-security-numbers-researcher-warning. Accessed 12 Sept 2020
14. ICT Professionalism. http://ictprofessionalism.eu/documents/. Accessed 5 Sept 2020
15. IFIP IP3 Application and Assessment Guidelines 2020. https://www.ipthree.org/wp-content/uploads/IP3-Application-Accreditation-Guidelines-v8.pdf. Accessed 5 Sept 2020
16. IFIP IP3 GIC 2015, GIC 2020 Skills Assessment, IFIP / IP3 GIC Directors, 2015. https://www.ipthree.org/ifipip3-global-industry-council/gic-2020-skills/. Accessed 5 Sept 2020
17. IFIP IP3 Key elements of a profession, https://www.ipthree.org/knowledge-portal/best-practice/, last accessed 2020/9/5
18. IFIP WCC 2008, Declaration on ICT Professionalism and Competences, IFIP WCC 2008, Milan. http://www.ifip.org/images/stories/ifip/public/Announcements/wcc08-ict-p&c-declaration.pdf. Accessed 5 Sept 2020
19. IT Professionalism Europe, Body of Knowledge. https://itprofessionalism.org/about-it-professionalism/body-of-knowledge/. Accessed 5 Sept 2020
20. Lindley, D., et al.: Educating for professionalism in ICT: is learning ethics professional development? In: Weckert, John., Lucas, Richard. (eds.) Professionalism in the Information and Communication Technology Industry ch 11, ANU E Press, The Australian National University Australia (2013). http://press-files.anu.edu.au/downloads/press/p223541/html/intro05.xhtml?referer=&page=24. Accessed 7 Aug 2020
21. Lynch, L.: VW emissions and the 3 factors that drive ethical breakdown, Business, Ethics & Society, University of Virginia. https://ideas.darden.virginia.edu/vw-emissions-and-the-3-factors-that-drive-ethical-breakdown. Accessed 7 Aug 2020
22. Patel, P.: Engineers, Ethics, and the VW Scandal, IEEE Spectrum, 25 Sep 2015. https://spectrum.ieee.org/cars-that-think/at-work/education/vw-scandal-shocking-but-not-surprising-ethicists-say. Accessed 7 Aug 2020
23. Professional Employees Award 2020. https://www.fwc.gov.au/documents/documents/modern_awards/pdf/ma000065.pdf. Accessed 7 Aug 2020
24. Thompson, C.: IT professional role today and tomorrow. In: Mazzeo, A., Bellini, R., Motta, G. (eds.) E-Government Ict Professionalism and Competences Service Science. IIFIP, vol. 280, pp. 69–80. Springer, Boston, MA (2008). https://doi.org/10.1007/978-0-387-09712-1_8
25. US Department of Justice, Office of Public Affairs, Friday, August 25, 2017. https://www.justice.gov/opa/pr/volkswagen-engineer-sentenced-his-role-conspiracy-cheat-us-emissions-tests. Accessed 7 Aug 2020
26. US District Court for the Northern District of Georgia, Atlanta Division, Consolidated consumer class action complaint, Case 1:17-md-02800-TWT Document 374 Filed 05/14/18. https://www.equifaxbreachsettlement.com/admin/services/connectedapps.cms.extensions/1.0.0.0/ed93e6d9-c6b0-4829-994c-a7687661917f_1033_Consolidated-Consumer-Class-Action-Complaint-20180514.pdf. Accessed 12 Sept 2020
27. US Federal Aviation Administration, Recommendation No 8, Joint Authorities Technical Review (JATR), US Federal Aviation Administration, Preliminary Summary of the FAA's Review of the Boeing 737 MAX, August 3 2020, p. 71. https://www.faa.gov/news/media/attachments/737-MAX-RTS-Preliminary-Summary-v-1.pdf. Accessed 8 Aug 2020
28. US House of Representatives, Committee on Transportation and Infrastructure, Final Report: The Design, Development and Certification of the Boeing 737 MAX, p. 19. https://transportation.house.gov/committee-activity/boeing-737-max-investigation. Accessed 21 Sept 2020
29. Ibid, p. 24
30. Ibid, p. 238
31. Ibid, p. 14

Digital Equity, Sustainable Development and the ICT Professional

Leon Strous[1]([✉]), Robert M. Davison[2] [iD], and Gabriela Marín-Raventós[3] [iD]

[1] Gistel 20, Helmond, The Netherlands
strous@iae.nl
[2] City University of Hong Kong, Kowloon, Hong Kong, China
isrobert@cityu.edu.hk
[3] Universidad de Costa Rica, San José, Costa Rica
gabriela.marin@ucr.ac.cr

Abstract. Digital equity and sustainable development are in the focus of attention nowadays. While ICT professionals and professional societies have contributed to supporting developing countries for many years, it is even more urgent nowadays to take responsibility. Technological and also societal developments are happening at an incredible speed with the risk that underprivileged persons and communities are lagging behind faster and further. A risk that is not limited to developing countries but also affects emerging and developed countries. This chapter describes some major UN initiatives and reflects on the options for ICT professionals and professional societies to contribute to achieving digital equity and sustainable development. These options are illustrated by a few examples of what has been done so far. Most of the efforts to contribute meet challenges and impediments and we list a number of them. Finally, suggestions are made to address the challenges and to increase the impact and long term effect of efforts.

Keywords: Digital equity · Sustainable development · MDG · Millennium Development Goals · SDG · Sustainable development goals · WITFOR · Developing and emerging countries · ICT4D

1 Introduction

Digital equity and sustainable development are in the focus of attention nowadays. While ICT professionals and professional societies have contributed to supporting developing countries for many years, it is even more urgent nowadays to take responsibility. Technological and also societal developments are happening at an incredible speed with the risk that underprivileged persons, communities and societies are lagging faster and further behind. This is a situation that is not limited to developing countries but also affects persons and communities in emerging and developed countries. The COVID-19 pandemic demonstrates even more the urgency of addressing digital equity. Differences in access to information and to technologies make a difference in chances for continuing education and for saving lives.

© IFIP International Federation for Information Processing 2020
Published by Springer Nature Switzerland AG 2020
L. Strous et al. (Eds.): Unimagined Futures, IFIP AICT 555, pp. 220–231, 2020.
https://doi.org/10.1007/978-3-030-64246-4_17

IFIP has been active in supporting developing countries for more than 40 years. In these 40 years the world has changed and some major UN initiatives have exerted a significant impact on efforts to address inequality. This chapter briefly describes these UN initiatives, reflects on some activities undertaken in the recent past and examines the role and involvement of professionals, both on an individual level and as members of societies.

The chapter is written from an IFIP perspective but most of the activities described, problems encountered, and roles and options for the future are also applicable to national and regional societies and associations.

In 2016 an appeal was made that "professionals, scientists and IT professionals and their organization should take a holistic approach for all ICT activities and projects to always include and monitor the effects of their work on the SDGs (Sustainable Development Goals)" [1]. We subscribe to that appeal.

2   Major UN Initiatives

As mentioned in the introduction, a number of major United Nations initiatives have exerted a significant impact on efforts to make the world a better place to live in. In this section, three of these initiatives are briefly described.

2.1   Millennium Development Goals (MDG's)

The Millennium Development Goals (MDGs) were eight international development goals established following the Millennium Summit of the United Nations in 2000 with a target achievement date of 2015 [2]. The MDGs are:

1. To eradicate extreme poverty and hunger
2. To achieve universal primary education
3. To promote gender equality and empower women
4. To reduce child mortality
5. To improve maternal health
6. To combat HIV/AIDS, malaria, and other diseases
7. To ensure environmental sustainability
8. To develop a global partnership for development

The Millennium Development Goals have galvanized unprecedented efforts to meet the needs of the world's poorest. [3] The MDGs can be regarded as one of the most important and successful initiatives to eradicate poverty in modern history. The Sustainable Development Goals (SDGs) [1] succeeded the MDGs in 2016.

2.2   World Summit on the Information Society (WSIS)

Following a proposal from the Government of Tunisia, the International Telecommunication Union (ITU) decided to hold a World Summit on the Information Society (WSIS) in two phases. The United Nations General Assembly in 2001 endorsed the holding of this WSIS. The first phase took place in Geneva in December 2003 and the second phase took place in Tunis, in November 2005.

The rationale for this WSIS was the acknowledgment that a global discussion was needed to bridge the digital divide which had increased as a result of fast technological and societal developments. Developing a clear statement of political will and identify concrete steps to achieve an information society for all was the objective of the first phase. The second phase put a plan of action into motion. The ITU website on the WSIS is a rich source of information [4].

After the second summit in 2005, in the context of the annual consideration by the UN Economic and Social Council (ECOSOC) of the integrated and coordinated implementation and follow-up of major UN conferences, the Commission on Science and Technology for Development (CSTD) was assigned to assist the Council as the focal point in the system-wide follow-up of WSIS. Starting in 2006, the annual WSIS Forum organized by ITU and co-organized/supported by almost all UN agencies, addresses progress of the actions and goals defined in the summits and the MDGs and the subsequent SDGs.

IFIP participated in most of the forums, in plenary sessions, with workshops and in preparatory meetings. IFIP has also been an official partner in the forum since 2014.

2.3   Sustainable Development Goals (SDG's)

With the end date of 2015 for achievement of the MDGs and the observation that there was still work to be done to achieve these goals, a new set of goals was defined.

These Sustainable Development Goals (SDGs) are a universal call to action to end poverty, protect the planet and improve the lives and prospects of everyone, everywhere. These 17 Goals were adopted by all UN Member States in 2015, as part of the 2030 Agenda for Sustainable Development.

The goals, presented graphically in Fig. 1, are: [5]

Fig. 1. Sustainable Development Goals. Wikipedia (access 13-08-2020)

1. No Poverty – End poverty in all its forms everywhere;
2. Zero Hunger;
3. Good Health and Well-being – Ensure healthy lives and promote well-being for all at all ages;
4. Quality Education;
5. Gender Equality – Achieve gender equality and empower all women and girls;
6. Clean Water and Sanitation – Ensure access to water and sanitation for all;
7. Affordable and Clean Energy – Ensure access to affordable, reliable, sustainable and modern energy;
8. Decent Work and Economic Growth – Promote inclusive and sustainable economic growth, employment and decent work for all;
9. Industry, Innovation, and Infrastructure – Build resilient infrastructure, promote sustainable industrialization and foster innovation;
10. Reducing Inequality – Reduce inequality within and among countries;
11. Sustainable Cities and Communities – Make cities inclusive, safe, resilient and sustainable;
12. Responsible Consumption and Production – Ensure sustainable consumption and production patterns;
13. Climate Action – Take urgent action to combat climate change and its impacts;
14. Life Below Water – Conserve and sustainably use the oceans, seas and marine resources;
15. Life On Land – Sustainably manage forests, combat desertification, halt and reverse land degradation, halt biodiversity loss;
16. Peace, Justice, and Strong Institutions – Promote just, peaceful and inclusive societies;
17. Partnerships for the Goals – Revitalize the global partnership for sustainable development.

The goals are interconnected and all have a strong link to ICT. For each goal it is not difficult to find examples of how ICT can help, or is even instrumental, in achieving the goal. To mention just a few: technology and applications that assist farmers in precision farming and in marketing and distributing agricultural products; health monitoring systems; promotion of healthy living habits using games and IoT; e-learning systems; use of IT to increase efficient use of energy; development of low cost technological products to support industries in developing countries; use of social networks to promote increasing citizen involvement.

Considering constraints in terms of available time and money, individuals and societies have to make choices and set priorities in order to make effective and meaningful contributions to society and mankind.

3 What Can ICT Professionals and Professional Societies Do

Many stakeholders can contribute to achieving digital equity and sustainable development, and are doing so. Among these stakeholders are governments, industry, academia and non-governmental organizations (NGOs). What are the distinctive features of individual ICT professionals and professional societies that (can) make their contributions different from other stakeholders and in particular from governments and industry? An important distinction is the non-political and non-commercial nature of professional societies. Vested interests and conflicts of interest generally are few. Another important feature is that many members that are active in professional societies live and work in the communities that are supposed to benefit from the SDGs. They are familiar with the on-the-ground realities and thus can advise which initiatives will work (or not) and what adjustments need to be made.

The goal of advancing digital equity, by promoting accessibility of ICT, promoting good practices, and promoting and enhancing appropriate access to knowledge and experiences, can be achieved in a variety of ways.

- Events. This category has a broad set of options in itself. It includes events from small (workshops) to very large (conferences, congresses) and events focused on a small set or a broad range of topics. It can be events organized by a professional body on its own or in cooperation with other organizations/stakeholders. It can also be contributions to events organized by others.
- Research. Scientific research can be of great support to develop cost effective and pertinent technologies, to adopt emergent technologies successfully, and to help communities draft well-founded policies. Supporting research in developing countries will help focusing on the specific needs and topics for their environment. Also research and comparison of good practices can be helpful.
- Publications. Publishing the results of scientific research and of good practices and making these publications easily available enhance knowledge sharing. Encouraging and facilitating contributions from developing countries in book series and journals, promotes researchers and broadens problem solving.
- Projects. Specific projects can have a quick impact but also have the potential for a longer term impact.
- Policies. Professionals and professional bodies can assist policy makers in drafting policies that include ICT. They can also influence policies by issuing and sharing policy statements and good practices and publish these.
- Professional bodies. Supporting the creation and positioning of national and regional professional bodies is a way to get ICT professionals in a better position to effectively contribute to their country/community and to promote ICT use to reach the SDGs.

4   Some Examples from IFIP

In a contribution to the Quarter Century of IFIP jubilee book, Narasimhan assessed that the strength of IFIP is its international, non-governmental character [6]. The lack of financial resources is a major limitation to providing assistance and to start essential projects. Despite this limitation significant contributions have been made. This section provides some examples. As stated in the introduction, the chapter is written from an IFIP perspective but most of the examples described are also found in other national, regional and other global societies or associations.

4.1 Committees

The role of "committees" essentially is to initiate, guide and/or coordinate various activities towards the realization /achievement of a specific strategic goal. Committees should create and safeguard conditions that support these activities. IFIP established in 1979, with assistance from UNESCO, the IFIP Committee: Informatics for Development (ICID). ICID's guiding philosophy was that emphasis should be given to events organized within developing countries. Topics would be selected in direct cooperation with organizations or individuals in those countries, and technical experts would be supplied by IFIP.

In 1987, ICID was transformed into the Developing Countries Support Committee (DCSC). The aim of the DCSC was to promote IFIP's cooperation with developing countries and to help developing countries/areas in their specific needs and requests. Specific tasks of the DCSC included among others identifying needs and requests from developing countries/areas that may be answered by information and skills available at present in IFIP. Another task concerned interfacing with Technical Committees, Working Groups and Affiliate Members to get involvement and expertise in the different work areas of these groups.

In 2015 another transformation took place. The activities of the DCSC, of the WITFOR Steering Committee and a separate digital equity initiative, were merged into the Digital Equity Committee (DEC). The activities of this Standing Committee are:

a. Promoting accessibility of ICT;
b. Promoting good practices;
c. Promoting and enhancing appropriate access to knowledge and experiences;
d. Organizing and contributing to activities aimed at achieving the UN Sustainable Development Goals (SDGs) and the goals of the World Summit on the Information Society (WSIS).

Looking at the various subsequent committees and their activities, aims, scope and guiding principles it is interesting to observe that, although using different terminology and despite new types of activities, there is still a strong base from the beginning that has not really changed.

4.2 Working Groups

Many of IFIP's technical committees and working groups pay attention to digital equity and sustainable development. In this section we list a few that are dedicated to these topics. Here we provide a brief summary. More information about aims and scopes can be found on the respective websites.

WG 6.9 Communications Systems for Developing Countries [7]
This working group aims to identify and study technical problems related to the access to, understanding of and application of network and telecommunications technology in developing countries or regions. It also encourages cross-fertilization of concepts and

techniques among developing countries, and between developing countries and developed countries. The areas of study include models and methods for transfer of concepts and methods in communication systems and the establishment of new applications in developing regions for existing technologies. The requirements of the users of those regions include cost-effective technologies for global access, rural access to services and social development in those regions through appropriate applications of communication systems. The problems of human resources, sharing of experience and cost of technology are particularly acute, and are to be examined in detail.

WG 9.4 – Social Implications of Computers in Developing Countries [8]
This Working Group is currently updating its' aims and scope and has proposed a name change to "The Implications of Information and Digital Technologies for Development". Subject to approval, the aims of the group are:

- To collect, exchange and disseminate the social, cultural, economic, environmental, and political experiences of information and digital technology implementation in all the contexts of the 'Global South' as well as disadvantaged groups in societies more generally.
- To develop greater awareness amongst professionals, policy makers and the public on the social and ethical implications of information and digital technologies.
- To develop criteria, guidelines, methods and theory (including indigenous ones) appropriate to the study of information and digital technologies.
- To establish international collaboration networks of researchers and practitioners interested in the use of information and digital technology for addressing the complex and pressing problems of society.
- To mentor academics and PhD students from across the international collaboration network.
- To promote sustainability and inclusion in all the arenas where we undertake research and practice.
- To enable open access to content wherever possible so as to ensure that all stakeholders can freely benefit from the research that we undertake.

WG9.9 ICT and Sustainable Development [9]
An important aim of this group is to be actively involved in the development of ICT applications which involve the goal of sustainable development. It wants to investigate the interaction among social, environmental and economic issues in the development of ICTs and their applications. A cluster of aims concerns the promotion of worldwide research and practice, the strengthening of interdisciplinary research efforts and the provision of a platform for presenting and discussing emerging ideas and trends in the intersection of the topics 'information society' and 'sustainable development'. Last but not least promoting and supporting the organization of meetings as well as easy access to high-quality data, information and knowledge in this area and related areas are within the scope of this group.

WG 13.8 Interaction Design for International Development [10]

WG 13.8 supports and develops the research, practice and education capabilities of Human Computer Interaction (HCI) in institutions and organizations based around the world taking into account their diverse local needs and cultural perspectives. It promotes application of interaction design research, practice and education to address the needs, desires and aspirations of people across the developing world. While researching and promoting interaction design practice in cross-cultural settings, with a special focus on new and emerging economies, the group develops links between the HCI community in general and other relevant communities involved in international development and cross-cultured aspects of ICT development.

WG 13.10 Human-centered Technology for Sustainability [11]

In the field of human-computer interaction, WG 13.10 promotes research, design, development, evaluation, and deployment of human-centered technology to encourage sustainable use of resources in various domains. These technologies would include interaction techniques, interfaces, and visualizations for applications, tools, games, services, and devices. The group brings together, and stimulates exchanges between, researchers, practitioners, and policy-makers from across different disciplines involved in sustainability through regular events. These disciplines would include computer science, engineering, design, social sciences, etc.

4.3   Activities and Services

Availability/Access to knowledge

By making the content of scientific event proceedings available for free in its digital library, IFIP contributes to the "access to high quality digital content" element of digital equity. Another way to increase access to knowledge is to promote open access publications. For instance, the Electronic Journal of Information Systems in Developing Countries [12] since its inauguration in 2000 has been online and platinum open access, which means that readers pay no fee for reading and authors pay no fee for submitting and processing articles. [13]

Encouraging and facilitating participation of researchers from developing countries in scientific events is also a good practice for many event organizers, and that creates more access and inclusiveness.

Events - WITFOR

In 2001 a proposal for the organization of a new IFIP flagship event, called the World Information Technology Forum (WITFOR) was accepted. The overall goal of WITFOR is to assist developing countries in developing and implementing sustainable strategies for the application of ICT and to share experiences that will help to bridge the digital divide and improve the quality of life. [3, 14] The specific goals are:

a. To share and discuss experiences in drafting and implementing ICT policies;
b. To share and discuss experiences in initiating and implementing ICT projects;
c. To present and discuss research concerning the overall goal.

WITFOR has been organized periodically since 2003 in cooperation with several stakeholders in each host country. The concept of WITFOR is to bring together senior policy-makers, academics, NGOs and GOs representatives, ICT experts, and the private ICT sector with the aim of discussing together ICT policies and practical experiences. WITFOR investigates ICT strategies in developing countries and examines different initiatives and projects on effective, context-sensitive development and use of ICT applications, access to quality relevant information, and the development of "fair use principles".

Fig. 2. IFIP WITFOR general logo

IFIP in cooperation with the host countries successfully managed to engage UN bodies and persons in WITFOR with high-level speakers, involvement in the organization and support, for instance, by making conference venues available. Linking WITFOR with a UN event is beneficial for both in terms of availability of speakers and participants, and sharing mutual topics of interest. An example of this is the Second Session of the Conference on Science, Innovation and Information and Communications Technologies of the Economic Commission for Latin America and the Caribbean (ECLAC) which was held as a joint event with WITFOR 2016 in Costa Rica.

Although the term WITFOR is usually linked to the big global conference, the idea is to undertake a number of activities under the umbrella of the World Information Technology Forum (WITFOR). Another idea behind WITFOR was to involve the national professional society of the host country not only in the event but in the network of IFIP relations for the longer term.

Events – Working Groups
The working groups with a focus on developing countries and digital equity have a long track record of conferences. This includes bigger events such as the WG 9.4 bi-annual conferences that are always organized in a developing country location with an average attendance of 150 registered participants. Also smaller events like working conferences as well as special sessions as part of other major conferences are organized regularly by the working groups. The groups strongly encourage the participation of both established researchers and PhD and Master students.

Participation Support
With limited general funds IFIP supports the participation of researchers from developing countries in conferences by partially covering expenses. This is a small effort to encourage such researchers to submit papers to scientific conferences and by doing so get

involved in international networks of scientists. Besides the general funds, some Technical Committees and Working Groups also provide, whenever possible, sponsorships, often for PhD students in particular, drawing on funds held over from past events.

5   Challenges, Impediments

In previous sections we have described how volunteers and volunteer societies can contribute to achieving digital equity and sustainable development goals. A limited number of examples was provided. In many discussions at all levels within IFIP and also outside, concerns are raised about the effectiveness and impact of our efforts. In this section we list some obstacles that volunteers face.

- Volunteers and volunteer societies in general have limited resources, both in terms of time and money. This prohibits for example investments in projects and solid continuous financial support for participation in events from developing countries.
- Working on a voluntary basis makes activities highly dependent on people whose time and commitment may change in time. Moreover, finding good successors is not always possible.
- Good working relationships with governments are dependent on the stability of governments and government policies. Governments change, therefore initiatives supported by one government may suffer from change in support and priorities of the new government.
- Involvement of people from emerging and developing countries, or underprivileged communities in general, can be hindered by lack of funding or lack of access to the information and communication technologies needed for being connected.
- The focus of activities can be too vague or too general which results in not attracting the participants that were envisaged.
- Many scholars, whether from developed or developing countries, are motivated primarily by the prospect of enhancing their curricula vitarum, not by making the world a better place. Thus, changes to scholarly agendas, and reward systems, are essential to the undertaking of research that makes a difference. Thus, the volunteer editors and reviewers of journals that focus on publishing research that ostensibly makes the world a better place nevertheless have to wade through the treacle of research that is broadly in scope, yet that makes no such contribution.

6   How Can We Address the Challenges

We strongly believe the activities described in the previous sections are valuable contributions to achieving digital equity and sustainable development. In our opinion ICT professionals and professional societies do have an important role to play in these goals. Despite the challenges in terms of financial and human resources, there is still a lot that can be done. The non-exhaustive list of activities in this chapter illustrates that there are many ways to contribute to achieving digital equity. However, in order to increase the impact and long term effect of efforts, it is important to:

a. set priorities; perhaps based on the experience of what works;
b. rethink how available funds are spent – and can be raised;
c. work with local and national bodies to create incentives, rewards and recognition for researchers who set out to make the world a better place via digital equity;
d. engage groups that are not purely focusing on digital equity but that can contribute due to the nature of their field and work;
e. increase cooperation with other societies/organizations;
f. decide what should be achieved with each event or activity and link this planned achievement/target to specific IFIP objectives;
g. leverage high level contacts and participation in high level events in order to secure funding, recognition, kudos or opportunities that we can leverage; and
h. change research agendas and research culture, enhance SDG awareness among researchers in order to increase SDG-relevant research and publications. [15]

Furthermore, we can give it another try for initiatives from the past that were not successful (but carefully select initiatives and set priorities):

a. assist in creating national professional ICT societies in those countries where no such societies exist;
b. engage these societies in international cooperation, regional and global;
c. initiate projects with a longer lifespan as a follow up to an event in a developing country; and
d. encourage more countries to belong to IFIP, especially those in less developed parts of the world.

In order to encourage volunteers, and in particular academics, to spend time on activities in the digital equity efforts, a way should be found to reward volunteers for contributing to "non-scientific" events with academic credits (comparable to accepted papers in conferences and journals).

COVID-19 has shown that virtual meetings are a solution to inability to travel; one of the obstacles for a bigger involvement of professionals from the developing countries to participate in activities and specifically in events is travel limitations (mostly in terms of funding). Here we have an opportunity to change at least part of the events that are annually organized to permanent virtual editions or combinations of physical and virtual meetings.

We are convinced that with some adjustments in our approaches ICT professionals and professional societies can make a difference and by doing so demonstrate the added value of such societies.

References

1. Tjoa, A.M., Tjoa, S.: The role of ICT to achieve the UN sustainable development goals (SDG). In: Mata, F.J., Pont, A. (eds.) WITFOR 2016. IFIP AICT, vol. 481, pp. 3–13. Springer, Cham (2016). https://doi.org/10.1007/978-3-319-44447-5_1
2. MDG. https://www.un.org/millenniumgoals/. Accessed 23 Aug 2020

3. Jha, S., Strous, L.: IFIP WITFOR 2007 – ICT for Development and Prosperity. IFIP Press (2007)
4. WSIS. https://www.itu.int/net/wsis/. Accessed 23 Aug 2020
5. SDG. https://www.un.org/sustainabledevelopment/development-agenda/ and https://www.un.org/sustainabledevelopment/sustainable-development-goals/. Accessed 23 Aug 2020
6. Narasimhan, R.: IFIP and the developing countries. In: Zemanek, H. (ed.) A quarter century of IFIP, pp. 245–251, North-Holland (1986)
7. IFIP WG 6.9. https://ifip.informatik.uni-hamburg.de/ifip/tc/6/wg/6.9/AnS. Accessed 23 Aug 2020
8. IFIP WG 9.4. http://ifiptc9.org/wg94/home/. Accessed 23 Aug 2020
9. IFIP WG 9.9. http://ifiptc9.org/wg9-9-ict-and-sustainable-development/. Accessed 23 Aug 2020
10. IFIP WG 13.8. http://ifip-tc13.org/working-groups/working-group-13-8/. Accessed 23 Aug 2020
11. IFIP WG 13.10, http://ifip-tc13.org/working-group-13-10/. Accessed 23 Aug 2020
12. Electronic Journal of Information Systems in Developing Countries (Wiley) https://onlinelibrary.wiley.com/journal/16814835
13. Open Access, https://en.wikipedia.org/wiki/Open_access. Accessed 23 Aug 2020
14. Khakhar, D. (ed.): WITFOR 2003 White Book, IFIP Press (2003)
15. Davison, R.M.: Sustainable Development Goals and the ISJ/EJISDC, Keynote Address at the pre-ECIS working conference on Sustainable Development Goals in IS Research: Opening the Agenda Beyond Developing Countries' Research, Stockholm, Sweden, 10 June 2019

Author Index